Rob Burns

# The Quest
# for Modernity

## The Place of Arno Holz in
## Modern German Literature

## PETER LANG
### Frankfurt am Main · Bern

CIP-Kurztitelaufnahme der Deutschen Bibliothek

**Burns, Rob:**

The quest for modernity : the place of Arno Holz
in modern German literature / Rob Burns. -
Frankfurt am Main ; Bern : Lang, 1981.
(Europäische Hochschulschriften : Reihe 1,
Dt. Sprache u. Literatur ; Bd. 431)
ISBN 3-8204-6225-2
NE: Europäische Hochschulschriften / 01

ISBN 3-8204-6225-2

© Verlag Peter Lang GmbH, Frankfurt am Main 1981

Druck und Bindung: fotokop wilhelm weihert KG, darmstadt

CONTENTS

The Quest for Modernity

# European University Studies

Europäische Hochschulschriften
Publications Universitaires Européennes

Series I

German Language and Literature

Reihe I    Série I

Deutsche Sprache und Literatur
Langue et littérature allemandes

Bd./Vol. 431

PETER LANG
Frankfurt am Main · Bern

Preface

I wish to acknowledge my indebtedness to Dr. Keith Bullivant for the invaluable contribution he made to this book in terms of both ideas and stylistic advice. I also benefited greatly from Professor Roy Pascal's expert knowledge of Holz and the Naturalist movement and the second chapter in particular owes much to the stimulus he provided. I would likewise wish to recall the valuable assistance given me by the Amerika Gedenkbibliothek in Berlin, and in particular by Herr Mehner, in allowing me unlimited access to their archival material on Holz. I also wish to record my appreciation of The British Academy's generosity in providing financial assistance for the publication of the book. Finally, a very special word of thanks is due to Brenda Waller (and Hattie!) for her many hours of labour and extreme patience in typing the original manuscript.

In the introduction to Volume 10 of his work, published in 1924/5 by
Dietz Verlag, Arno Holz wrote the following sentence:

> Dieses Werk setze ich wie einen Markstein in die
> Geschichte menschlicher Wortkunst als Grenzscheide
> zweier Zeiten.[1]

Although he himself had no doubts that he had made a greater contribution
to the development of German literature than any other of his contemporaries,[2] Holz nevertheless reconciled himself, albeit somewhat
reluctantly, to the fact that recognition of his achievements by his own
age would always be denied him, the inevitable fate of a man ahead of
his time:

> es handelt sich bei mir...um einen allerseltensten
> Ausnahmefall! Um den eines Menschen, der, auf seinem
> Gebiet, seiner Zeit weit voraus geht, und der grade
> deshalb, seiner abnormen Leistungen wegen, nicht von
> ihr verstanden und begriffen wird![3]

That Holz's critical judgement was not exactly one that tended to under-
value his own importance was a facet of his character of which even he
was aware;[4] and yet recent literary criticism has nevertheless proceeded
very much in the direction in which these two statements point. For if
the publication by Luchterhand in the years 1961 to 1964 of a new seven-
volume collection of Holz's work may be said to have initiated a modest
renaissance in Holz studies and thus to have rescued him, to a certain
extent, from what he considered the relative oblivion imposed upon him
by his own time, then it is also true to say that the focus of much subsequent research has revolved around the premise that Holz's work does
constitute a significant, if not indeed primary, landmark in the development of modern German literature. The "Nachwort" to the Luchterhand
edition, written by one of the editors, Wilhelm Emrich, and entitled
"Arno Holz und die moderne Kunst", is typical of numerous attempts to
re-evaluate Holz's work, the tenor of the argument being exemplified by
Emrich's opening paragraph:

> Es gehört zu den ausweglosen Erfahrungen unserer Zeit,
> daß sie ihre eigene Wahrheit und Wirklichkeit nicht
> begreift und daher gerade diejenigen ihrer Dichter

übersieht oder aus ihrer geistigen Diskussion ausklammert,
die diese Wahrheit und Wirklichkeit kompromißlos gestalten
bzw. selber anschaubar in ihrem Werk repräsentieren. Man
wäre heute, nach einem über sechzigjährigen hoffnungslos
verfahrenen Streit um das Wesen der modernen Kunst, bereits
sehr viel weiter fortgeschritten in der Selbstdeutung
unserer Zeit und ihrer Kunst, hätte man sich ernsthaft
bemüht, die Dichtung und Kunsttheorie von Arno Holz, die
am Anfang unserer sogenannten "modernen" Dichtung steht
und ihre Entwicklung vierzig Jahre lang begleitet hat,
wirklich von Innen her aufzuschließen und in unser
Bewußtsein zu heben.[5]

Emrich closes the essay by locating Holz at the beginning of a "tradition",

which encompasses, amongst others, Marcel Proust, Thomas Mann, James

Joyce, Robert Musil, Hermann Broch and Franz Kafka and concludes:

In diesem großen geschichtlichen Zusammenhang muß das Werk
von Arno Holz gesehen werden. Durch ihn wird es nicht nur
gerechtfertigt, sondern auch in seiner poetischen Schönheit
und Wahrheit gerettet.

In general, I would not wish to disagree with the premise underpinning

both Emrich's argument and many other similar studies;[7] that is to say,

in my opinion the work of Arno Holz is worthy of reconsideration and the

primary aim of such a reconsideration should be the contextual one of

defining his contemporary significance. Where I would disagree, however,

is with the specific authors and modes of writing that recent criticism

has sought to associate with Holz's work. In this respect Emrich's

essay provides a good example, for it is highly questionable whether

Holz's writing reveals any immediately discernible connection with that

of those writers cited by Emrich. His argument suffers, then, from a

double failing: firstly, it merely asserts rather than demonstrates the

connection – and detailed textual comparison is conspicuously absent in

all such studies of Holz's work – and secondly – and arguably as a

consequence of that omission – the authors he wishes to relate to Holz

are not, in fact, those whose work offers the best comparison with

Holz's writing. In a word, therefore, it is the aim of this

study to rectify these two failings in the hope that, by demonstrating

concretely certain literary relationships, we may then be in a position

to define more precisely the real significance of Holz's work for

modern literature.

2

Since the principal difference between other studies of Holz and my own
is a methodological one, it may be as well to identify briefly the basis
of approach.  Firstly, it lays no claim whatsoever to the status of
"Wirkungsgeschichte" in the accepted sense of empirical impact studies.
It is much less the extrinsic approach of documenting reception and
response processes than the intrinsic method, which focusses on the
absolute value of the literary text.  Secondly, although I will adduce
them where relevant, my main concern is not that of the recording of
artistic appreciations. That is to say, it is not my intention to
identify the influence of Holz on other writers:  firstly, because to
prove rather than to impute influence requires historical evidence
beyond the level of textual verification and secondly because, as
Macherey has observed, influence is in any case largely something
objective, existing independently of subjective acknowledgement,[8] so
that often analysis at this level may not transcend the status of
unprovable hypothesis.  For this reason I prefer to the idea of
influence the more cautious term "relationship", because this too is
something objective but something which can be demonstrated and also,
because it can be, but need not be, restricted to examination of the
text.

Holz once commented that "eine Definition..., die mehr umfaßt, als sie
umfassen soll, ist keine"[9] and accordingly it is necessary to define
more precisely what is meant by "relationship",if the term is not to
become so diffuse as to be almost meaningless.  Consequently, I propose
to differentiate between three types or stages of relationship, namely
a parallel, a tendential relationship and a relationship of substantial
identity.  The most arbitrary and least significant of these is a
parallel, for as Käte Hamburger has pointed out, strictly speaking the
term implies that there can be no point of intersection.[10]  By
parallel, therefore, is meant that largely incidental similarities
exist which do not derive, however, from a common starting-point.  A
tendential relationship, on the other hand, is one in which it is
possible to identify a common basis but where the differences, particularly as regards the text, are sufficiently great as severely to
relativise or limit the degree of relationship.  In contrast, a relationship of substantial identity refers to one which evinces a common

starting-point and which, despite inevitable differences, nevertheless develops substantially the core of that starting-point as reflected above all in the text. I hope that the levels of differentiation, which these terms are intended to denote, will become more apparent in the course of comparative analysis. For the moment, I would like to add just one qualification to this scheme: obviously we are not concerned with pure imitation, for there, indeed, one would need to speak of "influence", as was the case with those writers who formed around Holz under the name of the "Saßenbach-Kreis".[11] Clearly, too, no writer of any repute merely reproduces Holz's literary techniques and nothing more, for if that were so, the results would be so meagre or derivative as to be scarcely worthy of separate analysis, as in fact is the case with the "Saßenbach-Kreis". It follows, therefore that any comparison must necessarily be selective in that consideration of the work of other writers must restrict itself solely to discussion of that which is relevant to its relationship to the work of Holz. At the same time such writers should be seen in the main as representative, in the sense that what concerns us are relationships, not so much with particular individuals, as with certain m o d e s of writing.

Basically, there are three areas of Holz's work which I wish to examine: the early political poetry of B u c h  d e r  Z e i t, the prose-work commonly associated with the term "Sekundenstil" and the development of poetic form in his P h a n t a s u s poetry. I do not intend, however, to discuss his dramatic works because they either offer little in terms of relationships (as is the case with D i e S o z i a l a r i s t o k r a t e n or T r a u m u l u s, for example) or merely duplicate developments in other areas (as with D i e F a m i l i e  S e l i c k e or S o n n e n f i n s t e r n i s and I g n o r a b i m u s). Of the three areas under consideration it is true to say that recent studies have concentrated predominantly on Holz's later poetry, the implication being that this is, as it were, his most "modern" work and reveals the greatest affinities with other literature. Hopefully, this study will at least throw into question the validity of this particular emphasis, if not show it to be a view of Holz which substantially underestimates the significance for modern literature of other areas of his work.

# 1. BUCH DER ZEIT

## (i) Holz and the Socialist Tradition

> Holz...(hat) mit einer Reihe von Gedichten, über den
> bloß literarischen Naturalismus hinausgehend, zur
> Entwicklung der sozialistischen Lyrik in Deutschland
> beigetragen.[1]

Ursula Münchow's judgement is scarcely typical of the reception of
Holz's early poetry among the critics.  Indeed, the conventional wisdom
views B u c h   d e r   Z e i t as being wholly representative of the
vituperative nature of the earliest phase of Naturalism.  Regarded
merely as a product of the natural exuberance and rebellion of youth,
the work is thus seen as having little in common with what is held to
be the more mature mood of later Naturalism, whereas aesthetically it is
thought to be extremely derivative and as such to be hardly likely to
have exercised any great influence over succeeding generations.  Nor,
it must be added, has B u c h   d e r   Z e i t   fared any better among
the critics of politically engaged literature, for although most accounts
of the development of "Arbeiterdichtung", for instance, will generally
include a somewhat perfunctory reference to Holz, placing him in the
tradition of Heine, Herwegh or Freiligrath, little attempt has been made
to analyse the positive elements of the poetry or to relate it in its
historical context to the development of a socialist literature[2] in the
twentieth century.  Undeniably there were certain contradictions in Arno
Holz's position at the time of writing and inevitably these were reflected in the poetry.  But if, as regards Holz's contemporaries, we
assent to the basic differentiation between those who were engaged in
what was effectively no more than pseudo-protest and those whose avowed
aim was direct political action,[3] then we must agree with Jost Hermand's
assertion that Holz - or, at any rate, the Holz of B u c h   d e r   Z e i t
- is to be regarded as one of the relatively few writers whom one can
properly categorise as being a genuine political activist.[4]  This much
is apparent from Holz's contributions to M o d e r n e   D i c h t e r-
C h a r a k t e r e,[5] an anthology which, both through the substance of
the poems themselves as well as through the prefaces written by Conradi
and Henckell, sought to expound the new literary credo of the Naturalist

movement. The following year saw the first publication of B u c h
d e r  Z e i t.  L i e d e r  e i n e s  M o d e r n e n with which
Holz hoped to develop the literary and political impact of M o d e r n e
D i c h t e r - C h a r a k t e r e.

The work's main concern is conveyed by its title and expressed, in what
is effectively a programmatic statement, by the introductory poem
"Zum Eingang". Holz bemoans the purely aesthetic preoccupations of
contemporary poetry, regrets its lack of relevance to the modern world
and fears that in his present form the poet will quickly become an
anachronism. The writer, therefore, must discard obsolete classical
themes and confront modern reality in all its forms as the subject
matter of his poetry:

> Nein, mitten nur im Volksgewühl,
> beim Ausblick auf die großen  Städte,
> beim Klang der Telegraphendrähte
> ergießt ins Wort sich mein Gefühl.
>
> Denn süß klingt mir die Melodie
> aus diesen zukunftsschwangern Tönen;
> die Hammer senken sich und dröhnen:
> Schau her, auch dies ist Poesie!

To what extent modernity influences the nature of art is embodied in
the reflections expressed by the poet in "Meine Nachbarschaft", for
the classics provide him with no solution to the material problems he
surveys from his garret. Moreover, philosophy cannot explain why
wealth and poverty exist side by side and the poet's despair at his
felt helplessness thus informs his verse almost willy-nilly:

> Was half mir nun mein "Stückchen Philosoph"? (...)
> Die Armut bettelt um ein Stückchen Brot,
> O Gott, warum dies alles, o warum?
> Wie Zentnerlast dräckt mich die Frage nieder!
> In meinen Reimen geht sie heimlich um
> und ächzt und stöhnt durch meine armen Lieder[7]

In the poem "Die deutschen Denker an die deutschen Dichter" Holz has
moved from the level of this simple experience to a denigration of those
poets who either fail or refuse to come to terms with the immediate
reality, "denn was ihr singt, ist eitel / und was ihr sagt, ist nichts."[8]

The mood of the time, he argues, is one of strife and conflict and
no amount of poetry extolling the beauty and tranquillity of peace can
disguise the fact. Moreover, this is no parochial conflict but the
very struggle for existence, involving the whole of mankind, and the
solution does not lie with a passive belief in ostensibly eternal concepts such as truth, hope and faith. Not words alone but only the
positive action that words might inspire can help alleviate the misery
and iniquity of the present and establish a real and enduring peace. For
Holz this is clearly the supreme task facing the poet and only when he
has acknowledged this, can he feel justified in his activity:

> Und kehrt der Friede wieder
> dereinst nach Kampf und Streit,
> dann singt: Das Lied der Lieder,
> das ist das Lied der Zeit! [9]

Holz was well aware, however, that such a view of art was anathema
to the majority of his contemporaries and in the poem "Tagtäglich" he
anticipates the strictures of his critics. They will, he knows, attempt
to divert him from his concern with social and political matters, arguing
that such a subservience of art to politics can only be to the detri-
ment of poetry and, in any case, dismissing his work as merely reviving
the hapless idealism of 1848. The true purpose of art, they will say,
should be to elevate and to appeal to man's virtues, whereas the sole
effect of the poetry Holz composes is to incite hatred. Holz, however,
remains intransigent for although he knows that it would be financially
more rewarding to follow their advice, he adds caustically that he lacks
the talent to become such a "schwarzweißroten Hofpoeten". [10] To prostitute
his art in this way would be to sacrifice his integrity and instead he
offers the simple message:

> Die Welt, die sich um Liebe dreht,
> weiß auch das Hungertuch zu hassen. [11]

The contrast between the traditional conception of poetry and the
new one Holz proposes is further illuminated by the juxtaposition of
two poems of considerable length to be found in the section of the
work entitled "Großstadt". In "Phantasus" the poet sits alone in his
garret, seeking the creative inspiration that is rendered increasingly

elusive both by his own impoverished circumstances and by the misery
that is everywhere evident in the locality. His sole release is the
poet's imagination, but the illusions fostered there are shattered by
the harsh reality that attends each day-break. Misery, temporarily
concealed by the darkness, is once again revealed:

> die Nacht **verrint** und seufzend tut nun
> das Elend seine Augen auf![12]

His calling he still identifies as the furtherance of beauty and yet he
cannot remain impervious to those whose existence is debased by penury,
a fate which he can see little chance of improving:

> O sprich, wie lang noch soll es dauern,
> das alte Reich der Barbarei?
> Noch stützen tausen dunkle Mauern
> die feste Burg der Tyrannei.[13]

Not even his poetry can offer any real solace, for communication
between men has all but been eliminated by the dehumanising effect of
a life that has reduced man to the level of a machine:

> Denn auch der Mensch wird zur Maschine,
> wenn er mit hungerbleicher Miene
> das alte Tretrad schwingt.[14]

The sole response to his predicament is one of despondency and resignation. Phantasus is clearly not a man of his time, "mein Reich ist
nicht von dieser Welt", but "ein Träumer, ein verlorner Sohn"[15] and
ultimately all he demands of fate is one further night of life in the
service of his art. His tragedy resides in the fact that his laudable
determination to preserve those values he holds dear leaves him unable
to adapt a traditional but, perhaps, now outmoded view of life to suit
the exigencies of the present.

The poem "Ecce Homo" offers an alternative to the response of
"Phantasus", for here the poet is shown as a man of action, who combines his artistic talents with a practical involvement in politics.
He utilises his intellectual powers as the editor of a party newspaper
and in his role as member of parliament. In this account of the poet's
development it is the emergence of a political awareness which constitutes its focal point. Obliged to work in the heat and dirt of the
compositing room of a local newspaper, he quickly comes to recognise

the injustice of his own position as one common to millions of others: "es war sein eigenes Los, / das Los von Millionen"[16]. Thus, he uses the newspaper as the organ of the masses, channelling his revolutionary passion into converting the people through the power of his words and uniting them under the banner of "Die Freiheit und das Recht". Faced with the hostility of the propertied classes, he nevertheless remains secure in the knowledge that no harm can befall him, so long as he continues to represent the masses and does not consider himself superior to them. Indeed, this image of the poet as a man of the people is reinforced throughout the poem and yet his personal vision is no modest one, but prescribes radical social change:

> Ich will ins Morgenrot
> der nahen Zukunft sehn,
> und euer Schrei nach Brot
> wird in Erfüllung gehn.
> Der Knechtschaft Dorngesträuch,
> mein Schwert soll es zerkrachen,
> ich will aus Sklaven euch
> zu freien Menschen machen!
>
> Ich stoße von dem Thron
> das Wörtchen 'mein und dein',
> das brave Volk wird schon
> auf seinem Posten sein.
> Drum tanzt nur! Der Vulkan
> wird bald in Feuer kreißen,
> dann wird es Zahn um Zahn
> und Aug um Aug heißen![17]

These two poems are of further significance in that they probably reflect what was at one time Holz's own predicament. Undoubtedly the experience described in "Phantasus" was one familiar to Holz himself and yet his response to it was not one of despair but that of the resilience and commitment exemplified in "Ecce Homo". He states his position quite unequivocally in the poem "Selbstporträt" with the words "Ich bin nur ein Tendenzpoet!"[18] and although certain critics insist that in B u c h  d e r  Z e i t Holz was only practising social criticism, Jost Hermand is surely correct in defining the underlying intention as, in part at least, a propagandist one.[19] Certainly, at this time, Holz adhered to a radical socialism which, as a letter explaining his later rejection of this political position implies, viewed as essential and inevitable the idea of revolution:

> Seit ich aber diese (i.e. Social Democracy, R.B) und
> namentlich auch einige ihrer Vertreter näher kennen-
> gelernt habe, ist meine Begeisterung, meine kritiklose
> Begeisterung, für den 'Zukunftsstaat' usw. ziemlich
> erkältet. Ich habe einsehen gelernt, daß die
> Weltgeschichte, so sehr sie uns auch oft – scheinbar!
> – vom Gegenteil zu überzeugen versucht, keine Sprünge
> liebt.[20]

Certainly, in the poems themselves the spirit of revolution is everywhere most manifest and most assuredly it is this aspect of Holz's
poetry, and not just the acerbity of his social criticism, which won
for  B u c h  d e r  Z e i t  the lasting admiration of the contemporary
Marxist critic, Franz Mehring.  Thus, for example, "Die deutschen
Denker an die deutschen Dichter" concludes in its last three stanzas
with the call to revolution, unambiguously heralded by the words
"Doch nun genug der Schande, / auf, auf!  und greift zur Wehr,"[21] as
the only way to solve that most basic of struggles, "der Kampf ums
Brot."[22]  Thus, a predominant adjective is that of "rot", on the one
hand, suggesting blood and violence and, on the other, describing
the revolutionary flag, "das rote Banner",[23] as in "An unser Volk!"
The poem "An die 'obern Zehntausend'" continues this mood of defiance,
expressing a plea for solidarity in order to prepare for the violence
that must accompany the end of an era.  This notion of inevitability
is reiterated in "Noch eins!", for the age of the bourgeoisie, it
proclaims, is past and "unser Jahrhundert ist das Jahrhundert der
Revolution",[24] even if that class itself is unaware of the changes
taking place:

> Ihr aber tut, als wäre die Welt
> noch die Welt, die sie ehmals war; (...)
> und keiner merkt wie im Freiheitsbaum
> schon die Knospen gesprungen sind![25]

In these circumstances the masses must intervene in the process of
historical change and the poem ends on the familiar note of the call
to action:

> Dann ruft das Volk: Vermaledeit!
> He, Pulver her und Blei!

>      Die Porzellan= und Reifrockzeit
>      ist Gott sei Dank vorbei![26]

This revolutionary aspect of the poetry is reflected in the extent to
which the activist ideal supersedes all others. Indeed, some poems
actually point to the underlying deception of certain accepted ideals.
One example is "Das Volk an die Fürsten", which argues that the people
have served the nobility for too long, believing themselves instead
to have been pursuing the cause of freedom. Similarly, in "Essetai
Hemar!" we find reiterated the idea that traditional ideals may merely
foster illusions which serve to make the present more tolerable:

>      O Glaube, Liebe, Hoffnung, heilige Dreiheit,
>      Wir dienen dir, und du belohnst uns nie,
>      denn auch noch heut ist unsere deutsche Freiheit
>      nur eine schwarzrotgoldene Phantasie![27]

That is not to say, however, that a belief in ideals should merely
give way to unbridled pessimism and resignation for, as Holz declares
in "Zum Eingang", "sinnlos ist kein Traumgesicht."[28] Man must have an
ideal to strive for, but ideals can only have a genuinely dynamic
quality when they are defined by those whose interests they serve.

One idea that, for Holz, does not fall into that category is
nationalism. This theme occurs infrequently in B u c h   d e r   Z e i t,
but it is undeniable that it does contain certain poems which, in this
connection, appear problematical. One such poem is "Zum zweiten
September" with its generally chauvinistic attitude to other nations
and its uncritical reference to "schwarzweißrot". It has been Holz's
misfortune that subsequent critics have seized on elements such as
these as a vehicle for their own particular preconceptions. In an
article Hermann Ploetz, for example, published in 1934, these verses
are used in order to appropriate Holz for the cause of National
Socialism, the author adding disingenuously that Holz's patriotism
had not been officially recognised because "er galt zu sehr als
Sozialist, um rechtzeitig beliebt zu sein, denn die Summe von
Nationalismus und Sozialismus kannte man noch nicht."[29] Significantly,
however, Ploetz refrains from mentioning the poem immediately preceding

"Zum zweiten September", in which Holz pays rich tribute to France
and contrasts the universality of the struggle for freedom there with
the parochial and narrowly chauvinist nature of German patriotism:

> Doch ihr...verhöhnt mich immer nur,
> ihr biedern Knopflochpatrioten;
> ich weiß, ihr schwärmt nur für Dressur,
> für Kalbsfilet und Schweinepoten.
> Ihr sammelt Lumpen, sammelt Geld
> und träumt von längst verschollnen Tagen;
> was kümmerts euch, wenn durch die Welt
> der Zukunft Nachtigallen schlagen?
>     Ich aber rufe:  Vive la France!
> Honny soit, qui mal y pense![30]

Equally typical is Alfred Klein's assessment of Holz, which appears in
his contribution to L i t e r a t u r   d e r   A r b e i t e r k l a s s e
under the title "Zur Entwicklung der sozialistischen Literatur in Deutschland 1918-33":

> Wenn man weiß, daß Arno Holz nicht nur der Verfasser
> des B u c h   d e r   Z e i t ist, sondern auch an
> einem Gedichtbuch mit dem Titel D e u t s c h e
> W e i s e n mitgearbeitet hat, an einem Buche, das
> durchaus in der Nähe eines extremen deutschen
> Nationalismus steht, und wenn man außerdem weiß,
> daß sich Arno Holz genau in dem Augenblick, wo
> sein Rebellentum auf dem Höhepunkt angelangt ist,
> von der Sozialdemokratie und von der Arbeiterklasse
> abwendet, so kann nicht so sehr überraschen, daß
> er im ersten Weltkrieg mit nationalistischen
> Gedichten hervortritt.[31]

The questions posed by the latter part of this statement, relating to
Holz's withdrawal from Social Democracy, will be considered later, but
suffice it to say that they are more complex than Klein's view would
suggest. Similarly, the accusations concerning the patriotic
flavour of D e u t s c h e   W e i s e n[32] and inferring a chauvinist
consciousness on Holz's part are thrown into doubt not only by the
majority of the poems contained in B u c h   d e r   Z e i t but also
by general statements made by Holz at the time.  Even in 1884, as a
letter of that year makes clear, Holz was disclaiming all responsibility
for this particular aspect of his earlier work:   "Die allenfalls ein
wenig nach der verpönten "Tendenz" schmeckenden patriotischen Lieder

usw. gehören dem Gedanken nach s ä m t l i c h Jerschke an und haben
mir nur die Flüssigkeit ihrer äußeren Form zu danken;..."[33]   Moreover,
a precise analysis of the genesis of B u c h   d e r   Z e i t  reveals
that the poems which appear somewhat ambivalent in the light of
Holz's general attitude towards patriotism, were not in fact added
until later.  The poem in question, "Zum zweiten September", for
example, did not appear until the edition of 1892.  On the evidence of
such poems alone - and Klein's reference to Holz's nationalist poetry,
supposedly written during the First World War, remains a mystery - it
would be difficult to associate the Holz of B u c h   d e r   Z e i t
with the cause of ultra-nationalism.

Yet another indication of Holz's low regard for Wilhelminian nationalism
is to be found in his antipathy to the monarchy.  That Holz remained
irrevocably opposed to what he evidently identified as an inherently au-
thoritarian institution can be seen from a variety of statements
made between 1885 and 1929, the year of his death.  In the letter of
1885, for example, in which he seeks to redefine his position vis-à-vis
socialism, he nevertheless reasserts his allegiance to the principle
of the democratic republic:

> Aber eins bin ich geblieben, was ich war und was ich
> immer sein werde: Antimonarchist! Die Republik ist
> für mich die einzige ideale Staatsform und wenngleich
> ich auch das eingesehen habe: daß unser und wahrschein-
> lich auch die andern heutigen Völker für die wahre,
> ideale Republik noch lange nicht reif sind, so glaube
> ich doch, daß es für jeden rechtlichen Menschen mehr als
> Pflicht ist, für den unendlichen Sieg dieser Ideen, alles
> zu tun, was in seiner Macht steht.[34]

This attitude is reflected in many of the poems in B u c h   d e r
Z e i t  where the rejection of the monarchy is unequivocal and is
supplemented by the poet's prophecy that its power will be swept aside
by the age of revolution.

Holz's hostility to the monarchical state is not unrelated to his
rejection of the prevailing religious values.  For although, in
assessing Holz's overall position, it is necessary to differentiate

between religion as a metaphysics and the Church, its objectification,
there is little doubt that Holz was extremely critical of the supportive
function that institutionalised religion fulfilled in Wilhelminian
Germany. In the "Phantasus" poem he refers at one point to the protective walls that surround "die feste Burg der Tyrannei" and these
he names as "Kasernen, Kirchen und Kanonen".[35] This is the poetical
representation of a view which Holz formulated in a letter as "Von
der politischen zur religiösen Frage ist es nur ein Schritt".[36] That
is to say, the state and the Church are conceived of as an ideological
entity, a view which was by no means the sole prerogative of a radical
socialist perspective as is evidenced by Ernst Troeltsch's essay
"Die Religion im deutschen Staate", in which he discusses the interpenetration of religious and political ideas:

> Die beiden Konfessionellen Parteien (The Centre Party and
> the Conservatives, R.B.) sind Kräfte der Autorität, des
> realen Machtsinnes, dem dynastischen Monarchismus, dem
> militärischen Gehorsamgeiste und der metaphysischen
> Verklärung des Beamtentums innerlich verwandt. Sie sind
> es gerade im Zusammenhang mit ihren religiösen Ideen.
> So ist es natürlich, daß der von Bismarck geschaffene
> Staat heute auf sie in erster Linie sich stützt.[37]

Underpinning Holz's attitude to institutionalised religion in  B u c h
d e r   Z e i t  is his distaste for the disjunction between Christian
doctrine and the action that all too often has been justified in
Christianity's name. For those who question whether such a disjunction
exists, Holz offers the following advice:

> Und wagt sich frömmelnd pfäffische Sophistik an die
> Behauptung, daß mein Vorwurf hinkt, dann schlagt
> nur nach die grause Blutstatistik, die wie ein
> Schandpfuhl wüst zum Himmel stinkt![38]

Similarly, the satirical poem "Religionsphilosophie" attacks the
utilitarian character which religion can assume as justification for
a materialistic, predatory way of life. The poem is in the form of a
prayer, but this suppliant's belief in God extends only as far as the
fulfillment of his material needs:

Doch wenn du filzig bist,
dann dank ich für die Kur;
dann werde ich Atheist
und wähle bebelsch nur!
Dann mag Altar und Thron
nur dreist zusammenbrechen,
dann werd ich deinen Lohn
in Gold und Blut dir blechen![39]

Although Holz is at his most caustic when berating Catholicism - the
Pope is "Der alte Vizegott im Vatikan", his autocracy defended by
"Sankt Peters kahlgeschorne Schmutzkohorte"[40] - he exempts no
institutionalised religion from attack, for organised Christianity
as a whole is "der größte Schwindel dieser Weltgeschichte",[41] the
hypocrisy of which does not go unnoticed by the underprivileged masses:

Doch wer wird heute noch die Hände falten
wer ballt sie lieber nicht zur grimmen Faust,
Wer wird zum Rosenkranz Gebete plappern
wenn er verhungernd hintern Eckstein hockt,
wenn ihm vor Winterfrost die Zähne klappern
wenn ihm das Blut in allen Andern stockt.[42]

However, that Holz's opposition to the Church did not extend to an
atheistic rejection of religion as such can be seen from Holz's letters
of the time and the following passage probably defines most accurately
his overall position:

Aber gerade weil ich so viel "Religion", so viel
wahres Christentum in mir verspüre, bin ich gegen
unsere kirchliche Luderpfaffenwirtschaft! Ich
verwerfe jegliches Dogma! Zwischen mich und mein
Gefühl soll sich nichts, aber auch nichts drängen!
Das wäre wahrhaftig das Letzte, worin ich fremde
Einmischung dulden würde. Ich bin also aus
Religion gegen die Religion! D.h. g e g e n   d i e
R e l i g i o n   a l s   F o r m ![43] (my italics)

When, however, he adds that as yet he has not arrived at a "positive(n)
Weltanschauung" then this illuminates the ambivalence that informs some
of the poetry. For, on the one hand, it would seem that in certain
poems Holz has defused Christianity of a metaphysics to leave only a
humanist religion of love, as exemplified in his de-mythologisation
of Christ: "Für mich ist jener Rabbi Jesus Christ nichts weiter, als -

der erste Sozialist."[44]    Similarly, other poems suggest that religion, the realm of faith, is increasingly being diminished by science, the realm of knowledge:

> Schaut hin, schon hats an den Nagel gehängt
> Purpur und Hermelin
> und sitzt am Studiertisch tief versenkt
> in die heilige Schrift des Darwin.
> Ja, die biblische Spottgeburt aus Lehm
> b e s a n n  sich auf ihre Kraft,
> und die Wahrheit entschleiert ihr Weltsystem
> vor der Königin der Wissenschaft![45]

On the other hand, certain poems clearly affirm the validity and accessibility of religious experience, while another letter of 1885 conveys an almost pantheistic conception of the world, in categories, moreover, that were to remain central to Holz's thought for the following forty-five years:

> "Gott" ist die All-Einheit. Die Natur ist das Medium, durch welches sie uns zum Bewußtsein kommt. Die All-Einheit erfassen, packen und in ein großes  Wort drängen, ist Sache des Dichters. Um seine Mission erfüllen zu können, muß er sich also an die "Natur" halten. Die Natur ist demnach faktisch die p.p. All-Einheit für ihn. Der Natur gerecht werden, der Schöpfung, dem Schöpfer. Wir haben, also bisher glücklich gefunden, daß es nicht drei (!) ewige Grundlagen der Poesie gibt, sondern nur eine:  die Natur! Und ist das Menschenleben, das Völkerleben kein Stück Natur?[46]

This apparent wavering between the poles of atheism and pantheism is just one of the inconsistencies manifested in B u c h  d e r  Z e i t. For although, for the purposes of contextualising Holz's early poetry, the attempt has been made here to distil from the work a co-herent and seemingly unitary philosophy, it must be conceded that, quite apart from wholly irrelevant sections concerned with literary trivia, there are certain poems which quite clearly contradict any such viewpoint. The poem "Erkenne dich selbst" illustrates this ambivalence. While the prevailing tone of the work has demanded that art be revolutionised in order to meet the demands of the time, this poem evinces a degree of pessimism as to the overall usefulness of

16

art as such.  Similarly, the poet in "Rückblick" reaches the conclusion
not that aesthetic precepts need to be redefined, but that all poetry
must necessarily be a self-deception which can serve no useful purpose.
This mood of resignation even impinges on the writer's political prognosti-
cations, for whereas the unmistakable message of the "Vivos voco!"
section is that the people have it within their power to change their
own reality and create a more humane society, this, the most
aggressively optimistic of all the sections in the book, closes nevertheless not with the familiar call to action but on a discordant note of
defeatism:

> Die Zeit ist morsch wie ein Totenbein
> So ist es gewesen, und so wirds sein.[47]

Similarly, the poet's professed solidarity with the oppressed masses
suddenly counts for nothing in "Ein für allemal" as the idealisation of
the free individual reasserts itself:

> doch zehnmal lieber schwarzweißrot
> als mit dem M o b  fraternisieren![48]

The poet who expresses himself here is one who not only rejects the
dictatorship of the few but who also fears the rule of the majority with
its restrictive effect on individuality.  This statement was, of course,
prophetic in that Holz was shortly to be one of the first among the
writers of the Naturalist movement to sever his allegiance to the Social
Democrats, a decision which has undoubtedly played no small part in the
subsequent summary dismissal of B u c h   d e r   Z e i t by certain
critics.  Undeniable though the imperfections and contradictions of
B u c h   d e r   Z e i t  are, such an unqualified rejection nevertheless
constitutes an over-simplification, which does scant justice to the
complexities of the situation that faced those intellectuals who
attempted to unite their literary aims with the cause of socialism.

The superficial view of the relationship between Naturalism and
socialism would tend to see the period of collaboration in two distinct
phases, the 1880s representing a seemingly unproblematical and
productive harmony only to be followed by the visceral antagonisms and

mutual disillusionment of the 1890s. What such a view disregards,
however, is the fact that the tensions and conflicts which were ultimately responsible for the dissolution of the alliance, did not merely
surface in the 1890s but were present all along. That is to say, they
were temporarily concealed by a conjucture of circumstances peculiar to
the 1880s. Of central importance in this respect was the anti-
socialist legislation introduced by Bismarck in 1878, the effect of
which was to impose on the Social Democrat Party a homogeneity and
unity of purpose that it did not in reality possess. Singled out in
this manner as a party regarded as hostile to the national interest,
its survival was thus contingent upon an appearance of solidarity and as
a consequence all overt controversy, whether of a political, ideological
or cultural nature, was precluded in the interest of presenting a united
front. Furthermore, as these laws effectively prohibited direct
political activity, the energies of the working class and the party's
other membership came more and more to be channelled into organisations
of an essentially cultural nature, the most immediate result of which
being the foundation of the "Volksbühnen". Thus, the image arose of
middle-class intellectuals and working-class activists united by common
aims and strategy. In truth, however, as both Georg Fülberth and
Herbert Scherer have adequately documented,[49] this was always a somewhat
insecure and precarious relationship and, indeed, the case of Arno
Holz himself provides an index for the latency of the conflict which was
to emerge so openly at the beginning of the 1890s.

The antinomy that lay at the heart of this conflict was the problem of
reconciling the general individualism of the intellectuals with the
collectivist tenets of Marxism, which, at that time, still underpinned
the political perspective of the SPD. Typical of the attempts to effect
this reconciliation was Heinrich Hart's essay of 1890, "Die Moderne",
which contained the following passage:

> Nur scheinbar zielt der Sozialismus auf Uniformierung, auf
> eine noch drückendere Einzwängung in ein Staatganzes hin.
> Sein Zweck ist es, das Individuum von der Sorge um das
> tägliche Brot zu entlasten, ihm seinen Lebensunterhalt
> unbedingt zu sichern, durch eine gleichmäßige und gerechte

> Verteilung von Arbeit und Arbeitsertrag, die materielle
> Arbeit selbst aber zu erleichtern und zu vermindern. Auf
> diese Weise kann es erreicht werden, daß der Mensch Zeit
> und Kraft gewinnt, sich in höherem Maße als heute der
> Ausbildung alles dessen zu widmen, was ihn wahrhaft
> erst zum Menschen macht.[50]

Underlying this argument is the – for Heinrich Hart – fundamental but
ill-defined idea of "Mensch sein", a theme which, it is true, has in
one form or another dominated literature  both before and since
Naturalism, but which, in itself, is sufficiently abstract as to be
virtually meaningless in political terms. That precisely this concept
should occupy such a predominant position in his political thought is
symptomatic of the extent to which Hart's individualistic idealism
outweighed any pretensions to historical materialism. It is, however,
also symptomatic of the general dilemma confronting the intellectual
at this time[51] and it is surely this dilemma above all to which can be
attributed the inconsistencies in Holz's writing, namely:  the vacilla-
tion between sympathy and revulsion for the oppressed masses, the un-
resolved ambivalence towards religion, the professing of a deterministic
credo and yet the quasi-metaphysical conception of man as a social
being.  Holz himself expressed his basic predicament at the end of
B u c h  d e r  Z e i t :

> Zwar mein Kopf hat sich schon längst
> radikal emanzipiert;
> doch in meinem Herzen blühn noch
> alle Blumen der Romantik![52]

That is to say, Holz experienced this dilemma but was unable to resolve
it.  It is not, however, peculiar to him – rather, one could argue, he
merely recognised its irreconcilability earlier than some of his fellow
intellectuals – for, as Franz Servaes formulated it, it was clearly felt
to be the dilemma of Holz's generation as a whole:

> sich selbst zu finden, ohne in die Einsamkeit zu flüchten –
> sich mit anderen zu vereinigen, ohne sich selbst zu verlieren;
> das ist das Problem, das jeder Schaffende zunächst bei sich zu
> lösen hat, und das im großen Ganzen dann noch einmal gelöst
> werden – muß 'Genosse und Einsiedler sein', wie Bruno Wille sagt[53]

However, an explanation of the rift between the two groups which stopped short at a unilateral apportionment of blame - such as Klaus Scherpe's dogmatic assertion that "der bürgerliche Literat setzt moralisches Engagement an die Stelle politischer Agitation"[54] - would remain but a partial one.[55] For, in truth, the fact that a complete integration of the intellectuals into the party structure was never properly effected was due as much to the open hostility of party members as to the intellectuals' undisguised individualist tendencies. These tensions finally erupted in the year 1891 in the form of a quarrel, which was to seal once and for all the polarisation within the party, between the older national party leaders and a group known as "Die Jungen" - a group which contained, in addition to such figures as Bruno Wille and Paul Ernst, a number of intellectuals associated with the Naturalist writers. August Bebel, the leader of the Social Democratic Party, was himself particularly active in the ensuing debate, the outcome of which was the withdrawal of Wille and his adherents from the SPD and the forma-tion of the "Verein Unabhängiger Sozialisten".[56] Typical of the almost anti-intellectual stance of the party at this time was the debate in the following year concerning the organisation of the "Freie Volksbühnen" (of which Wille was chairman). Osborne quotes Paul Dupont as demanding that a greater control be exercised on the committee by workers and, even more significantly, as questioning the need for any intellectuals at all.[57] Wille was succeeded as chairman of the "Volksbühne" by Franz Mehring, who was explicitly critical of Naturalism as such and favoured instead productions of classical dramatists such as Lessing and Schiller. Given this particular climate, it is not especially difficult to understand how certain intellectuals might have come to the view that ultimately the alliance with socialism and its disciples was counter-productive as far as their artistic development was concerned.

Mehring, in fact, is a significant figure in the context of this debate in that he is fairly representative of the negative attitude amongst socialist critics - both then and since[58] - towards Naturalism. In general, Mehring held to what, from the present position of Marxist

aesthetics,[59] could be considered a static and undialectical conception
of the relationship of ideas to social reality, believing that the
emancipatory effect of any art would necessarily be minimal while
ever it operated within a bourgeois culture. This is the essence
of the argument he espoused in his essay "Kunst und Proletariat"
and to which he adhered in all his critical writings: "Die Kunst darf
ihre Wiedergeburt erst von dem ökonomisch-politischen Siege des
Proletariats erwarten; in seinen Befreiungskampf vermag sie nicht tief
einzugreifen."[60] Mehring's appraisal of Naturalism was, consequently,
particularly negative, for although he conceded that the Naturalists
were indeed extremely critical of certain aspects of bourgeois
society, he insisted that their work reflected only the decline of a
disintegrating system and that their positivism and exclusive preoccupation with their immediate reality denied them any possibility of
mediating artistically the new forms of social organisation that could
develop out of that existing reality:

> (Dagegen) ist die moderne Kunst tief pessimistisch. Sie
> kennt keinen Ausweg aus dem Elend, das sie mit Vorliebe
> schildert. Sie entspringt aus bürgerlichen Kreisen und
> ist der Reflex eines unaufhaltsamen Verfalls, der sich in ihr
> getreu genug widerspiegelt. Sie ist in ihrer Weise...ehrlich
> und wahr;...aber sie ist durchaus pessimistisch in dem
> Sinne, daß sie im Elend der Gegenwart nur das Elend sieht.[61]

This was interpreted at the time as dismissing all art of bourgeois
provenance and, with some justification, Mehring was accused by Paul
Ernst of elevating class-consciousness to the status of being the sole
aesthetic category and of thereby neglecting any consideration of the
social and psychological situation of the individual writer and its
mediation in the work of art.[62]   Fülberth cites one example of this
anti-bourgeois attitude in the campaign of 1908 against Richard Dehmel,
which was instigated by Mehring in his capacity as editor of  D i e
N e u e  Z e i t.   In it he attempted to defuse Dehmel's poetry of any
positive elements, categorising it pejoratively as "soziale bürgerliche
Dichtung", and to refute those members of the SPD who saw in it an
expression of solidarity with the oppressed.[63]   The relationship of the
Naturalists to organised socialism was thus an extremely complex one,

of which a cursory analysis such as this only begins to scratch the
surface, but there is nevertheless considerable justification for
sharing Roy Pascal's view that the waning of the radicalism of Holz
and his contemporaries was at least in part due to this sectarian and
dogmatic rigidity of the Marxists.[64]

This acquires further significance when one considers that contemporary
socialist criticism has, if anything, been even more hostile and that
since the Naturalist period there has been virtually no attempt to
re-evaluate Holz's early work, other than in a purely negative light.
Typical of this trend is the essay by Klein, quoted above, in which
he pursues the quite common and undifferentiating practice of developing
a formula vis-à-vis Naturalism and then applying it without modification
to any writer belonging to the period, as in this case with Holz. Klein's
general thesis runs as follows:

> Die starke nationale Komponente, die im Naturalismus mit
> sozialen Fragestellungen vermischt wird, war von vornherein
> der Gefahr ausgesetzt, in eine nationalistische Tendenz
> umzuschlagen, weil es viele Schriftsteller nicht vermochten,
> ihre Weltanschauung von reaktionären Einflüssen frei zu machen
> und den Traum von einer großen deutschen Zukunft mit den Zielen
> der Arbeiterklasse zu verknüpfen.[65]

As a general statement this is not without a certain validity, relating
as it does to the development out of Naturalism of Neo-romanticism
and "Heimatkunst"; but when Klein attempts to project it on to Holz as
being the supreme example of this assertion, he merely achieves a lack
of differentiation that borders on caricature. As argued earlier,
there is little evidence in Holz's work to substantiate such a claim.
Even when he uses a word such as "Volk" (which appears frequently in
B u c h  d e r  Z e i t), it is clear that he does so in the sense of the
underprivileged masses rather than identifying with the chauvinistic
connotations which the word acquired in the romantic-conservative
ideology of writers such as Lagarde. Furthermore, it is significant
that Holz did not contribute to the general euphoria which surrounded
German's participation in the First World War and which could evoke
from a writer such as, say, Heinrich Lersch – whom socialist critics

have traditionally regarded in a much more favourable light than
Holz - the nationalistic sentiments which inform much of his war
poetry.

On the other hand, an accusation of a quite different order is made
by Armin Kesser in his review of "Arbeiterlyrik":

> Das Anwachsen der sozialdemokratischen Partei, die
> Verteidigung des liberalen Kunstinteresses gegen die
> Wilhelminische Aera...haben den Sozialismus eines
> Arno Holz hervorgebracht...Man formulierte nicht die
> Interessen der revolutionären Klasse, sondern man
> benutzte den "Arbeitsmann", den deklamatorischen
> "Proletar" (Holz) für die Formulierung der eigenen
> Interessen, die eng und kunstzünftlerisch genug waren.[66]

What Holz is charged with here is apparently a form of literary
opportunism, of jumping, as it were, on to the "proletarian bandwagon",
a claim which, given the particular socio-historical circumstances in
which Holz was writing, is only worth consideration in so far as it
illustrates the extent to which the attempt is sometimes made to dis-
credit bourgeois writers.  Whatever the merits and demerits of Mehring's
argumentation, his critique did at least emanate from a consistent
position, it never descended to the level of crude and unsubstantiated
denigration.

In fact, just how little doubt there was at the time in the genuineness
of Holz's socialism can be judged from the reaction B u c h   d e r
Z e i t evoked upon publication.  Indeed, Mehring himself, for all his
strictures, expressly exempted B u c h   d e r   Z e i t   from
criticism, adjudging it to be one of the very few examples of revolutionary
art that Naturalism had produced.[67]  Nor did Mehring's admiration for the
work contradict his general view for in his opinion B u c h   d e r
Z e i t  was almost unique in the way that it transcended what he felt
to be the intrinsic pessimism of Naturalism.  Clearly, what attracted
him to Holz's poetry was "the call to action" so evident in B u c h
d e r   Z e i t which, for Mehring, symbolised "das siegfreudige
Bekenntnis zum Banner einer neuen Welt."[68]  The poetry positively
exuded what, for him, was otherwise totally lacking in the literature of

the Naturalist writers, namely "jenes freudige Kampfelement, das dem klassenbewußten Proletariat das Leben des Lebens ist."[69] The reasons for Mehring's positive evaluation of B u c h   d e r   Z e i t  are further illuminated when related to one of the few other works of the Naturalist period that aroused his enthusiasm, Hauptmann's  D i e  W e b e r.  When, in his remarks on the play,[70] Mehring refers to the weavers' song as forming "das Rückgrat des Schauspiels", then the affinity between the two works becomes obvious.  In "Das Blutgedicht" the weavers are given a simple but articulate assessment of their real situation which serves to galvanise them into action, and although, as stated earlier, at no time did Mehring ever adhere to the utopian view that art can by itself induce a change of political consciousness, it is clearly this aspect of the poems in B u c h   d e r   Z e i t  that Mehring holds in such high regard.

Of significance also is the fact that even in the twentieth century Holz's poems were felt to be relevant to the purposes of political struggle and continued to be published in various journals such as M ä r z  and  D e r   S t u r m.  Similarly, another area where  B u c h  d e r   Z e i t  has continued to exert an influence, perhaps even more so than in the journal, is the anthology.  Along with Dehmel and Henckell Holz's poems were incorporated in a large number of anthologies, which appeared round about the turn of the century and after, and which were clearly aimed at a working-class readership.  Typical of this trend were the two volumes,  S t i m m e n   d e r   F r e i h e i t  of 1899, which has been described as "die reichste Quelle der frühen Arbeiterlyrik",[71] and  V o n   u n t e n   a u f,  which originally appeared in 1911 and was republished in 1928.  Another prominent anthology with which writers in the twenties were undoubtedly familiar was Karl Hoppel's  D a s   E r w a c h e n.   R e v o l u t i o n ä r e  D i c h t u n g e n,  which was first published in 1920 and included such poems by Holz as "Mein Herz schlägt laut", "An unser Volk" and "Das Volk an die Fürsten".  Perhaps the most important of all, however, was the anthology B u c h   d e r   F r e i h e i t  which was commissioned by the SPD itself and appeared in the party's Vorwärts-Verlag in 1893.  Compiled by Henckell it included Holz's poems "Den Franzosenfressern", "Phantasus" and "Weltgeschichte" alongside the poems of early socialist writers such as Jakob Audorf, Ernst Klaar, Rudolf Lavant and August Geib. It has been revised several times since then and an edition appeared as recently as 1956.[72]

Of course, just how broad Holz's audience was and precisely what influence he exerted on other writers through these early poems, is merely a matter for speculation. We do have a certain barometer, however, in the volume compiled by Friedrich Avenarius to commemorate Holz's sixtieth birthday and entitled A r n o   H o l z   u n d   s e i n W e r k.   D e u t s c h e   S t i m m e n   z u   s e i n e m   6 0 G e b u r t s t a g e. Naturally such a work covers a diversity of political sympathies and the spectrum ranges from Hermann Hesse to Kurt Tucholsky, from Gustav Stresemann to Karl Kautsky. Of significance, however, is the fact that, although by the year of publication (1923) the great body of Holz's work was complete, it is for   B u c h d e r   Z e i t, the earliest major work, that Holz is remembered and admired by a great many of the contributors. Karl Kautsky, for instance, refers primarily to the Holz of   B u c h   d e r   Z e i t   in his statement:

> Arno Holz ist mir sehr sympathisch als Mensch wegen seiner Tapferkeit und Bekenntnisfreudigkeit, wegen seines steten Suchens und Ringens nach Höherem. Ich schätze ihn hoch als Dichter, der nicht nur die Form beherrscht, neue Formen schafft, sondern auch ihnen einen bedeutsamen Inhalt gibt.[73]

Particularly illuminating is the statement of Konrad Haenisch, who belonged to the radical Marxist wing of the SPD. He recalls how   B u c h d e r   Z e i t   was a constant companion for him when he was imprisoned for his socialist activities and he goes on to stress the importance which he considered   B u c h   d e r   Z e i t   to have for the working-class movement:

> Saß ich, was erfreulicherweise immerhin für den sehr viel größeren Teil meines Redakteurdaseins galt, nicht im Gefängnis, so tat ich mein Möglichstes, um durch

Besprechungen in der Presse, durch Rezitationen bei
Arbeiterfesten usw. Arno Holz den großen Massen des
deutschen Volks nahe zu bringen.[74]

Statements such as this would surely testify to the relevance of B u c h
d e r  Z e i t to the development of a socialist and working-class
literature. That much subsequent criticism has often sought to diminish
or even deny that relevance must be attributed in part to a basic antipathy in Marxist circles to the bourgeois intellectual as such, an antipathy, moreover, which has persisted throughout the twentieth century
and which, as this brief discussion has shown, even today informs much
of the reception of such literature. It is, then, perhaps hardly surprising that one of the more sympathetic analyses of Holz's position at
this time - and, by extension, that of those writers of Holz's generation
who shared his outlook - should, in fact, come from an intellectual
who could be said to have been in a similar situation in the Weimar
Republic to the one in which Holz found himself in the 1890s. I refer
to Alfred Döblin.

Although not without his criticisms of B u c h  d e r  Z e i t - which
will be discussed in detail in the following chapter - Döblin wrote of
that work in 1930: "Dieser Gedichtband zeigte an: die soziale Gärung
in Deutschland, die Arbeiterbewegung ist in das Blickfeld der
Literatur getreten".[75] For Döblin, however, the crucial question was:
what was it that stifled the "revolutionary advance" so clearly marked
by the work of Holz and other writers of similar persuasion, for, he
remarks, "Die Arbeiterbewegung konnte den Naturalismus gebären, aber
sie konnte ihn nicht am Leben erhalten".[76] In small part, Döblin concedes, this was the fault of the writers themselves, in that like Holz,
despite their political attachments, they still remained in effect
"between the classes", trapped, as Schulz puts it, between the two
fronts of the economically powerful bourgeoisie and the organised labour
movement.[77] The solution for Holz Döblin formulates emphatically as
"Hinwenden zur breiten Volksmasse!",[78] predicated on the realisation
"daß Literatur etwas anderes ist als ein Ding an sich oder ein Lehrfach
der Universität, sondern daß sie Funktion des Volkskörpers ist."[79]

But,Döblin immediately concedes, such a conception of literature, namely
what he terms "eine organisch-funktionelle Beziehung zwischen Volk
und Literatur",[80] simply was not realisable in the historical circumstances in which Holz was then writing and this for reasons which
Döblin identifies as the primary cause of the "defeat" suffered by Holz
and his contemporaries: "das starke deutsche Bürgertum konnte zwar die
Geburt des Naturalismus nicht verhindern, aber es vermochte ihn langsam
zu erdrücken...weil es das Bildungsmonopol hat."[81] Döblin, in fact,
intends this as a general statement but he could also have made mention
of the specific problem that confronted writers such as Holz in the
1880s, namely that of reaching any sort of public at all. The Anti-
Socialist Laws, for example, meant that the Social Democratic press
was illegal. What journals existed were of a generally literary
nature, such as D i e   G e s e l l s c h a f t   or   K r i t i s c h e
W a f f e n g ä n g e, and apart from D i e   N e u e   Z e i t   the
forum for socialist writers was extremely limited. The first volumes
of Karl Henckell's work, for example, were banned in Germany in accordance with the anti-socialist legislation. Not surprisingly this fate
also awaited B u c h   d e r   Z e i t   so that Holz could only get it
published originally through the Swiss firm of Jacob Schabelitz. Such
copies as there were, were circulated in clandestine manner in Germany,
but this state of affairs could scarcely be considered a positive
stimulus to the young writer such as Holz.

In more general terms, however, what Döblin refers to is the problem
which has faced working-class literature from its inception and which
even today continues to confront it, namely the problem of creating
its o w n audience, publication network and means of distribution,
in short, of actually reaching the public to which the literature is
specifically addressed. B u c h   d e r   Z e i t   can thus be seen to
stand at the beginning of a whole tradition of working-class literature
in Germany, to which it is related not only by its very style and tone
but also by the problems which surrounded its development. The lesson
that Döblin drew from his analysis of Holz was the bold message,
"Der unterbrochene Weg von Arno Holz ist weiterzugehen", but history has

shown that the specific solution he proposed, namely "Verbreiterung der Bildungsbasis durch Beseitigung des Bildungsmonopols"[82] was no easy one.

(ii)    B u c h   d e r   Z e i t   a n d   t h e   D e v e l o p m e n t
        o f   "G r o ß s t a d t l y r i k"

B u c h   d e r   Z e i t   must also be considered in one other respect,
namely  in the light of Holz's claim to have been the first writer to
give lyrical expression in any sort of consistent manner to the theme
of the "Großstadt".[1]  As with so many of Holz's statements this assertion
is not without a certain validity but nevertheless needs to be qualified
by viewing the work in its proper historical perspective.

In fact, almost a century before  B u c h   d e r   Z e i t  William
Blake had written poetry which described quite unsparingly the dehumanising
effect of existence in the city.   In contrast the Romantics, although
depicting certain facets of that existence, seemed scarcely aware of en-
countering a qualitatively new reality, their somewhat limited response
to the city being typified by William Wordsworth's famous "London
Sonnet" of 1802:

> Earth has not anything to show more fair:
> This City now doth, like a garment, wear
> The beauty of the morning; silent, bare
> Ships, towers, domes, theatres and temples lie
> Open unto the fields and to sky
> All bright and glittering in the smokeless air
> Ne'er saw I, never felt, a calm so deep![2]

The first poet to develop a more differentiated conception of the city,
however, was Baudelaire with the poems of  L e s   F l e u r s   d u   M a l
and L e   S p l e e n   d e   P a r i s, which he wrote in the 1850s.
Baudelaire was not blind to the Romantic attraction of the metropolis,
but nor was he oblivious to the other side of its character as represented, in particular, by the effects on mankind of technology and
advanced mechanisation.   In giving expression to modern alienation, with
its complementary nostalgia for harmonious experience, Baudelaire - as
Walter Benjamin has well shown[3] - thus stands, as it were, at the
beginning of contemporary European poetry.   From this follows Rimbaud's
call for modernity, the city poems in his I l l u m i n a t i o n s  and
the verse of such writers as Verhaeren and Alexander Blok.

If it is only at this point that German literature, in the form of Holz's B u c h  d e r  Z e i t, has something equatable to offer in the development of this quasi-genre "Großstadtlyrik", then for this there are certain clearly definable reasons.  Correlatively, those self-same reasons help to explain why for the next forty years the theme of industrialisation in general, and the metropolis in particular, were to dominate literature in Germany as in no other contemporary European culture.  Of most significance is the fact that historically the transformation of German society consequent upon industrialisation came at a relatively late point in time.  During the second half of the nineteenth century the German population almost doubled, a dramatic increase that was reflected primarily in the growth of the cities. Just how late this process took place in Germany can be illustrated by the fact that whereas even by 1800 London had nearly one million inhabitants - a figure Paris reached by 1850 - it was not until the turn of the century that Berlin could boast a similar population and then the growth was such that by 1910 this number had doubled to two million.[4]  The impact of this process was naturally all the greater for being telescoped in such a manner.  Consequently, it was the metropolis that constituted the predominant social and cultural experience of the time for, as Pascal explains, it was there, in the great city, "that the industrial and social forces that were creating a new Germany took the tangible shape of a living area in which they impinged on personal experience in countless ways".[5]  Although in Holz's poems of the "Großstadt" section the city as such tends to be in the background, rather than the expressedly focal point that the title would imply, nevertheless what the poems do consistently reflect are these multiple levels of existence and experience that are inherent in the very nature of the metropolis.

As would be perhaps expected, the note of protest so prominent in other parts of B u c h  d e r  Z e i t is also evident.  But here the mood is more muted, the tone less abrasive and overtly polemical.  Description replaces exhortation and the scenes described are often allowed to speak for themselves without the authorial voice being superimposed.  Thus,

the simple montage of the first two poems in the cycle, "Ein Bild" and
"Ein Anderes", makes it unnecessary for the poet actually to articulate
his condemnation of the situation he depicts. The first poem portrays
the stately residence of a prominent member of the nobility. An air
of mourning prevails as the servants move silently about the corridors
so as not to disturb the almost holy aura of the house, a subservience
emulated by the house physician who is a frequent visitor. Even in the
sick-room the luxury is evident, "düstre Teppichpracht, rötliches
Geflimmer", while the invalid herself lies listening to the music of
the fountains outside and satisfies her hunger with "Eis und Himbeer".
The final lines reveal the reason for the anxiety, "Die gnädige Frau hat
heut-Migräne".[6] The scene in the second poem is the top floor of a
tenement block. In stark contrast there is no grand approach to this
residence, just worm-eaten stairs, while within the roof and walls are
riddled with holes. Possessions are limited to the bare essentials for
survival: a piece of black bread, a water jug, a stool and a work-
table. There are no sumptuous curtains, just a board nailed across the
window and amid this austerity a young woman lies prone on a bed of
straw, not simulating illness but on the verge of death. Here there
reigns not the pious calm of the first scene but the tangible silence
of her onlooking children, while the husband can only anaesthetise his
misery with the palliative of alcohol. The "Armenhilfsarzt" finally
arrives only to find the patient already dead. In this image of the
"Vorderhaus/Hinterhaus" dichotomy Holz formulated a simple but credible
symbol of the social inequalities that the metropolis harboured. In
other poems, too, Holz presents further evocations of the squalor and
misery of the penurious, but this is not his exclusive concern, rather
it is just one of a multiplicity of images. There is, however, an
element in these descriptions that borders on the bathetic and Holz
is distinctly more successful when he treats urban phenomena in a more
dispassionate vein. Typical of this is Holz's approach to the themes
of alcoholism and prostitution.

The drunkard and the prostitute figure in a number of poems but in
a matter-of-fact rather than sensationalist manner. Clearly, they are

considered to be just as much a part of the city as the factories and
the tenement blocks and to omit them would be to present but a partial
picture.  Consequently, they are not described from the point of view
of either condescension or revulsion but reveal a synthesis of empathy
and a concern to show reality.  Thus, for example, the poem "Paysage
intime", which relates events of a night spent with a prostitute,
succeeds in conveying both the vulgarity of the experience and the
fact that it is nevertheless an intrinsic part of existence in the
metropolis and generally accepted as such.  The first stanza sets the
scene, the early hours in Berlin.  The street light is not bright
enough for the man to be able to distinguish the woman's face properly
and only when she strikes a match in the brothel corridor does he
realise how unattractive she is.  It is too late to escape, however,
for the door is locked;  the process is both inevitable and irrevocable.
It is clearly a working-class district for he hears the distant sounds
of a bawdy party and on one of the doors he reads the sign
"Baltrutsch Knopfarbeiter".  On entering the woman's room he is a
little surprised to find how cosy it is, with its glowing fire and
clean blinds.  A couple of broken chairs recall memories of previous
none too successful encounters, "Memoiren ohne Worte", and completing his
mental inventory of the prostitute's room with the observation "Auch die
Marmortoilette fehlte selbstverständlich nicht"[7] reveals that despite
his apparent lack of enthusiasm he nevertheless makes a habit of such
visits.  Later when intercourse has duly been mechanically enacted, his
only thoughts are that he must get away and to his embarrassment on
leaving he bumps into the woman delivering newspapers  who, however,
registers no visible response.  With his coat collar buttoned up to
try and preserve anonymity he emerges into the frost and fog of a
winter morning, the final lines succinctly condensing his reaction to
the entire experience:

> "Brrr!" und vor sich selbst aus Ekel
> spie er mitten in die Gosse[8]

The prostitute in Holz's poetry is an incidental figure, significant
above all else for its typicality and thus surely does not emanate from

what Jost Hermand designates as a "Dirnenkult",der alles Erotische
in das Getriebe der rein physiologischen Vorgänge zerrt".[9] Nor, on the
other hand, is it intended as the symbolic representation of the curse
of the metropolis as, for instance, are the prostitutes in Stadler's
"Heimkehr", humiliated and degraded figures who drag their bodies "wie
eine ekle Last in arme Schenken".[10] This is not to say, however, that
Holz remained totally uncritical of an ethos that reduced human beings
to sexual objects but, on the other hand, it is too undifferentiated a
statement to assert, as Roy Pascal does, that the city was of
experiential significance for Holz only in the sense that he could
share the revolutionary protest of the deprived.[11] Such an assessment
would imply a consistency of attitude to the metropolis which is, in
fact, not borne out by the poems of B u c h   d e r   Z e i t.  In
truth, Holz manages to be at once both optimistic and pessimistic in his
relationship to the city and if, as Pascal implies, it is the mood of
pessimism which ultimately prevails, then it must be added that nevertheless this does not amount to an unqualified and total rejection of the
city as such.  That Holz's poetry should paradoxically evince both, on
the one hand, a pronounced anti-urbanism and, on the other, a positive
embracing of the metropolis as the new and undeniable reality, is not
something peculiar to Holz;  rather it is, as Fritz Hofmann argues,[12]
a feature common to Holz's generation, a paradox that endured well into
the twentieth century.  Thus  Becher, for instance, can express his close
identification with the chaotic and revolutionary challenge of the city
in a poem such as "De profundis III", while also being the author of
such apparently unequivocal statements as "Hoffentlich gehen Städte bald
zu Grund.  Hier lebe ich...versunken im Anschauen der kommenden Morgen-
röte".[13] It is above all in this ambivalence towards the city that
B u c h   d e r   Z e i t  reveals an affinity with the "Großstadtlyrik"
that developed both in and after Naturalism.

Undeniably, the attitudes of writers to the city were many and various,
but in one central respect they were united.  For from the unproblematical
affirmation of the city evident in Bölsche to the unmistakable revulsion
and pessimism of Heym or Rilke, they all recognised the great city as

being the decisive and inescapable reality of their time. If for no
other reason, then, B u c h  d e r  Z e i t  deserves attention for
being, along with the anthology M o d e r n e  D i c h t e r -
C h a r a k t e r e, the first work to formulate this awareness pro-
grammatically. The first four stanzas of "Berliner Frühling", for
instance, reiterate the notion that man's concept of beauty has changed
as his surroundings have altered. The old concepts of poetry are effete.
The language of past poetry is no longer adequate for the depiction of
a changed reality and the new muse of poetry resides in a different
milieu, "die blaue Blume ist ihr längst verblüht".[14]  The poet is a
"Kind der Großstadt und der neuen Zeit" and he must use this experience
as his subject matter, for "Auch dies ist Poesie!"[15]  Thus, spring in
the city is just as much an object of poetry and beauty as its reflection in nature; it merely manifests itself in forms other than
"Vogelsang" and "Vollmondschein". It announces itself in the form of
the south wind which howls around the rooftops only to give way to the
sunshine as it breaks through the clouds. Melted snow flows in the
street gutters and these and other signs are perceived by all, even
the poorest beggar. The women discard their long dresses and the
children play noisily in the streets, while in the women's magazines
the new spring fashions from Paris appear for the first time. Not for
months has the city seen such a hubbub of activity for the spring has
made its impression on city life in the form of a medley of sights
and sounds. This mosaic character of the city, compounded of myriad
disparate elements, is hinted at in many of these poems, but one of
the most positive evocations is the poem "Samstagsidyll". This is
essentially a portrait of the city seen from without, for the poet is
in the countryside looking down upon the city, perceiving it as an
entity. The working-day is drawing to a close and as an example of
this healthy vitality he singles out the smith, draped in his protective
apron and with sparks flying from the red-hot iron as he operates the
powerful hammer:

> Hier wars ein Eisenwagen, dort ein Schiff,
> der Schornstein rauchte und der Dampfhahn pfiff,
> und alles drehte sich im alten Gleise.[16]

Meanwhile dusk has fallen and the city acknowledges this with the mellifluous tones of the city bells. As the poet looks down on the city silhouetted against the sky-line, he is struck by its darkness and uncertainty, its amorphous complexity and power. Every now and then the darkness is punctuated by shafts of light from house windows and the reflection of the moonlight on the metal roofs of the factories. This pleasing visual experience is complemented acoustically by the sounds of a "frommer Nachtgesang" from the suburbs, its notes carried to the poet's ears by the warm evening breeze. The poem ends in a vision of complete harmony, the poet in total accord with the surrounding beauty of the city and its poetry which, the poet claims in a final flush of optimism, "... speist die Armen, und (sie) stärkt die Schwachen / sie kann die Erde uns zum Himmel machen".[17] This comforting image is not dissimilar to that evoked by Ernst Stadler in "Dämmerung in der Stadt". From the same perspective as the Holz poem the individual houses appear as ships, collectively forming the great ocean, "Meer", which is the city:

> Die Häuser sind im Grau
> durch das die ersten Lichter branden
> Wie Rümpfe großer   Schiffe
> die im Meer die Nachtsignale hissen.[18]

Recalling Holz's "frommer Nachtsgesang" the sea is calmed with "lindem Schmeichelwort...und der Süße alter Wiegenlieder" and the final image of the city is that of a "lichtgepflügten Hafen", a place of sanctuary and repose. Indeed, the positive attitude to the city asserts itself sufficiently in Stadler's work for Helmut Uhlig to be able to describe him as a poet "der...in den wachsenden Großstädten, in den allmählich aufkommenden neuen Lebensformen, das Schöne, das Große,   das Gewaltige sieht",[19] which again would suggest certain parallels with Holz.

Holz's optimism, however, never reaches the adulatory heights of August Endell, who in his D i e   S c h ö n h e i t   d e r   g r o ß e n S t a d t   would even extol the privation and physical ills of industrial labour. Much closer to Holz's conception is the anthology   I m s t e i n e r n e n   M e e r,   in the introduction to which the editors

Oskar Hübner and Johannes Moegelin quote Holz's "Auch dies ist Poesie"[20] to endorse their assertion that nature can no longer serve as the exclusive or even primary inspiration for modern poetry. The anthology includes six of Holz's own poems but his significance would appear to extend beyond his individual contribution, for some of the other poems appear decidedly derivative. By far the most positive attitude to the city, however, was that adopted by the "Werkleute auf Haus Nyland" as expressed in the poems of Josef Winckler, collected under the title of E i s e r n e   S o n n e t t e,  and in their programme of 1912 which embraces the following sentiments:

> Nicht sentimentales Bedauern erweckt in uns der Rauch der Schlote und der Hochöfen, die menschenverschlingende Großstadt ...wir grüßen die tausend Kräfte, die an der Arbeit sind, um unsere Zeit von sich selbst zu erlösen...Einer atzenden Verneinung (of the city and technology, R.B.) setzen wir unsere entschlossene Bejahung entgegen, unseren unbesieglichen Zukunftsglauben.[21]

The poetry reflects this euphoric tone so that the debilitating effects of mechanisation, squalor and poverty, the concomitants of rapid industrialisation, are in these verses scarcely acknowledged as a valid reality.

For Holz, however, the city was far too complex a phenomenon to allow of such unproblematical affirmation. Indeed, even if there were in B u c h   d e r   Z e i t  no explicit condemnation of certain facets of the city, there would still be sufficient evidence of an implicit kind to foster this feeling of ambivalence and to suggest that Holz's admiration for the city was less than absolute. One particular pertinent example is the way Holz conceives of the relationship of the city and nature. For although, as we have seen, certain poems proclaim that the city has a beauty of its own particular kind, in other poems there is nevertheless a tendency to identify beauty with nature and the countryside. In "Nachtstück", for example, the poet insists that even in winter, despite the cold and the poverty, the city still possesses a degree of beauty. But when he goes on to delineate that beauty in terms of stars, trees, rivers etc., it is clear that this

is still a conventional conception of beauty which in no way necessarily
relates to the essence of the metropolis. The poem "Großstadtmorgen"
portrays this at its most explicit. It shows the poet walking along
Friedrichstraße on his way home in the early hours of the morning and
describes the thoughts that the scene arouses in him. He does not
recoil from specifying the vulgarities that Friedrichstraße has to
offer - the drunks and the whores - but he does so dispassionately and
not in a language suffused with revulsion. Nevertheless, the poet is
aware that something is on his mind and suddenly the mood changes.
Gradually his thoughts wander from the immediate present and in a dream
he is transported from the mundane surroundings of Friedrichstraße to
a verdant hill in the countryside. Bathed in sunlight he is galloping
on horseback through the fields, consuming voraciously nature's many
treasures. But the dream is an ephemeral reality and he is jolted
back to the austerity of Friedrichstraße by the freezing cold and the
piteous cry of a beggar selling matches. Elsewhere in B u c h   d e r
Z e i t Holz refers quite frequently to the idea of the city walls
and the city gates - in "Berliner Frühling", for instance, we read:
"Doch **drauß** vorm Stadttor rauscht es in den Bäumen"[22] - and this would
seem to represent both a real and symbolic divide between two worlds,
between two different realities. Certainly, it would also appear that
whereas nature penetrates into the city, the effects of industrialisation
are restricted to within the city boundaries. This is similarly the
case in the poems of I m   s t e i n e r n e n   M e e r, for despite
the editors' categorical claim that nature is no longer the main
source of poetic inspiration, it is nevertheless in nature that beauty
would appear to reside.

Stadler occasionally eschews even this minimal differentiation and a
poem such as "Kleine Stadt" suggests that city and countryside blend
and merge together harmoniously:

> Die vielen kleinen Gassen,
> die die langgestreckte Hauptstraße überqueren,
> Laufen alle ins Grüne.
> Überall fängt Land an.
> Überall strömt Himmel ein und Geruch von Bäumen

und der starke Duft der Äcker
Überall erlischt die Stadt
in einer feuchten Herrlichkeit von Wiesen.[23]

The emphatic repetition of "überall" suggests that the city is so
embedded in nature as almost to preclude the possibility of looking
upon it as a separate entity.  In contrast, Heym effectively inverts
this relationship, for clearly in his poetry it is the city which
impinges on the countryside, industry and technology, which encroach
upon and eventually suffocate the realm of nature.  Typically, therefore, the image of the sea, "Meer", used so positively in Holz and
Stadler, assumes negative connotations in Heym's work, for as Heinz
Rölleke argues,[24] it signifies above all the elimination of any
city / countryside dichotomy in that the immeasurability and unres-
trainable power of the ocean is for Heym paralleled in the vastness and
irresistible growth of the metropolis.

As well as the city/nature dichtomy there is another factor which would
tend to relativise Holz's attitude to the city.  That is to say, Holz
does not imbue it with one definite character, rather it assumes various
guises.  Thus, as we have seen already, nature itself, in the form of
the seasons, makes a substantial difference to the character of the
city.  Winter exacerbates its negative aspects, spring and summer
emphasise the positive.  Holz often makes a similar differentiation
between night and day, as can be seen from the "Phantasus" poem in
particular.  Here night appears as the comforting guardian against
the harshness of reality, for then it is that man can escape from his
alienated existence either into the pleasures of the urban night-life
or into his own dreams ("die Nacht verrinnt, der Traumgott ruht nun").
As in "Samstagsidyll" it is at night that the city can attain a tran-
quility and splendour comparable to that evident in nature, but with
the dawn that tranquillity is disturbed.  Life takes its inevitable
course once more and misery, temporarily concealed by the darkness, is
revealed again ("die Nacht verrinnt und seufzend tut nun / das Elend
seine Augen auf").[25]  The morning is a curse to the worker for it
means toil and hardship until he can again find respite in the night.

For other writers, who experienced the city as a more oppressive reality
than Holz, the night offers no such refuge. In Engelke's "Die Fabrik"
he shows that the industrial city does not recognise nature's laws,
night and day are one and the same:

> Tag und Nacht:  Lärm und Dampf
> Immer Arbeit, immer Kampf.[26]

In fact, if anything, the night is felt to intensify the oppression of
the city; it seems lifeless, its inhabitants "erstarrt im Stadtnacht-
Schweigen".[27] For Heym, too, darkness is a prevailing mood, serving
only to underline the inherently apocalyptical nature of the city as
typified by the opening of "Stadt der Qual": "Ewige Dunkelheit hängt
über mir."[28]

These various dichotomies – the metropolis and the countryside, the
city by day and the city by night – are, as stated, symptomatic in
Holz's B u c h   d e r   Z e i t of a basic ambivalence towards the
city. Often apparently contradictory viewpoints will be expressed
within the same poem. The crucial thing, however, is that this ambivalence both derives from and is compounded by the fact that the city
never appears absolutely before the reader but is always mediated
through the perspective of the lyrical self. The focal point of the
poem is not so much the metropolis itself as the ego depicting what
surrounds it.[29] The images of the city, therefore, are almost without
exception contingent upon the mood of the speaker and his emotional
responses. Thus, for instance, the idyllic evocation of life in
"Samstagsidyll" is relativised by the fact that here the city is viewed
through the eyes of the poet basking in the warmth of an idyllic love
relationship, as epitomised by the closing line "nicht wahr mein
Herz, das Leben ist doch schön",[30] a remark which only tangentially
relates to the great city as such. Thus, the city is not evoked
directly but indirectly and so changes its character according to the
situation and mood of the experiencing subject. This is demonstrated
in extreme form in the two poems, "Osterbitte"[31] and "Meine Nachbarschaft".
The former shows the transformation of the poet from a state of almost
suicidal depression to one of metaphysical rebirth. Significantly, the

winter / summer and city / countryside dualisms are particularly in
evidence and the poet is rescued from his melancholy when, looking
down from outside the city, the pealing of the Easter bells reminds him
that the misery of winter is past.  This is sufficient to banish all
nihilistic notions and convince him that life and the city have after
all much to offer.  In "Meine Nachbarschaft", on the other hand, the
poem still revolves around the relationship of the poet to his
surroundings but the pattern is reversed.  Initially he seems to
suggest that oppressive though certain aspects of his environment are,
he can nevertheless derive considerable consolation and self-fulfilment
through his writing.  But later in the poem he says that it does not
really help being a philosopher.  It is not just a question of his
surroundings disturbing him in his creative work, for tremendous
metaphysical questions are involved.  What, he asks, can he, the
writer, do in such conditions?  At the end of this poem, therefore,
there is apparently a change of position, for he says that his environment cannot be compensated for by his work, but on the contrary pre-
empts his writing.  It is clear, therefore, that no definitive statement vis-à-vis the city can be extracted from these poems.  This point
is reinforced all the more if comparison is made with Georg Heym.
The latter's view of the city is almost monolithically negative and it
is surely no coincidence that in Heym's poetry the city is evoked more
directly and the form of the reflecting self is rarely deployed.  In
Holz's poetry, however, the view of the metropolis is determined by
the mediating ego and it is to this above all that the mood of ambivalence is attributable.

If, as argued, Holz was at times both optimistic and equivocal in his
attitude to the metropolis, then it must be added that certain poems
also reveal a pronounced pessimism.  Holz's social conscience was too
strong for him to ignore the social misery and poverty attendant
on industrialisation.  But whereas in other parts of B u c h   d e r
Z e i t   he was able to rationalise this in his belief that such
misery could be overcome by the solidarity of the masses and a re-
structuring of society, in the "Großstadt" cycle this optimism tends

to give way to an anti-urbanism which would see these evils as being
basically endemic in the great city. This is particularly evident in the
"Phantasus" poems which centre on the apocalyptical image of the city
rendered by the lines:

> Ja, jede Großstadt ist ein Zwinger,
> der rot von Blut und Tränen dampft.[32]

Emphasis is laid in these verses on the coldness of the city, a cold
which is experienced not only as a physical sensation but above all as
a state of mind and which no amount of sunlight can counteract. Ultimately this induces such a state of helplessness and resignation that
all the individual can do is to curse the city which denies him all
possible escape. Crucial to this description is the humiliation the
city inflicts on man, a sense of degradation that is underlined by
Holz's frequent use of the concept "vertiert"[33] – man dehumanised and
rendered bestial, caged and trapped in his primitive surroundings,
devoid of freedom and volition and bound to the inexorable law of survival. The final stage in this process of dehumanisation deprives man
of even these animal instincts, reducing him solely to the level of
automaton:

> Denn auch der Mensch wird zur Maschine,
> wenn er mit hungerbleicher Miene
> das alte Tretrad schwingt.

The factory completes the process by fragmenting and destroying his
mental powers:

> Das ewige Rädern der Maschinen
> hat mir das Hirn zerpflückt, zerstückt.[34]

It is indicative of the extent of the prevailing pessimism in the
"Phantasus" poems that only in death is there envisaged any escape from
such a crushing reality. This pessimistic strain in Holz's poetry
assumes greater relevance when it is remembered that some German
Naturalists came positively to fear the city. Bölsche's attitude at
the turn of the century, for example, is an unmistakable echo of the
sentiments expressed in certain of Holz's poems:

> (Ich) bin heute nicht nur der Weltstadt entfremdet, sondern

> ich meine auch, daß sie ein wahrer Kraken ist, der
> an unserem geistigen Leben saugt. Je höher die Etagen
> unter den Rauchhimmel steigen, desto flächer wird die
> Gemütsbildung und desto mehr keucht jede Geistesäußerung
> vom Treppensteigen. Der Sinn geht verloren für die
> feinen Werte in Natur und Kunst, also gerade für das,
> worin die Entwicklung ansteigt.[36]

Indeed, these precise sentiments are given poetic expression in the
opening verses of Holz's work:

> Weit hinter mir liegt die Millionenstadt
> ihr wildes Leben hielt mich wild umkettet,
> nun aber hab ich, ihrer Wüste satt,
> in meine grüne Heimat mich gerettet![37]

B u c h  d e r  Z e i t  thus reveals that even at its inception German
Naturalism, although committed to the modern reality of the metropolis,
nevertheless betrays a latent anti-urbanism that prefigures the unequivocal rejection of the city by the Expressionists.

On the evidence of Holz's "Großstadt" cycle, therefore, it would be
difficult to deny  B u c h  d e r  Z e i t  a place in the tradition of
"Großstadtlyrik". Moreover, I would argue that its significance is more
than just a chronological one, for in respect to both the general positions it adopts vis-à-vis the metropolis and the themes and motifs it
develops which express those positions, Holz's cycle of poems reveals
definite affinities with later poetry. However, any evaluation would
remain incomplete without discussion of that element of Holz's early
poetry which has done most to limit its overall significance, namely
its form.

Reference has already been made to the great limitations inherent in the
perspective of the lyrical self. Essentially this restricted the potentially vast panorama of the metropolis to the subjectivised reflections of an individual - in most cases, a poet - which had important
repercussions on the content of the poems. Holz gives expression to
the individual's sense of isolation and mood of despair, but nowhere
in  B u c h  d e r  Z e i t  do we find conveyed the alienating

42

disorientation so peculiar to the modern city. Typical of this narrow
perspective is the fact that Holz rarely uses the image of the crowd,
the amorphous mass of anonymous individuals brought together by urbani-
sation and technology. Where people appear in profusion it is merely
to denote the multiplicity of activity; nowhere does one sense the
presence of the crowd as the unstructured welter of unhappy consciousnesses that can be found in, say, Baudelaire. It is this sense of
the confusing heterogeneity and felt purposelessness of mass existence
in the city that is conveyed so forcibly in Georg Heym's poetry. It
expresses the conviction that man's relationship to the city is not of
his own determining but rather that he is consumed and absorbed by it
to such an extent that he is no longer distinguishable from it. Consequently, the perspective of the reflecting self is of little concern
to him. Moreover, where Heym does introduce individual figures, they
tend to be, as Rölleke observes,[38] beggars, alcoholics, prostitutes,
cripples, invalids, lunatics – unconsoling existences from life's
periphery representing in extreme form the response to a reality beyond
comprehension.

The stylistic deficiencies of B u c h   d e r   Z e i t, however, extend
beyond the narrowness of the perspective. For in this early work, the
stress had fallen on the necessity to modernise content and had neglected
any proper consideration of a concomitant transformation of form. This
resulted in a sharp disparity between form and content, a weakness to
which Holz himself later readily admitted[39] and which was succinctly
summed up by Döblin as "revolutionärer Inhalt, alte, abgelebte Form."[40]
Indeed, the very title of the work, with its undoubted allusion to
Heine's B u c h   d e r   L i e d e r, in a sense corroborates Helmut
Scheuer's view of what Holz was attempting:

> Einerseits blickt er schon nach den neuen literarischen
> Sujets, aber andererseits will er auch nicht alle Brücken
> zur anerkannten Lyrik der Gegenwart abbrechen. Er glaubt
> diese Pole sogar verbinden zu können.[41]

A poem such as "Mein Nachbarschaft" provides a good illustration of the
problems involved in this attempted synthesis of modern content and

traditional form. The poem focuses on the relationship of the poet to his environment, underlying which is the basic assumption of B u c h d e r Z e i t that revolutionary social changes have rendered anachronistic the old conception of the poet. Ironically, however, these thoughts are expressed in a language that recalls only too readily precisely those poets from whom Holz wished to dissociate himself. Lines such as the following, for example:

> und all mein Tun ist nur ein wenig Schreiben

or

> bis endlich, endlich es auch mir gelang,
> was ich gefühlt zum Wohllaut zu gestalten.[42]

Similarly, the poet also has a propensity for words with religious associations, at one point comparing writing with a religious act. However, if the poet's intention is to question the modern world, then classical metaphors and quasi-religious vocabulary hardly provide the appropriately modern vehicle.

Two other examples illustrate a further problem. The poem "Deutsche Literaturballade" begins with the line "Kennt ihr das Lied, das alte Lied",[43] which is undoubtedly intended as a parody of Goethe's "Mignon". Similarly, the poem "Religionsphilosphie" is constructed in the form of a prayer:

> O Herr, aus tiefer Not
> schrei ich zu dir hinauf:
> Gib mir mein täglich Brot
> und etwas Butter drauf!

The satiric effect behind such use of quotation, however, is considerably diminished by the fact that elsewhere in B u c h d e r Z e i t Holz himself frequently deploys uncritically the very style which he here seeks to parody.

A further characteristic of this poetry which makes it seem particularly epigonic is Holz's rigid adherence to traditional rhyme, rhythm and stanza pattern. That is to say, not only does the choice of language reflect an inappropriately traditional propensity for the rhetorical, but also that language itself is then structured within a more or less

conventional poetic framework. This, too, could be seen to have had
serious repercussions on later poetry, for the pattern established in
B u c h   d e r   Z e i t   remained more or less standard for the
following two decades[45] and, in many cases, with even worse consequences
for the quality of the poetry. The anthology I m   s t e i n e r n e n
M e e r  suffered particularly from this overemphasis on content, some
of the contributors apparently being blissfully unaware that even
though a poem may be suffused with vocabulary from the industrial
world, that in itself may not be sufficient to render it modern.

However, not all of Holz's "Großstadt" poems are straitjacketed by
conventional form. Indeed, some even evidence the attempt to develop
a more original and personal style, whether it be with the neologisms
of "Auf der Straße" or a poem like "Ninon" which dispenses with rhyme
in favour of prose-like, staccato statements. Moreover, where Holz
does begin to reveal some awareness of the importance of form, then
arguably he is at his most successful. For this reason it would seem
to me that the poems "Großstadtmorgen" and "Paysage intime" are more
effective than most, for the dispassionate and non-lyrical tone is much
more appropriate than the rhetorical style of the majority of the
other poems. "Großstadtmorgen", although still conventional in its use
of rhyme, does at least break out of the formalised stanza pattern
deployed elsewhere and occasionally varies the rhythm to good effect,
the rupture of the final line "Mich...fröstelte",[46] for example, providing a jarring reminder to the reader of the actual reality on which
the poem centres. More than this, however, the poem operates at a
wholly different level linguistically, for no longer is it the impassioned
and somewhat bathetic outcry of the poet that addresses the reader.
Here the picture is presented through the eyes of a slightly cynical
Berliner and as a result is permeated with colloquial, slangy language
which in lines such as

> Halb zwei. Mechanisch sah ich nach der Uhr.
> An was ich dachte, weiß der Kuckuck nur[47]

at least begins to convey in an appropriate tone the mundane and everyday existence of Berlin. Similarly, the cry of the beggar selling

matches not only disrupts the rhythm but at the same time represents
the actual reality of Friedrichstraße interrupting the man's ephemeral
escape into dream.  This quasi-reportage style is also effectively
used in "Paysage intime", where the description of a man's experience
with a prostitute is punctuated by fragments of their perfunctory
conversation and by his thoughts at the time:

> 'Kommst du wieder?'  Gott sei Dank!
> Jetzt nur noch den Rock und −
> 'Kommst du wieder?  − jetzt 'Adieu!''[48]

In addition, Holz for once eschews the use of rhyme, the rhythms are
less repetitious and insistent and the stanza lengths less rigid, all
of which makes for a much less lyrical description and provides one of
the few examples in which form and content approach anything like
compatibility.

In truth, however, it was only with the Expressionists − and in
particular with the striking, eruptive and original images of Georg Heym
− that the lyric of the metropolis acquired a form that corresponded to
the modernity of its content.[49]  The achievement of Holz's  B u c h
d e r  Z e i t  and Naturalism in general was to effect the actual
revolutionisation of the content and thereby to provide a stimulus for
those writers who were later to change the form.  Without further
qualification, however, such a judgement would suggest that that achievement was essentially an historically limited one and thus prompt the
conclusion at which Schulz, for example, arrives:  namely, that the
status of  B u c h  d e r  Z e i t  in literary terms is solely that of
an historical document,[50] i.e. without significance beyond the context
of its own time.  I would argue, however, that the history of German
literature suggests otherwise.  The relationship between literature and
social reality has in Germany always been a rather uneasy one and
German Naturalism is a case in point.  For according to one view, as
represented, for example, by Jost Hermand, the impetus underlying
Naturalism did not of its own accord simply wane towards the end of the
century as is commonly assumed;  rather its development was, as it
were, broken off or interrupted.[51]  As we have already seen, this idea

that the Naturalists had set themselves tasks which they had been
unable to complete and which, therefore, it was incumbent on later
generations to take up, is one which inspired an important debate in
the 1920s and which led Döblin, for example, in referring specifically
to Holz, to proclaim his own time to be the age of Naturalism.[52]
Significantly, too, when this debate surfaces yet again in the 1960s,
the Naturalist writer who comes to the forefront of literary
discussion is Arno Holz. That is to say, the acknowledged need for
the involvement of imaginative literature in a constantly changing
social reality has been a characteristic of the development of
German literature in this century and if we agree with Pascal's view
that "the modern movement in literature arose from the will to make
art serve the purpose of changing the social world, or at least the
ethical consciousness of men",[53] then Naturalism and B u c h  d e r
Z e i t's radical significance within that movement can be seen to
have had an enduring relevance for the orientation of modern German
literature as a whole.

## 2. CONSEQUENTIAL NATURALISM

Apart from B u c h  d e r  Z e i t  Holz's literary contribution to
Naturalism was, in purely quantitative terms, a relatively minor one.
It consisted of a volume of sketches, N e u e  G l e i s e[1] (1892),
which is commonly associated with a style of prose-writing known alternatively as "consequential Naturalism" or "Sekundenstil" and a work on
aesthetics, D i e  K u n s t.  I h r  W e s e n  u n d  i h r e
G e s e t z e[2] (1891), which, in attempting to define the relationship
between art and nature, provided in the first instance the theoretical
underpinning of this new literary style.  This small body of material
has nevertheless given rise to an acute polarisation in terms of its
critical reception.  On the one hand, the traditional view, ranging from
some of Holz's contemporaries such as Heinrich Hart to modern critics
like Klaus Scherpe and Günther Mahal, sees Holz's writings as representing an extreme verism that aims at a strictly mimetic reproduction of
reality.  Thus, Wilpert's S a c h w ö r t e r b u c h  d e r
L i t e r a t u r  describes Holz's method as essentially "Wirklichkeit
kopierende(n) Technik".[3]  On the other hand, however, an alternative
view has recently gained currency which denies Holz any restrictive,
purely imitative aim and which locates the major achievement of his
writing not in any drive towards objectivity but, on the contrary, in
the way his work opened up new possibilities for a differentiated
representation of complex subjectivity.

Before considering these two views and their implications in detail,
however, it is as well to try and discover the source of this interpretational divergency, for which, I would argue, there are two explanations.
The first concerns Holz's theoretical pronouncements, since their
reception parallels in many ways the dichotomy of views already
described.  Hence Marianne Kesting can call Holz's "Kunstgesetz" "silly",[4]
whereas Wilhelm Emrich insists that it has been misunderstood and that
it is, in fact, much more elastic and subtle than has been commonly
assumed.[5]  Roy Pascal explains this by arguing that Holz's writing is so
ambiguous and inconsistent that it easily allows of various, even

antithetical interpretations.[6] This is certainly true but more crucial, in my opinion, is the failure to observe fully the relationship between theory and literary practice. Thus, on the one hand, there is the tendency for critics merely to extrapolate from the creative writing and either to dismiss Holz's theory as ill-conceived or to reduce it to the level of a platitudinous, mathematical formula without discussing its possible, wider ramifications; while, at the other extreme, writers like Emrich focus on the theory, abstracting from it as if it were a totally coherent, uncontradictory entity, rather than counterposing it to the prose-writing which derives from it. Nor, in my view, is this relationship grasped in its entirety if it is limited merely to the assertion of the identity or non-identity of theory and practice. That is to say, it would be as undifferentiated to argue that Holz's prose-writing bears little resemblance to his theoretical propositions[7] as it would be to see in those prose-works merely the simple realisation of his aesthetic theory. Essentially – and this is, I think, the second explanation for the emergence of contrary interpretations of Holz's work – this is because the ambiguity that Pascal identifies in the theoretical writings is also present in Holz's prose-works. Or, to put it another way, there are stylistic tendencies in Holz's sketches which simultaneously point in differing directions. More concretely, therefore, it is necessary to draw a distinction that has as yet nowhere been made, between the types of sketch in the N e u e  G l e i s e volume: the first category, which comprises "Die papierne Passion",[8] "Ein Tod" and "Die Familie Selicke", corresponds to the tendency towards a veristic reproduction of empirical reality, while the second category, consisting of "Papa Hamlet" and "Der erste Schultag", although deploying a similar basic representational method, contains techniques not evident in the other sketches which ultimately lead in a direction different from that of purely mimetic realism. For the sake of convenience these two categories will from now on be referred to as, respectively, the objectivist and the subjectivist tendency, since this distinction, both in respect to the sketches themselves and the literary developments they suggest, will hopefully be substantiated and elaborated in the course of the following analysis.

(i)   T h e   O b j e c t i v i s t   M o d e


Attention has already been drawn to the necessity of seeing the relationship between Holz's theoretical statements and his literary practice.
The view advanced by some critics [1] that the main motivation for developing his theory was Holz's **constant** opportunist desire to make a name for
himself, however much it might reveal of Holz's enigmatic personality,
nevertheless tells us precious little about the nature of that relationship.  It seems appropriate, therefore, to provide first of all a brief
exposition of Holz's aesthetic writings, if for no other reason than
that Holz himself claimed that his creative writing developed from his
theory and not vice versa:  "(ich) modelte mein Werk nach meiner
anfänglich von mir 'intuitiv' aufgestellten und dann später mir von mir
selbst bewiesenen 'Theorie'". [2]

In fact, it is not unreasonable to assume that the first impulse for
Holz's theoretical reflections was the idea that theorising the problems
he encountered in literary production would actually help improve his
creative writing. [3]  Holz himself relates how in 1887 he had begun an
autobiographical novel, entitled G o l d e n e   Z e i t e n, and how
a dissatisfaction with the work in general, and in particular  his
inability to define the source of the charm that certain of his sentences
exerted over him, caused him to turn instead to aesthetic studies.  There
he found the second source of his theoretical interest, Zola's conception
of the work of art as "un coin de la nature vu à travers un tempérament".
To Holz this formulation appeared a trivial commonplace.  Similarly, he
dismissed Zola's concept of the "experimental novel" arguing that whereas
in science the experiment is conducted in reality, in literature it only
takes place in the novelist's head and that "Ein Experiment, das sich
bloß im Hirne des Experimentators abspielt, ist eben einfach gar kein
Experiment, und wenn es auch zehn Mal fixiert wird." [4]  Although he rejected this method of writing as still being essentially embedded in
the subjective imagination, Holz nevertheless reacted positively to the
idea of empirical analysis as a literary process that Zola's juxtaposition
of literature and science implied.  In order to achieve the theoretical

clarity which, in his view, Zola's ideas lacked, Holz turned, as the
second stage of his studies, to the work of the English and French
positivists such as Mill, Spencer, Comte and Taine.

As his basic premise Holz borrowed from Mill the notion that "Es  ist
ein Gesetz, daß jedes Ding ein Gesetz hat",[5] deducing from this that art
too must be subject to a definable law of development.  A little further
on in the argumentation Holz adumbrates the idea of the social determinacy
of art as a possible basis for that law  when he asserts "daß die Kunst
als ein jedesmaliger Teilzustand des jedesmaligen Gesamtzustandes der
Gesellschaft zu diesem in einem Abhängigkeitsverhältnis steht, daß sie
sich ändert, wenn dieser sich ändert."[6]  Had Holz ever written the
S o z i o l o g i e   d e r   K u n s t  which he had planned, this idea
could usefully have served as his starting-point.  Instead Holz concluded
that  since art as a totality was not reducible to an object of
empirical analysis, he should focus on an individual manifestation of
art in the sense of it being a microcosmic reflection of that totality:

> liegt ein Gesetz einem gewissen Complex von Tatsachen zu
> Grunde, so liegt dieses selbe Gesetz auch jeder einzelnen
> Tatsache desselben zu Grunde.  Liegt der Kunst in
> ihrer Gesamterscheinung ein Gesetz zu Grunde, so liegt
> eben dieses selbe Gesetz auch jeder ihrer Einzelerscheinungen
> zu Grunde.[7]

Assessing Holz's aesthetics as a whole, John Osborne, in an acute
observation, has pointed to what he considers the underlying contradiction of Holz's theory.  For, he argues, on the one hand his theory
amounts to a programmatic demand for Naturalism, while  on the other
hand  aspiring to be a scientific aesthetic that claims to reveal a law
applicable to all art, whatever its particular style.[8]  The quote
above illustrates that Holz was oblivious to this tension between the
general and the specific and believed that the law he sought to discover
governed not only Naturalism, his immediate object, but all forms of
art, past and present, high and low:  "Das Gesetz...begreift ein altes
japanisches Götzenbild nicht minder, als eine moderne französische
Porträtstatue, einen Böcklin nicht minder, als einen Menzel".[9]  From
the simple example of a young boy's scribblings on a slate, which Holz

is unable to recognise as the soldier the boy thinks he has drawn,
Holz deduces that the essence of artistic achievement lies in the discrepancy between artistic aim and its realisation. Holz then devises a
formula which seeks to quantify that discrepancy: "Kunst = Natur − X".[10]
By analysing the reasons for the discrepancy Holz can then formulate
his law: "Die Kunst hat die Tendenz, wieder die Natur zu sein. Sie
wird sie nach Maßgabe ihrer jedweiligen Reproduktionsbedingungen
und deren Handhabung".[11] Whereas Zola's definition of the work of
art as "un coin de la nature vu à travers un tempérament" retains
the idea of the artist's imagination as the decisive factor in artistic
production, Holz's law seeks to minimise the subjective element by
shifting the emphasis on to the means the artist has at his disposal.
As these will necessarily never be perfect, the approximation of art
to nature can likewise never be complete:

> Eine völlige exakte Reproduktion der Natur durch die Kunst
> ist ein Ding der absoluten Unmöglichkeit, und zwar − von
> allen anderen abgesehen − schon aus dem ganz einfachen ...
> Grunde, weil das betreffende Reproduktionsmaterial, das
> uns Menschen nun einmal zur Verfügung steht, stets unzulänglich
> war, stets unzulänglich ist und stets unzulänglich bleiben
> wird.[12]

In so far as these thoughts, when applied to literature, point to an
awareness of the limitations of language, they are of significance
since, as will be shown later, they place Holz in a particular tradition
that has developed from a dissatisfaction with traditional language
as a meaningful means of expression. More problematical for the
present discussion, however, is Holz's concept of "nature", all the more
so since Holz nowhere actually defines precisely what he means by it.
Klaus Scherpe's analysis of Holz's aesthetics stresses Holz's indebtedness to and absorption into a scientistic positivism to the extent that
he argues it was never Holz's intention to concretise the notion of
nature. Rather it represented a methodological category, signifying
merely "object of the sciences", and correlatively the call for an exact
reproduction of nature was basically only a formal principle. By
Naturalism, therefore, Scherpe concludes, Holz meant essentially what
he calls "die Verwissenschaftlichung der Kunstproduktion",[13] meaning the

idea of scientific objectivity and stressing observation and empirical
inquiry as the basis for literary technique. More specifically Pascal
argues that by "nature" Holz means its external phenomena that are
susceptible to direct perception by the senses,[14] whereas Rasch contends
that Holz effectively defines artistic activity as the exact
reproduction of a physically perceivable object.[15] Certainly when, in
the quotation above, Holz argues that a totally exact reproduction of
nature through art is an absolute impossibility, the implication is
that it is nevertheless desirable. Similarly, Osborne argues that
since Holz "had dismissed as an unsound dogma the view...that the essence
of art does not consist in the exact imitation of nature...the implication behind these words is reasonably clear: art does consist in the
exact imitation of nature".[16] Given the ambiguities of Holz's
theory, the question as to whether these judgements are unjust or not is
of less relevance than the implications they have for an analysis of
Holz's creative writing.

The literary characteristic most readily associated with the
"Sekundenstil" is probably that which Wyndham Lewis has, in another
context, nicely termed "the law of fanatical scrupulosity",[17] meaning
the meticulous attention to the minutiae of description. Heinrich Hart
quotes probably the most illuminating example of the effect Holz was
trying to achieve:

> Er entwickelte seine Absicht am Beispiel eines vom Baume
> fallenden Blattes. Die alte Kunst hat von dem fallenden
> Blatt weiter nichts zu melden gewußt, als daß es im Wirbel
> sich drehend zu Boden sinkt. Die neue Kunst schildert
> diesen Vorgang von Sekunde zu Sekunde; sie schildert,
> wie das Blatt, jetzt auf dieser Seite vom Licht beglänzt,
> rötlich aufleuchtet, auf der andern schattengrau
> erscheint, in der nächsten Sekunde ist die Sache
> umgekehrt, sie schildert, wie das Blatt erst senkrecht
> fällt, dann zur Seite getrieben wird, dann wieder lotrecht
> sinkt, sie schildert - ja, der Himmel weiß, was sie sonst
> noch zu berichten hat.[18]

While eschewing the tendentiousness of Scherpe's conclusions, Roy
Pascal nevertheless endorses his view that the overriding influence
on Holz was that of scientific positivism and contends that this led him

to see the chief purpose of literature in the uncovering of causal laws.[19] Similarly Fritz Martini, in explaining how this influence was reflected in his creative writing, argues that Holz extended his conviction as to the ultimate determinacy of all things into the belief that even the smallest individual phenomena are causally linked to that whole which constitutes life as a totality. Since, then, even the apparently most insignificant detail reflects an underlying causality, a true application of scientific method to literature thus demands that as far as possible everything, no matter how insubstantial or contradictory, be recorded by the artist.[20] Holz himself expressed his belief in the law of causality in the following terms:

> Erst durch sie (i.e. die endliche, große Erkenntnis von der durchgängigen Gesetzmäßigkeit alles Geschehens, R.B.) ist uns die Welt aus einem blinden, vernunftlosen Durcheinanderwuten blinder, vernunftloser Einzeldinge, dessen Widersinnigkeit unserer wachsenden Erkenntnis um so empörender dünken mußte, je ernsthafter wir in ihm das Walten eines uns gütigen Wesens verehren sollten, das uns Hunger und Pest, Tod und Krankheit erleiden ließ, um uns seiner 'Liebe' zu vergewissern, zu einzigen, riesenhaften Organismus geworden, dessen kolossale Glieder logisch ineinander greifen, in dem jedes Blutskügelchen seinen Sinn und jeder Schweißtropfen seinen Verstand hat.[21]

Consequently, Mahal terms Holz's style "eine(r) auf Totalität abzielende(n) Mimesis"[22] and there is indeed evidence to support the view that Holz was advocating art as the reproduction of physically perceivable reality. After all, the examples that Holz himself cites (the leaf, the young boy's soldier) were, significantly, drawn from the physical world, while the particular use of the words "Reproduktion" and "wieder" in his "Kunstgesetz" inevitably suggests the idea of copying reality, an impression enhanced furthermore by the description of Holz's method given by his collaborator, Johannes Schlaf: "...nur das Sinnfällige, Positive, tatsächlich Wahrnehmbare und Kontrollierbare (wird) gegeben..."[23] Thus, by far the most common view of consequential Naturalism is one which equates it with a "photographisch und phonographisch exakten, räumlich und zeitlich lückenlosen, sprachlichen Bestandaufnahme der Wirklichkeit".[24] This typical emphasis[25] on the "photo-phonographic" element of depiction imputes to Holz, above all, a confidence in the

power of language to convey material reality. Indeed, in D i e  K u n s t.
I h r  W e s e n  u n d  i h r e  G e s e t z e  Holz constructed a
hierarchy of the arts in which literature has primacy since its artistic
means, words, are, he argues, more comprehensive ("...kein Mittel ist
umfassender als das Wort").[26] Clearly, therefore, the aspect of language
that Holz was embracing was its powers of concreteness, not its powers
of abstraction.

By "photographic" depiction is meant the evocation in words of visible
realities. The actual empirical nature of description this meticulous
faithfulness to actuality often involved is illustrated by the
circumstances surrounding the composition of the final scene of "Papa
Hamlet". Interwoven into the details of Thienwiebel's brutality, his
wife's hysterical responses and the child's death is the minute
description of the light effects caused by an old oil lamp that is
gradually burning out. Before they were able to complete this scene,
Holz relates,[27] he and Schlaf decided it was necessary actually to enact
the process with the oil lamp in their room so that they could record
all the various effects as they occurred. In general stylistic terms,
however, what this emphasis on concrete details tends to produce is
a proliferation of adjectives. The following short passage from "Ein
Tod", in which eight nouns merit no less than thirteen different
qualifying words, is typical of Holz's simple descriptive method:

> In dem matten Schein der Lampe jetzt ein blaurotes, gedunsenes
> Gesicht, das mit seinen kleinen, verschommenen Augen blöde im
> Zimmer umherglotzte. Unter dem eingedrückten Hut vor dünne,
> flachsblonde Haare in die rote, fette schweißtriefende Stirn.[28]

Such an unrelenting compilation of adjectives could quickly become tiresome if its sole purpose were the amassing of random detail. At certain
moments, such as those describing the interior of Thienwiebel's room in
"Papa Hamlet", the myriad heterogeneous elements may melt together into
a visual picture that Martini calls a "still life".[29] But, as will be
shown elsewhere, this "still-life" technique at the same time produces
quite the opposite effect of an objective reproduction of external
reality and constitutes, on the contrary, a subjectivising tendency.

The most important feature of mimetic realism, however, is the idea of
phonographic reproduction, by which is understood the use of language
to register auditory realities. Often this involves the translation
of acoustic effects into linguistic form; for example, the crackling
of the oil lamp and the dripping of the thawing snow in the last
scene of "Papa Hamlet", the creaking of the cupboard in "Ein Tod" etc.
In a, perhaps, slightly comic moment in "Die papierne Passion" an
object is even allowed direct speech, for instead of the reader being
informed by the narrator that there was a ring at the door, in the
text he finds" ""Zing, zing! ... zing, zing!""[30]  In the main, however,
the idea of phonographic reproduction refers to the detailed recording
of human speech. The emphasis on everyday language - which produced what
Holz was quite happy to have described as "die Mimik der Rede"[31] -
was essentially, as Holz explained, a reaction against an artificial,
literary language, particularly that of the pre-Naturalist theatre:

> Die Sprache des Theaters ist die Sprache des Lebens. Nur
> des Lebens! ... Ihr Ziel zeichnet sich klar: die aus dem
> gesamten einschlägigen Reproduktions-material sich nun einmal
> ergebenden Unvermeidlichkeiten möglichst auf ihr Minimum
> herabzudrücken, statt des bisher überliefert gewesenen
> posierten Lebens damit mehr und mehr das nahezu wirkliche
> zu setzen, mit einem Wort, aus dem Theater allmählich das
> 'Theater' zu drängen.[32]

The resultant stress on authenticity had particular consequences for the
style of language Holz developed. The main effect - and sadly the one
for which Naturalism in general is most often remembered - was the
reproduction, despite the attendant dangers of incomprehensibility, of
jargon and dialect in all their phonetic complexity. "Die papierne
Passion", for example, is written almost entirely in the following
manner:

> Det wah'n Kind! - Jott! Ick sage! - Se hätt'n man bloß ihre
> Ogen sehn solln! - Na! - Ick ... wenn ... mit eenem Worte ...
> Sehn Se! So'nn Kind muß mir nu sterben un mit det riedije,
> ruppije Froonzimmer muß ick mir zu Schanden ärjern!
> Nee! ... Ick ... Jott! - Ick sag schon! ... Nee![33]

This is not intended as an aim in itself. Rather it serves to capture

the natural inarticulateness and incoherence of ordinary people by
recording all their repetitions, interjections, hesitations and
incomplete utterances, in short, all the human sounds irrespective of
their value as direct communication.

The obvious effect of such a style is an intensification of realism in
the simple sense that people are presented, or rather present themselves,
as they really speak.  This allowed Holz the means with which to
differentiate between various linguistic registers and to translate
different levels of consciousness into basic, ordinary language.  "Ein
Tod" provides a good example of this technique.  In the sketch two
students are watching over a companion who has been fatally wounded in
a duel.  A drunk staggers into the room by mistake:

> "Sie sind fehlgegangen!"
> Wa. ..hbf. ..wa. ..waas? Hof! .."
> "Sie sind fehlgegangen".
> "Ah! ...En. ...Hbf! ...schul. ...Jen. ..i ...
> hbf! ...ich".
> "Bitte!"
> "Hb! Hbf! ..."[34]

This contrasts with the delirium of the dying student:

> "Ja! - Ja. ..Die Sonne scheint so wunderschön. ..Draußen. ..
> Heut abend bei Bergenhauus. ..an Strand. ..Nicht wahr, Nora? ..
> Ach, schön Morgen. ..Bloß ein Frasch! ...Nicht doch. ..bloß
> ein Frasch. ..Hier! Hier! ..Das Gras ist so schön. ..Oh,
> nicht wahr? Wir werden uns nie vergessen? ...Nie. ..Nie. ..
> Oh, nicht wahr? ...Noch ein Kuß?. ..Hm? ..Gute Nacht. ..
> Der Mond. ..so schön. ..dort. ..über der See. ..so rot. ..
> so groß. ..so grooooß. .."[35]

Finally, Holz records the sense of shock experienced by the students
at the moment of their friend's death:

> "Man. ..man spürt - den Puls gar nicht - mehr. .."
> "Was??"
> "Ach. ..Er. ..er ist ja - tot??!"
> W. ..?"
> Tot!!!"[36]

That this serves to heighten the realistic effect is clear.  There is,

however, another less obvious benefit. For Jost Hermand this method
of writing lowers language to the level of a "Begleitinstrument des
Mimus",[37] which has the effect of reducing characters to the status of
"bloße Sprechapparate".[38] In so far as this means that Holz rejected
the role of characters as bearer of ideas, it is undoubtedly true; the
term Hermand employs, however, is less apposite, since the analogy
with the machine implies insensate beings devoid of spontaneous reaction
and emotional response. That this fragmentation of language could,
on the contrary, effectively evoke mental states and reveal the pre-
conscious and instinctual realms of the psyche   perhaps even the
subconscious, was a stylistic feature of which Holz himself was clearly
aware:

> Jene kleinen Freiheiten und Verschämtheiten jenseits aller
> Syntax, Logik und Grammatik, in denen sich das Werden und
> Sichformen eines Gedankens, das unbewußte Reagieren auf
> Meinungen und Gebärden des Mitunterredners, Vorwegnahme von
> Einwänden, Captatio benevolentiae und all jene leisen Regungen
> der Seele ausdrücken...über die, die Widerspiegeler des
> Lebens sonst als 'unwichtig' hinwegzugleiten strebten, die
> aber gerade meist das 'Eigentliche' enthalten und verraten.[39]

In "Ein Tod", for example, the dialogue is intended to shed light on the
relationship between the two characters, for their conversation hardly
ever reaches the level of meaningful communication but rather is simply
a means of concealing their obvious pained embarrassment. Or, again,
in the final scene of "Papa Hamlet" Holz uses spoken language to
similarly good effect:

> Er hatte den Lutschpfropfen gefunden und wischte ihn sich nun an
> den Unterhosen ab.
> "So' ne Kälte! Na? Wird's nu bald? Na? Nimm's doch, Kameel!
> Nimm's doch! Na?!"
> Der kleine Fortinbras jappte!
> Sein Köpfchen hatte sich ihm hinten ins Genick gekrampft, er
> bohrte es jetzt verzweifelt nach allen Seiten.
> "Na? Willst du nu, oder nich?! - - Bestie!!"
> "Aber-Niels! Um Gottes willen! Er hat ja wieder den - Anfall!"
> "Ach was! Anfall! - - Da! Frißt!!"
> "Hergott, Niels ..."
> "Friß!!!"
> "Niels!;
> "Na? Bist du - nu still? Na? - Bist du - nu still? Na?! Na?!

"Ach Gott! Ach Gott, Niels, was, was - machst du denn bloß?!
Er, er schreit ja gar nicht, mehr! Er ... Niels!!"
Sie war unwillkürlich zurückgeprallt. Seine ganze Gestalt war
vornüber geduckt, seine knackenden Finger hatten sich krumm in
den Korbrand gekrallt. Er stierte sie an. Sein Gesicht war
aschfahl.
"Die ... L-ampe! Die ... L-ampe! Die ... L-ampe!"
"Niels!!!"[40]

The actual drama of this scene, the ostensible climax of the whole
sketch, is conveyed exclusively by the vocal responses of the two
characters. For whereas the narrator's interventions are markedly
dispassionate and restricted to a clinical description of Thienwiebel's
behaviour and the child's reactions, the direct speech records the
emotional progression in Thienwiebel from mild annoyance to brutal
loss of self-control to a state of paralysed mortification, and in Amalie
from irritation to apprehension to total horror at her husband's actions.
In this way Holz allows the diverse nuances of psychological characterisation to emerge through the characters' own speech. Klaus Scherpe argues
that Holz's exclusive emphasis on a stylised "Umgangsprache" and on a
language expressing involuntary psychological response merely underlines
the subordination of his characters to milieu.[41] Of course, like most
of the Naturalists Holz accepted more or less without qualification that
there existed a relationship of determinacy between human beings
and their milieu and his characterisation was, indeed, intended to
reflect that relationship: "Menschen ohne Milieu, konstruierte,
Abstrakte, kann ich für meine Zwecke nicht brauchen".[42] However, when
Scherpe asserts that Holz presents his characters as passive products
of their environment, seemingly deprived of individual rationality and
will, his comments represent not so much descriptive observation as
prescriptive criticism and as such they come, as will be shown later,
within a particular tradition in the critical reception of Naturalism
as a literary movement.

The "photo-phonographic" representation of reality, namely the
insistence on circumstantial precision and exact reproduction of human
speech that Hauptmann likened to the observing of life through a
magnifying glass,[43] is one aspect of the objectivity it is claimed Holz

achieved in his prose-writing. The objectivising tendency of this
characteristic of Holz's style, however, is clearly contingent on the
other feature of his imaginative prose that is commonly singled out in
this context, namely the suppression of an authorial subjectivity.
H.H. Borcherdt writes for example: "Es kann...gar kein Zweifel
bestehen, daß Holz damals wirklich an eine Kunst höchster Objectivität
gedacht hat, die das Subjekt des Künstlers völlig ausschalten sollte."[44]
Too often, however, such judgements appear to have been derived merely
from Holz's aesthetic writings and without reference to his prose-
works. It is above all Fritz Martini who, in his comprehensive and
often perceptive analysis of "Papa Hamlet", has done most to develop
this line of argumentation with regard to the creative writing. Perhaps
mindful of Holz's claim that literary representation should develop
"aus den Dingen selbst",[45] Martini says of "Papa Hamlet":

> Diese Prosa zwingt ihren Leser in diese abstoßende
> Wirklichkeit, ohne sie durch irgendeine erzählerische
> Distanz zu relativieren oder einzuschränken;[46] ...
> Holz erstrebte ein Maximum an Objectivität des Erzählens,
> in dem jede Fälschung der Realität durch das subjekti-
> vierende Dazwischentreten des referierenden Erzählers
> vermieden und so daß Leben unmittelbar zu Wort gebracht
> wird.[47]

In two crucial essays on the prose-style of Naturalism, Roy Pascal has
done much to correct what he considers to be a mistaken judgement of the
narrative perspective in Holz's work.[48] My own view is that despite
the many valuable insights which Pascal's analysis affords (and which
will be elaborated later) his case is nevertheless something of an
over-correction. That is to say, I believe it is possible to rehabilitate many of Martini's propositions if, as I argued earlier, one
differentiates between two types of sketch in the N e u e  G l e i s e
volume. As Pascal has clearly demonstrated, certain of Martini's
observations are simply not valid in relation to "Papa Hamlet" (or to
"Der erste Schultag" for that matter). They could, however, be applied
with much less difficulty to those of Holz's sketches I have placed in
the objectivist category where the narrator, although in Pascal's words,
always to a certain extent "irrepressible", is nevertheless not so
manifestly in evidence.

Clearly, any meaningful discussion of narrative perspective necessitates
a distinction between a direct and an indirect authorial presence.
When, therefore, Martini speaks of the narrative proceeding without the
mediating presence of the narrator, or of the ascetic eradication of the
self on the part of the writer,[49] he clearly means by that in the first
instance the elimination of any direct authorial comment. Furthermore,
he underscores the point by comparing "Papa Hamlet" with the sketch that
provided the basis for it  and which was the sole work of Johannes
Schlaf. It is, of course, true that in "Papa Hamlet" Holz does succeed
in reducing the obtrusive authorial prominence revealed in the patently
moralising stance of the narrator in Schlaf's "Ein Dachstubenidyll".
It is, however, equally untrue to maintain that Holz excluded all
direct narratorial intervention. The conclusion drawn at the end of
Section VI of "Papa Hamlet", for example, is in part at least, if not
in its entirety,[50] that of the narrator: "Der große Thienwiebel hatte
nicht so ganz unrecht: Die ganze Wirtschaft bei ihm zu Hause war der
Spiegel und die abgekürzte Chronik des Zeitalters".[51] Similarly, the
"epilogue" of Section VII is consciously structured in such a way as
to make a particular point. Martini himself lays great emphasis on
the function of this epilogue since, he argues, the conclusion it
provokes betrays not the bourgeois moralising characteristic of
Schlaf's first draft but an underlying doubt and cynicism that constitutes an important relativisation of the unsuppressed narratorial
distaste for the bohemian expressed elsewhere in the sketch. However,
the fact that such a corrective is necessary merely testifies to the
intrusion of the narrator's values in the first place.

More subtle, perhaps, but no less obtrusive than direct intervention
is the pervasive irony of the narratorial description. The repeated
use of a phrase like "der große Thienwiebel" ironising the actor's
delusory self-importance or the describing of a character as "der alten,
lieben, guten Frau Wachtel", when she is in fact the very opposite,
are not the objective statements of a detached observer. Rather they
are symptomatic of a caustic irony which is directed against the
characters the narrator describes and of which the reader cannot help but
be aware.

Another argument advanced to support the claim to objectivity deriving from the exclusion of the authorial voice is what many critics have referred to as the marked tendency to dialogue form.[52] In dialogue, it is argued, the author apparently stands back to let the characters, as it were, introduce and define themselves through their own words. I have already quoted examples from Holz's sketches illustrating how this works. Certainly, when in 1890 Holz wrote to Schlaf "Keine Verse mehr, keine Romane mehr, für uns existiert nur noch die offene, lebendige Szene",[53] then this enthusiasm stemmed from the belief that their development of a new form of dialogue pointed inevitably in the direction of drama and thus, by implication, to the redundancy of the narrator. Significantly, however, "Papa Hamlet" and "Der erste Schultag" are not the best examples of this tendency (in fact, the latter hardly exhibits it at all since it contains relatively little dialogue). On the other hand, "Ein Tod" consists almost entirely of fragments of dialogue, whereas in "Die papierne Passion" Holz emphasises the prominent role of speech by presenting all other parts of the narrative in small print very much in the style of stage directions. Altogether, therefore, as far as the question of a direct authorial presence is concerned, the case for its elimination would appear to be more substantial with regard to the sketches representing the objectivist tendency since not only do they dispense with all direct, moralising or interpretative, narratorial intrusions but they are also free of the critical irony that informs "Papa Hamlet" and, to a lesser extent, "Der erste Schultag".

I believe this is equally true of the role of the narrator as an indirect presence, that is to say, in respect of those elements of narration that cannot simply be identified as the narrator's explicitly subjective experience of the reality he relates. Essentially this concerns the problem of the overall structure of the narrative and the question of selectivity. Most commonly one encounters this in the popular "slice-of-life" conception of Naturalist fiction, that is, the idea that, as Martini puts it, life itself is being rendered in words. Holz himself uses precisely this image in relation to D i e   F a m i l i e   S e l i c k e:

> Mit kleinen völlig absichtlosen Studien direkt nach der
> Natur, ohne uns sozusagen um Gott und die Welt zu
> kümmern, hatten wir angefangen und schließlich mit der
> "Familie Selicke", durch die man in eine Stück Leben
> wie durch ein Fenster sah, aufgehört.[54]

The crucial word here is "absichtlos". For all his professed dislike of
the idea of the experimental novel, writing, as Holz understands it,
still seems to display more than just a vague affinity with Zola's
conceptualisation of it, since both imply that once the literary process
begins (i.e. in Zola's metaphor, once he has initiated the chemical
reaction, in Holz's metaphor, once he has chosen which window to peer
through) the author no longer in any way controls events and all he can
do is record what he sees. This has two consequences for the structure
of the narration:  firstly, the events and characters described must
essentially remain random and should not get together to form a
"story" and secondly, if the narrator's function is n o t  one of
a discriminating selector of events, it follows that the passage of
time in the narrative should reflect as faithfully as possible the time-
sequence of actuality.  That is to say, it presupposes the identity
of narrative time and narrated time and demands that the narrator forgo
the chronological mobility he is normally permitted in traditional
prose.  Martini sees the realisation of both these demands in "Papa
Hamlet".  And yet, of all the sketches this is surely, despite its
unremitting focus on the idea of the bohemian environment, the one with
the most easily recognisable story-line, complete in fact with dramatic
climax and authorial conclusion.  As regards the question of time-
sequence David Turner remarks in his discussion of  D i e  F a m i l i e
S e l i c k e  that Holz and Schlaf have not only made the inevitable
concession to choice in giving their play an end;  they further divided
it into acts, thus ignoring that part of reality, however trivial, which
occurs in the gaps.[55]  This comment applies equally to the temporal
disjunctions of "Papa Hamlet".  Moreover, as Pascal shows, there is a
clearly structured time-scheme indicated, on the one hand, by events
such as the birth of the child and the details of its growth  and, on
the other hand, by temporal allusions by the narrator such as "seit Wochen",
"heute abend", "mit der Zeit", which constantly remind the reader of the
uneven passage of time.  By comparison, however, one of the main features

of "Ein Tod" is precisely the way in which it communicates to the reader
the extremely regular, almost directly experiencable passing of time.
Similarly, "Die papierne Passion" appears as a unitary moment extracted
from "life", which - while I do not wish to descend to the fatuous level
of "when is a plot not a plot?" - nevertheless seems to me in no meaningful sense to constitute a story, a fact which surely underlies Turner's
view that of all the sketches only "Die papierne Passion" conveys a real
sense of random presentation.[56]

It has not been my purpose in this summary discussion of "Papa Hamlet"
to argue that those elements of narrative perspective I have referred to
represent major stylistic deficiencies. Rather I have been concerned to
point out that they militate against Martini's claim of the unassailable
narratorial objectivity of "Papa Hamlet". Moreover, in addition to those
aspects already discussed  there are two further stylistic characteristics
common to both "Papa Hamlet" and "Der erste Schultag" which weaken the
imputed objectivity. I refer to Holz's use of symbolism (of which
Martini's "still-life technique" is one example) and his use of the
"free indirect style" (which Martini fails to remark on at all). For
the moment it suffices to say that by this latter technique I mean the
narratorial mode of the shifting perspective, i.e. the alternating of
perspective from the narrator to the consciousness of one or other of the
characters and the assertion thereby of a multiplicity of viewpoints.
Again it is not my aim to portray these techniques as inherent stylistic
weaknesses;  on the contrary, as I hope to show later, I believe they
make for a substantial enrichment of the text. It is not, however, an
enrichment pointing in the direction of objectivity and, significantly,
it is only these two texts in the subjectivist category where Holz
deploys the techniques. In so far as the narrator can ever disappear
from view, therefore - and even in "Die papierne Passion" the contrast
between the literary, articulate language of the narrator, albeit after
the fashion of stage directions, and the chatty, jargonesque dialect of
the characters does ultimately remind the reader of his presence - I
would argue that the sketches of the objectivist type achieve his
elimination as successfully as will ever be possible within the framework
of simple realism.

To illustrate the objectivist interpretation of the "Sekundenstil" I
would like, in conclusion, to look in detail at one of the sketches I
have ascribed to the objectivist category, namely "Die papierne
Passion", since so far I have asserted rather than demonstrated the
validity of that ascription. In my discussion of the text I intentionally
reproduce many of the points made in Günther Mahal's analysis since he
regards "Die papierne Passion" as stylistically a paradigm of consequential Naturalism in which "mit einem ausgefeilten Instrumentarium
exaktheits – und totalitätsbemühter Reproduktion, mit einer nahezu
perfekten Mimesis Realität (wird) "Natur" "wieder" gezeigt".[57] Mahal's
analysis, then, is in turn a paradigm of the objectivist interpretation
of Holz's prose-style.

The action of the sketch is minimal:  it takes place in Mutter Abendroth's kitchen where, busy with her cooking, she expresses her impatient
concern over the growing sexual awareness of Wally, her maturing eleven-
year-old adopted daughter;  she gives hot food and drink to one of her
tenants, a shy student who asks for and gets a two-week extension
during which to pay his rent, and is amused by the jokes of her other
student tenant who consciously plays up to her;  Olle Kopelke, an old
suitor of hers, relives some of the memories of his youth and to amuse
Wally cuts out from a folded newspaper the symbols and figures of the
crucifixion;  this tour de force, however, is interrupted by the sounds
of a drunken husband beating his wife and by the noise of the crowd that
gathers to watch in the yard;  when the characters return from watching
the activity outside, they find the draught from the window has ruined
Kopelke's creation.  Schulz's view that this obviously symbolises the
increasing secularisation of industrial society[58] is rather far fetched
since this would be much too heavy a moral for such a light-weight sketch
to bear.  The title,says Mahal, has no special significance and could
just as easily be "Küchengespräche", "Untermietersorgen" or "Krach im
Hinterhof", since the sketch does not set out to impart any "message"
or pose any questions.  Rather it is "open-ended" in the sense that its
beginning and end are totally arbitrary, possessing no significance as
beginning and end other than as the means of encapsulating what is

described: "Alltag, bloße Durchschnittlichkeit, Wohnküchenroutine".[59]

This emphasises that the real "theme" of the sketch is the mileu, which
is the kitchen ("der ständige gegenwärtige Fokus")[60] on the fourth floor
of the tenement, and the surrounding localities of the "Hinterhof", a
basement bar and the large nearby factory. The interpenetration of the
kitchen milieu and the reality beyond it is presented in the text in the
following manner:

> Unten, vier Treppen tiefer aus dem Budikerkeller, jetzt
> deutlich der dünne Ton einer Ziehharmonika: "SISTE WOLL,
> DA KIMMT ER, LANGE SCHRITTE NIMMT ER"...Mutter Abendroth'n
> hat sich, die Hände in die Seiten, mitten in die dunkle
> Küche gestellt..."SISTE WOLL, DA KIMMT ER SCHON, DER
> BESOFFNE SCHWIEGERSOHN..." (...)
>
> "H a c h,  J o t t,  n a' I c k  s a g  s c h o n!"
> Mutter Abendroth'n hat sich wieder auf ihren Stuhl
> gesetzt, wieder kratzen die Kartoffeln über das
> Reibeisen. Draußen tappt es faul die Treppen hinunter.
> Eine Weile vergeht. Das kleine, blitzende Pünktchen
> auf dem Zinkdeckel der langen Pfeife hinten in der
> Schrankecke tanzt, zwischen den beiden blutroten Troddeln
> oben am Mundstück flinkern ein paar Goldfäden...Eben
> ist unten durch den Torweg wieder ein schwerer, mit Eisen
> beladener Wagen in den Hof gerasselt. Ein paar Arbeiter
> rufen und lachen, unten im Budikerkeller muß man unter-
> dessen die Fenster geöffnet haben, die Ziehharmonika ist
> verstummt, deutlich klappern ein paar Billardbälle.
> Dazwischen, regelmäßig, von der Fabrik her, die Dämpfe.[61]

Reference has already been made to how the narratorial details take
on the appearance of stage directions. Mahal, however, dislikes this
comparison since it suggests that the sketch was nothing more than a
preparatory exercise for Holz and Schlaf before turning to the drama
proper. Moreover, he argues, many details - like those relating to
smells or to effects of such minimal acoustic or visual intensity as
those in the above passage - are totally impracticable and could never
be realised in a stage production. Nor, he points out, is it merely
non-dialogue information that is presented in small print for, in the
passage quoted, for instance, the typographical form of the singing in
the basement is distinguished from both that of the narratorial
details and the dialogue in the kitchen. The text, therefore, constructs

a hierarchy in the following order: firstly, the dialogue between the characters in the kitchen; secondly, the narrator's description and thirdly, the talking, shouting and singing from the other floors of the building, the courtyard or the factory. The effect, Mahal claims, is to emphasise the kitchen as the locus of narration ("ständigen Bezugsort") while, at the same time, conveying the simultaneity of the many disparate but contiguous moments beyond that immediate experiential reality.

"Die papierne Passion" is, however, more than just a study of milieu; in addition it draws five miniature portraits of typical Berlin figures. As well as a wealth of concrete physical details there are hints at certain characterological traits such as Mutter Abendroth's basic generosity, the precociousness of Wally and Kopelke's pretensions to human insight in his love of dispensing advice. These are colourful, sympathetically drawn figures, comfortably and inconspicuously rooted in the reality the sketch reproduces. However, the two main "participants" in that reality never, according to Mahal, actually appear in the sketch itself. The first and more obvious of the two is the narrator. This is no omniscient figure carefully structuring his material to make a calculated point; rather it is the meticulous observer totally immersed in the reality of his characters and concerned only to record in the minutest detail all the possible sense-perceptions those characters experience. This, for Mahal, constitutes the basic paradox of the author's role: on the one hand, Holz has totally eliminated the narrator as a distinct presence, has hidden him behind or merged him into the various characters in such a way that the sketch appears to narrate itself; on the other hand, the author is omnipresent, his five senses of perception working overtime, as it were, to register the slightest physical sensation so that the sketch is down to the last detail his own unique product. The ultimate effect from either point of view is, Mahal argues, total objectivity:

> die Wieder-Gabe, die Reproduktion eines Beobachtungsfelds, das Wiedererstehenlassen eines minuziös als experimentelle Modellsituation 'erfaßten' bestimmten Raumes in einer

> bestimmten Zeit...ein derart ausgefeiltes Arrangement
> subjektiver Einzeleindrücke, daß diese qualitativ in
> objektive Totalität umschlagen.[62]

Moreover, this qualitative transformation has, according to Mahal, a
unique effect on the reader. For the process of, as it were, re-enacting,
recreating reality – an effect heightened both by the identity of
narrated and narrative time and by the immediacy of the present tense
which is used throughout – draws the reader irresistibly into that
reality itself, not just as an observer but as an actual participant. In
Mahal's words: "Der Leser schaut...nicht in eine Wohnkrüche hinein,
sondern befindet sich in ihr,...integriert und miterlebend..."[63] For
the reader this is the ultimate literary experience, "Kunstkonsumption
über alle fünf Sinne";[64] for the writer, who has therefore not merely
produced a photographic copy of reality but has succeeded in actually
recreating reality, this is by Holz's own criteria the optimal artistic
achievement: "der Nachvollzug totaler Mimesis...die Rückverwandlung
des aus der 'Natur' 'Kunst' Gewordenen in 'Natur' mit einer Vollständig-
keit, die schlechthin nicht mehr zu überbieten ist."[65] Günther Mahal
thus claims for "Die papierne Passion" what Holz himself maintained was
impossible: the reduction of the "-x" factor in his equation to an im-
perceptibility, that is to say, the exact reproduction of nature through
art.

Before examining the wider possible ramifications of Holz's style it is
as well firstly to clarify the relationship of that style to German
Naturalism as a whole and in particular to its most successful practitioner,
Gerhart Hauptmann. It is sometimes claimed – not least of all by Holz
himself – that Hauptmann was directly influenced by Holz in the development of his early dramas and in support of this claim it is common
practice to adduce the dedication to Holz that Hauptmann included in the
first edition of V o r  S o n n e n a u f g a n g: "Bjarne P. Holmsen,
dem konsequentesten Realisten, Verfasser von 'Papa Hamlet' zugeeignet, in
freudiger Anerkennung der durch sein Buch empfangenen, entscheidenden
Anregung."[66] Subsequently, however, Hauptmann withdrew this dedication
and denied that Holz's influence had ever played a decisive role. The

facts of the relationship between the two men are already documented[67] and the most likely explanation is that their collaboration did help Hauptmann refine certain ideas (particularly the reproduction of human speech) on which he had already begun to focus his attention. Clearly, therefore, Holz's later view that the style of the P a p a  H a m l e t volume is qualitatively different from anything that Hauptmann achieved is an exaggerated claim. As Osborne observes, it represents a difference in degree, not in kind.[68] Furthermore, this is equally true of Holz's relationship to Naturalism as a whole. Far too often German Naturalism has been erroneously equated with Holz's aesthetic theory whereas, as Roy Pascal rightly insists, Naturalism is actually characterised by a whole range of motifs and motivations, social, intellectual and aesthetic, for some of which the theory of Holz provided an important impetus but others of which it neglected.[69] In fact, Hauptmann's dedication of 1889 is an accurate assessment of Holz's relationship to Naturalism: that is to say, he was stylistically "the most consequential" of the Naturalists and it is precisely for that reason that his prose-style suggests certain relationships with subsequent literary developments.

The exclusive identification of German Naturalism with the theory and practice of Arno Holz betrays an undifferentiated use of the term. There is, however, another and, to my mind, more serious misuse of the word and one which is not, incidentally, restricted to the German context. This is the tendency, when analysing prose stylistically similar to Holz's "Sekundenstil", to deploy the term "naturalistic" in an intentionally pejorative sense, either to denote merely naive or trivial realism or, as is sometimes the case, simply as a euphemism for stylistically bad writing. This is particularly true of analyses of proletarian literature, probably since realism is, for obvious reasons, the style which many working-class writers turn to as the most easily accessible means of artistic expression. Roy Johnson has recently written an article on "The Proletarian Novel", which I quote at some length since it provides a good illustration of this kind of criticism:

> The sad fact of most 'proletarian writing' is that whilst
> it is motivated by the honourable intention of registering
> the existence of the working class within the fictional
> universe and counterbalancing the weight of middle-class life
> and thought which dominates literature,...invariably the
> political impulse behind the writing is stronger than the
> artistic. There is usually a fervent desire to explain
> for what seems to be the first time ever what it is like to
> endure the social, economic and cultural hardships of
> working-class life - but unfortunately this frequently
> results in a catalogue of trivial details, naturalistic
> descriptions and an absence of experience which has been
> artistically synthesised.[70]

While I would wish to contest the implication of Johnson's analysis

that naturalistic description is in itself "unfortunate" - and one can

well imagine that were he to look at Holz's prose he would make more

or less the same criticisms since, significantly, he does, elsewhere

in the article, apply precisely these strictures to certain contemporary

German developments[71] which, as I shall argue, do reveal a basic

affinity with Holz's prose - it is nevertheless undeniable that the

style and method of Naturalism has on occasions been taken over and

applied uncritically. No less uncritical, in my view, however, is the

way Johnson chooses to regard the style. For to dismiss Naturalism

as the failure to "synthesise experience artistically" is an abuse

of the term which seems to deny that the style, as essentially a mode

of perception, could ever be usefully appropriated by subsequent

writers. One of the purposes that such an appropriation might in

fact serve is indicated in Jost Hermand's expansive conception of

Naturalism:

> Man tut dem Naturalismus darum einen schlechten Dienst,
> wenn man seine revolutionären Elemente verabsolutiert und
> zu einem zeitlosen Stil erhebt. Es ist seinem ganzen
> Wesen nach eine Durchgangsstation, eine Wendemarke, deren
> Aufgabe lediglich darin besteht, das Stagnierende oder
> Erstarrte bewußt formalistischer Epochen auseinander-
> zusprengen und an ihre Stelle das Postulat der
> ungeschminkten Wahrheit zu setzen.[72]

Against this it is, of course, possible to argue that Hermand's view is

so general as to deprive the term Naturalism of all specificity,

historical or stylistic;  its undoubted merit, however, is its emphasis

on the primary concern of Naturalism with truth, in the sense of
**striving for objectivity,** for it is precisely that which also underpins
two types of contemporary literature that can, I believe, be related
to consequential Naturalism.  I refer to reportage and documentary
prose which could be seen as representing, respectively, the photographic
and phonographic elements of Naturalism.  This basic affinity is suggested
in the first instance by the sort of terms commonly used to describe
Holz's style:  significantly, in referring to Holz's example of the
falling leaf, the word Heinrich Hart uses to define the process of
descriptions is "berichten";  similarly, Hermand talks of a
"dokumentarische Echtheit"[75] and Martini says of Holz's prose:  "es
kommt...in die Nähe der nur noch Beobachtungen arrangierenden Reportage".[74]  Essentially, the similarity of style derives from the fact
that the striving for truth in Naturalism is reflected in reportage
and documentary prose in a concern with authenticity.

In documentary prose, which in the sixties has meant, in general,
non-fictional, mostly autobiographical accounts of ordinary people's
experiences, the search for authenticity is evident in the attempt to
reproduce as exactly as possible the actual language of the people whose
experiences are being related.  Documentary prose is, in fact, a
progression beyond Naturalism in the methodological sense that it
overcomes the contradiction at the heart of, for example, Holz's
writing.  That contradiction resides in the fact that while striving
for the highest degree of objectivity, his work nevertheless remains an
essentially fictional construct.  That is  to say, however  consistently
or, some may say, rigidly he implemented the principle of verism, the
literary product could at best only ever reveal what Martin Walser -
who played a large part in encouraging the development of documentary
prose - has termed a "nachgemachte Authentizität".[75] Documentary prose
substitutes for this a genuine authenticity as regards not only the
mode of narration but also the experiences related in which, as Walser
says in the introduction to one of these documentary accounts, "(hier)
wird endlich einmal **berichtet,** nichts als berichtet".[76]  In particular,
this development has been made possible by the technological improvement

of "the means of reproduction" since it was quickly recognised that
linguistic authenticity could be heightened by getting people to record
their experiences directly on to a tape recorder and then producing a
transcript. Günter Wallraff, for example, says of this method:
"Derartige Tonbandabschriften weisen oft erstaunliche Sprachkraft auf,
sind der reinen Schreibsprache an Intensität, Informationsgehalt und
sozialer Wahrheit überlegen..."[77] Similarly, when Erika Runge, the editor
of taped texts such as B o t t r o p e r  P r o t o k o l l e  und
F r a u e n. V e r s u c h e  z u r  E m a n z i p a t i o n, defines
the aim of her editing as "das Wesentliche des gesprochenen Stils zu
bewahren",[78] this then entails in its reproduction of the speaker's
hesitations, his or her mistakes and pauses etc., a phonographic depiction of speech similar to that of consequential Naturalism.

As I stressed earlier, however, the exact recording of human speech is
not by any means the only or even the most important aspect of Holz's
style. Rather it is as essentially a mode of perception that consequential Naturalism derives its significance. This is equally true of
reportage,[79] for like consequential Naturalism its commitment to
empiricism as the basis of literary production defines it primarily as
a method of perceiving and recording reality. The similarity of method
is evident from Wilpert's description of reportage as a style which is
characterised by "Nähe zur objektiven und dokumentarisch nachprüfbaren
Wirklichkeit und leidenschaftslos sachliche Schilderung des Details ohne
einseitige Tendenz, allenfalls aus der Perspektive des Berichters".[80]
The fact that in modern usage the term reportage is applied to accounts
of reality, irrespective of whether they are fictional or actually drawn
from real life, merely underlines its relationship to consequential
Naturalism. That reportage emphasises the photographic element of
depiction is suggested by Siegfried Kracauer's claim that "die Reportage
fotografiert das Leben"[81] or Günter Wallraff's comparison of himself as
the narrator with a camera.[82] Wallraff, arguably the most successful
post-war exponent of the reportage, describes in the following way how
he developed the technique:

> Zu Beginn war alles nur in der Ich-Form und ich notierte alles
> von meinem subjektiven Empfinden her und nur, was mit mir
> geschah. Allmählich veränderte sich das aber und ich schrieb
> auch, was mit den anderen passierte, unabhängig von mir. Ich
> wurde also zum teilnehmenden Beobachter.[83]

Wallraff alludes here to the apparent contradiction that Mahal identified
in his discussion of "Die papierne Passion": the account of reality is
clearly the product of a narrator while at the same time laying claim
to objectivity. In fact, in Wallraff's own reportage the narrator
intervenes in a way that his comments above do not suggest. However,
that the aim of the reportage is "to let events and conditions speak
for themselves" and that its primary concern is with the "Darstellung
von Realitätsausschnitten" and "die genau beobachtete und registrierte
Wirklichkeit"[84] - terminology which is, of course, equally applicable to
the aim of consequential Naturalism - can be demonstrated by considering
a text such as Klas Ewert Everwyn's "Beschreibung eines Betriebsunfalls".[85]

The accident to which the title refers involves a Greek "Gastarbeiter"
whose hand is caught between the rollers of a large printing press. The
report concentrates on the accident itself and the long process of freeing
the man from the machine. The way the machine functions, the man's
reactions and the various comings and goings of factory personnel are
related simply, in detail and without narratorial comment. Moreover, the
chronology of the events is strictly adhered to and further enhanced by
the use of the present tense and the precise recording of time ("Es ist
22.50 Uhr...Um 23 Uhr sind acht Menschen um den Mann im Halle III versam-
melt: drei Polizisten mit umgeschnallten Pistolen, vier Feuerwehrmänner
in weißen Kitteln und mit einer Bahre sowie der Wachmann...Es ist
23.10 Uhr.")[86] Throughout the narrator resists any temptation to sensa-
tionalise or comment on the action and nowhere is the mood of dispassionate
restraint more effectively deployed than in the description of the actual
accident:

> Er hat lediglich einen Blick auf die Stapel geworfen, die
> neben der Maschine lagern und dort auf ihren Abtransport
> warten. Der Blick hat nicht ganz eine Sekunde gedauert.
> Er hat jedoch ausgereicht, die Aufmerksamkeit und die

Wachsamkeit des Mannes zu mindern. Seine Lappenhand ist
dabei in den Bereich der Greifer geraten, die plötzlich
nicht mehr ins Leere zu greifen brauchen. Sie ziehen den
Gegenstand unwiderstehlich in die Richtung ihrer Bewegung.
    Der Mann hat nicht den Bruchteil einer Sekunde lang
die Möglichkeit, sich zu befreien. Statt dessen muß er
zusehen, wie seine Lappenhand mit der ersten Walzenumdrehung
zwischen oberer und unterer Walze verschwindet.[87]

To restrict discussion of this text to its intended objectivity, however,
is to omit a crucial dimension of reportage.  I referred earlier to the
fact that Naturalism and reportage shared a common concern with objective truth and authenticity.  There is, however, a further underlying
motivation which paradoxically both further relates and yet distinguishes
the two styles:that is to say, both are concerned to reveal the relationship of cause and effect.  But whereas Holz understood by this the idea
of natural causality which, he believed, was not susceptible of any
totalising conceptualisation, more often than not the writers who employ
the technique of reportage are concerned with social or political
causality, in other words, with phenomena whose relationship to life as
a totality it is in men's power to grasp and explain.  This necessarily
has certain consequences for the mode and structure of narration.
Firstly, the effect of total randomness, so characteristic of "Die
papierne Passion", for example, is not the aim of reportage.  Certainly,
it aims at typicality but in Everwyn's text, for instance, he presents not
a random "slice of life" but a specific event that serves a particular
critical intention.  Similarly, the clinical description which helps
create the effect of objectivity is not for the sake of random detail but
often fulfils a definite function.  Thus, it is precisely the objectivity
of Everwyn's report which itself reflects, and seems appropriate to, the
efficiency of the printing-works and the strict dividing of responsibility,
which makes the accident seem so much more outrageous, so much more
difficult to account for.  Similarly, Everwyn's precise recording of the
way the machine functions does not simply testify to his knowledge of
mechanics, his particular competence to make this report;  it also serves
to show, by implication, just how remote the efficiency is from the real
needs of the workers, in this case their safety.  It is precisely the

efficiency of the machine which prolongs the worker's suffering since
it cannot be turned back to enable him to withdraw his hand. Furthermore,
all this wealth of knowledge, useful in terms of productivity, is of no
use at all to the doctor. Everwyn, characteristically, does not make
this comment himself but it is implicit in the following observation:
"Ungefähr diese Auskunft (i.e. the way the machine works, R.B.) erhält der
Arzt, der nach einer Dreiviertelstunde als erster zur Unfallstelle
kommt."[88] Another example is Everwyn's precise recording of time. This
is not just for the purpose of signifying the inevitable passage of
time but is an example of how Everwyn lets the facts draw their own
conclusions. The hand becomes caught at 22.50. The worker does not
receive a morphium injection until 23.50 and his hand is not removed until
0.25. These facts need no commentary. Everwyn's supreme comment,
again implicit, is contained in the last four sentences of the passage:
"Die Männer verlassen den Schauplatz. Zigaretten werden angezündet.
Die kleine Blutlache ist vor der Maschine zurückgeblieben. Wenn alle
anderen gegangen sein werden, wird sie der Wachmann aufwischen".[89]

Furthermore, in addition to the problem of selectivity the intention
to illustrate social causality often has consequences for the structure
of the reportage. As I argued earlier, it is of course impossible to
eliminate totally the structuring presence of the narrator - a fact which
Holz himself was surely aware of when referring to his "arrangierendes
und Alles umkrempelndes and zurechtbastelndes Ich"[90] - but in Holz's
objectivist sketches at least, that presence rarely imparts to the events
described the degree of overall meaning and coherence that the narrator
of the reportage often seeks to impose on his material. Thus, Everwyn's
division of his report into four sections, "Die Maschine", "Der Mann",
"Der Mann und die Maschine", and "die anderen", clearly invites the
reader to draw certain conclusions about the incident. Similarly
Wallraff, while continuing to stress the need for authenticity, empirical
inquiry and precise observation, quickly realised that the structural
principle of montage, while not detracting from those qualities, would
help him achieve the interpretative (i.e. political) effectiveness he
was aiming for in his reportage.[91] That is to say, by structuring

his material in a certain way he could lead the reader to the conclusion he wished him to reach, without himself directly articulating
that conclusion.

These distinctions are naturally very important. However, they do not,
I believe, invalidate the relationship between Holz's consequential
Naturalism and reportage as a mode of perceiving and creating a
fictional reality. The real paradox is to be found in the fact that
whereas Holz's concern with form and consequential Naturalism was
accompanied by (and was, perhaps, even to a certain extent determined
by) the decline of his earlier political aims, it was in the pursuit
of precisely those political aims that certain writers subsequently
turned to a literary style similar to that which Holz had pioneered.
In fact, I regard as not totally untenable the definition of reportage
as the method of consequential Naturalism allied to a political or
social intention.

If, as I believe they are, the objectivist tendencies of Naturalism
are restricted in their resonance in the twentieth century to the
quasi-genre of reportage, then it is surely not an irrelevant question
to ask why this should be so. At least three reasons can be identified.
The first can be located in the actual critical reception of Naturalism
in which, as I hinted earlier, there is at least one particular tradition that has displayed an unremitting hostility. The tradition to which
I refer is that of Marxist aesthetics which, significantly, first began
to emerge in any vaguely systematised form in Germany as a result of the
Naturalism debate in the 1890s. While certain of the criticisms have
often been made by non-Marxist writers as well and although there is
obviously no one unitary Marxist theory on Naturalism, it is nevertheless
useful to summarise the main points of the Marxist critique since it
perhaps indicates certain characteristics of Naturalism which may have
discouraged later writers from appropriating and developing its style.

In broad terms it is possible to identify two major variants within
Marxist aesthetics in the twentieth century and while they may diverge
radically as regards the forms of artistic practice they prescribe, they

nevertheless converge in their rejection of Naturalism as a literary model. The first of these, associated primarily with Bertolt Brecht, is a theory stressing the direct cognitive relevance of art and which intentionally transcends the confines of literature as a passive object with which the reader has a purely contemplative relationship. It sees literature less as a simple refraction of reality than as a mode of practice which aims at changing that reality. Art should, therefore, portray the relationship between men and the external forces which determine men, in such a way as to show that, through social action deriving from the knowledge of that relationship, man can in turn master those external forces. Naturalism, it is claimed, cannot do this for two reasons: firstly, the Naturalist belief in mechanical causality resulted in a portrayal of man as a purely passive product of circumstances without the knowledge or power to change those circumstances; secondly, by striving to create the total illusion of reality Naturalism aims at the identity of subject and object in the sense that the reader (or spectator) is invited to identify only with the consciousness of the characters and obtains no supra-fictional awareness.

The second branch of Marxist aesthetics derives from Marx's model of base and superstructure which posits a degree of correspondence between ideas and social formations. These aesthetics explore the work of art as the reflection of this relationship. Even within this group the model has led various theorists to differing conclusions. However, I would like to consider briefly one particular model, namely Lukács's theory of reflection, not only because Lukács's writings contain a systematic critique of Naturalism but also because they illuminate further the suggested relationship between Naturalism and reportage.[92]

Lukács recognises as his basic premise the existence of an objective reality independent of human consciousness. Bourgeois epistemology, he argues, fails to grasp this relationship by one-sidedly emphasising the priority of one over the other. This results in the "twin errors" of mechanical materialism and philosophical idealism, since in both there is an irreconcilable separation between the ideal and the material world. For whereas the latter isolates the world of ideas from material reality as an autonomous entity, the former remains solely on the surface of the material world never transcending the level of appearances. Moreover, both tendencies have their counterparts in aesthetics: the subjectivism of idealism is reflected, for example, in Expressionism, the "denial of reality by 'abstracting it out of existence'", whereas mechanical materialism in art is represented by Naturalism.

Crucial to an understanding of Lukács's asethetics, and in particular to that of his critique of Naturalism, is the concept of totality which he introduced into dialectical philosophy early in the twenties. Essentially, this is an epistemological category based on the distinction between the isolated fact and overall reality, that is to say, between the empirical existence of an individual fact and its meaning within a network of relations. For, Lukács argues in G e s c h i c h t e u n d K l a s s e n b e w u ß t s e i n : "Erst in diesem Zusammenhang, der die einzelnen Tatsachen des gesellschaftlichen Lebens als Momente der geschichtlichen Entwicklung in eine T o t a l i t ä t einfügt, wird eine Erkenntnis der Tatsachen, als Erkenntnis der W i r k l i c h k e i t möglich."[93] From this relationship of the individual fact to the totality Lukács developed the category of "typicality" in which the individual fact, seen from the perspective of the laws and relationship in which it is embedded, acquires a status which raises it from the individual and empirical level to a position where it is seen to contain within itself the laws and relationships which are external to it or is seen to be an illustration of those relationships. The part becomes, as it were, the mirror of the whole. All reflections of reality, he argues, rest on this contradiction between the particular and the universal, the concrete and the abstract and it is the special quality of great art to be able to reconcile this contradiction. Every significant work of art, therefore, creates its own "self-contained" world in which "the universal appears as a quality of the individual and the particular" and in which the process of life is reflected "in motion and in concrete dynamic context". The great work of art, therefore, is the one which unites the two concepts of totality and typicality:

Indem der Künstler Einzelmenschen und Einzelsituationen
gestaltet, erweckt er den Schein des Lebens. Indem er
sie zu exemplarischen Menschen, Situationen (Einheit des
Individuellen und Typischen) gestaltet, indem er einen
möglichst großen Reichtum der objektiven Bestimmungen des
Lebens als Einzelzüge individueller Menschen und
Situationen unmittelbar erlebbar macht, entsteht seine
"eigene Welt', die gerade darum die Widerspiegelung des
Lebens in seiner bewegten Gesamtheit, des Lebens als
Prozeß und Totalität ist, weil sie in ihrer Gesamtheit
und in ihren Details die gewöhnliche Widerspiegelung
der Lebensvorgänge durch den Menschen steigert und
überbietet.[94]

This "common reflection of life" is the limit of Naturalism's achievement; that is to say, it strives to reflect not an intensive but an
extensive totality of life which Lukács deems necessarily beyond the
possible scope of any artistic creation. It aims, therefore, at the
mechanical imitation of the immediate world of phenomena which Lukács
considers merely a "pseudo-objectivity". Nowhere is this better
illustrated than in Naturalism's attitude to detail. The artistic
correctness of a particular detail is not, he says, contingent on its
authenticity, i.e. whether it corresponds to any similar detail in
reality, but rather on its relationship to the total process of objective
reality, in a word, on its degree of representative significance. This
notion of typicality is, of course, alien to Naturalism since its method
of photographic reproduction of reality is based on the idea that all
details are of equal significance. Furthermore, Naturalism aims at
randomness, not selectivity and a restrictive typicality.

If we now turn to Lukács's critique of reportage[95] - although we must
be mindful of the historical circumstances in which it was written[96] -
we notice a striking similarity with that of Naturalism. Lukács begins
by establishing a relationship between the emergence of the documentary
form and the development of the late bourgeois novel. He argues that
the ever widening dichotomy of the individual and society led the
bourgeois novel to concentrate on individual psychology and left it
incapable of relating this to the wider configuration of social
relationships. Reportage with its fixation on the factual he sees as a
further manifestation of that tendency; its "fetishistic dissection" of

reality evidences only an inability to perceive in the phenomena of
social life relations between men. In short, it fails to reflect life as
a totality. Nor can reportage meet the demand of typicality. In his
critique of reportage Lukács distinguishes two forms of typicality,
namely scientific and artistic typicality. Scientific typicality serves
to enlighten the relationships surrounding the individual fact and makes
this individual fact an example or illustration of them, whereas in
artistic typicality the individual is not an example of general laws
but contains them ("In der Gestaltung muß das Individuum, das individuelle
Schicksal als solches typisch erscheinen, d.h die klassenmäßigen Züge
als individuelle enthalten").[97] The essential thing about these two
forms of typicality, Lukács insists, is that they are not mutually
interchangeable but are restricted to their respective spheres of science
and art. This insistence on the separate identity of science and art is
at the heart of his critique, both of reportage and Naturalism:

> eine künstlerische Darstellung mit wissenschaftlichen Zielen
> wird stets sowohl eine Pseudowissenschaft wie eine Pseudokunst
> sein, und eine 'wissenschaftliche' Lösung der spezifisch
> künstlerischen Aufgaben ergibt ebenso inhaltlich eine
> Pseudowissenschaft und Formell eine Pseudokunst.[98]

The preoccupation of Naturalism and reportage with the factual and the
empirical reveals only surface reality and conceals the "real and
essential driving forces of social reality in its totality". It is
not that their artistic representation lacks authenticity; it is simply
that they provide an uncritical, incomplete and static reflection of
reality.

Clearly, the terminology of these essays is peculiar to Lukács; his
conclusions, however, are not. That is to say, Lukács's fundamental
dichotomy of Naturalism and realism as a differentiation between a style
which describes at surface reality and one which penetrates through and
beyond appearance to an essentially significant reality, is a distinction
which many writers have asserted, however differently they may have
chosen to formulate it.

The second reason why consequential Naturalism as an objectivist tendency

appears to have remained a more or less unique literary phenomenon
is that essentially literature is not the medium to which this style
is inherently suited.  It is surely not incidental that the literary
form which best accommodates the style is that of the short prose-form,
namely  the sketch or the reportage.  Significantly, Holz abandoned his
own attempt to write a novel and undoubtedly, when applying this style
to longer fiction   the main problem is that the continual amassing of
detail becomes either overpoweringly disorientating or merely wearisome.
Similarly, its concern with the random and the everyday makes it a most
hazardous theatrical proposition since it would be almost impossible to
sustain dramatic interest.  In any case, the obvious artificialities of
the stage make drama a medium which is, in many ways, the least amenable
to creating the illusion of reality.  That illusion is surely most
successfully evoked not in drama but in film and it is a nice irony
that historically it was, in fact, with the end of Naturalism that film
emerged as an art form.  Indeed, the historical relationship of
Naturalism and film could well serve to illustrate Walter Benjamin's
thesis on the genesis of new art forms: "Die Geschichte jeder Kunstform
hat kritische Zeiten, in denen diese Form auf Effekte hindrängt, die
sich zwanglos erst bei einem veränderten technischen Standard, das heißt
in einer neuen Kunstform ergeben können".[99]  Thus, one need only think
of the technique of "cinema vérité", of the Naturalist style of a
director such as John Cassavetes or Ken Loach or, more specifically,
of a film like Walter Ruttmann's B e r l i n ,  d i e  S y m p h o n i e
e i n e r  G r o ß s t a d t[100] to recognise just to what extent film
is the real artistic province of consequential Naturalism.

There is, finally, a third reason why the objectivist tendencies of
Holz's style have historically been restricted in Germany to
Naturalism.  In my discussion of Martini's analysis of "Papa Hamlet"
I suggested that the objectivist tendencies which he identifies are only
present in some of Holz's sketches and that "Papa Hamlet" is not, in
fact, one of those.  The obvious question, therefore, is:  why did
Martini not illustrate his argument with a sketch such as "Die papierne
Passion", which would have substantiated his thesis with much less

difficulty? The answer is equally obvious: basically "Papa Hamlet" is a substantially richer and more complex, artistic achievement. This is, I believe, also true of the respective tendencies these two sketches represent. Holz developed the objectivist possibilities of consequential Naturalism almost as far as is conceivable within literature. Lukács - although, of course, he intends it as a criticism - has not been alone in observing that the real legacy of Naturalism lies in a quite different area:

> Die Methode der Beobachtung und der Beschreibung ensteht
> mit der Absicht, die Literatur wissenschaftlich zu machen,
> die Literatur in eine angewandte Naturwissenschaft, in eine
> Soziologie zu verwandeln. Aber die sozialen Momente, die
> durch Beobachtungen erfaßt und durch Beschreibung gestaltet
> wurden, sind so ärmlich, so dünn und schematisch, daß sie
> sehr leicht in ihren polaren Gegensatz, in einen vollendeten
> Subjektivisimus umschlagen konnten.[101]

It is the aim of the following section to illustrate in what direction those subjectivist tendencies can be developed.

> Ob ich eine Statue meißle, oder ein lyrisches Gedicht schreibe
> – der eigentliche Mechanismus ist in beiden Fällen genau
> derselbe.  In beiden Fällen reproduziere ich mit dem und dem
> Material ein "Stück Natur".  Denn ein solches ist nicht bloß,
> im Original, jener "Hirtenknabe, die Flöte blasend", den ich hier
> als erste, vorläufige Skizze in Ton knete, sondern ein solches
> ist, genau so, auch jene eigentümliche Stimmung, die mich
> überrieselt, wenn ich zufällig so einen Burschen auf seinem
> Rohr spielen höre.  Und inwiefern ich mich nun mit meinen
> beiden Werken, der Skulptur und dem Gedicht, der Natur
> gegenüber in dem einen Falle "bildend" verhalten habe, in dem
> anderen aber nicht, ist mir nicht recht einleuchtend.  In beiden
> Fällen, sagt mir mein Wissen, habe ich nachgemacht.  Oder, wenn
> das so besser gefällt, wiedergegeben.  Es kommt hier auf
> eins heraus.  Und mein Werk erscheint mir infolgedessen auch
> um so vorzüglicher, je mehr ich mir glaube einreden zu dürfen,
> daß diese Prozedur mir gelungen ist.  Was sagt da "subjetiv",
> was sagt da "objektiv"?  Nichts!  Das sind hier Messer ohne
> Klingen, die keinen Griff haben.  Ich will Ihnen einen
> Vorschlag machen:  nämlich lassen wir diese beiden Wörtchen
> "subjektiv" und "objektiv" doch lieber ganz aus dem Spiel.
> Sie drücken Werte aus, die in der Kunst keinen Kurs haben.[1]

This quotation, from an essay that Holz published in 1896, illustrates
once again two central aspects of his writing.  Firstly, it emphasises
how imprecise was Holz's conceptualisation of the relationship between
subjectivity and objectivity.  Certainly whether, as in other statements,
insisting on their crucial importance[2] or, as on this occasion, denying
their absolute validity for the process of literary creation, Holz's
at times blatantly contradictory theoretical writings are nevertheless
informed by the need to come to terms with these two concepts.  Secondly,
the above quotation testifies once more to the primacy of nature for
Holz as the object of artistic production.  As far as the subjectivist
interpretation of Holz's work is concerned, these two points are both
of significance.  For if it is Holz's theoretical ambiguity which has,
perhaps, suggested to certain writers a subjectivist understanding of
Holz's work, then it is his concept of "nature" that has provided the
starting-point, from which they have sought to demonstrate the validity
of their analysis.

Raymond Williams has said of "nature" that it is, perhaps, the most
complex word in the English language. Moreover, of the three areas of
meaning that Williams distinguishes, it is his third definition, namely
"nature" as "the material world itself, taken as including or not
including human beings",[3] which points to precisely what has proven
problematical in Holz's usage of the term. In the previous chapter I
showed that the conventional wisdom understood Holz to mean by "nature"
those external phenomena that are directly perceivable by the senses
and that it thus saw his law as defining art as the mimetic reproduction
of those phenomena. In the last twenty years an alternative critical
reception, deriving primarily from the work of Hans-Georg Rappl,[4] has
developed that rejects this mode of analysis. It points out that not only
was Holz himself aware that an exact reproduction of reality was
impossible ("das strittige "x" wird sich niemals auf Null reduzieren"...
"Eine völlig exakte Reproduktion der Natur durch die Kunst ist ein Ding
der absoluten Unmöglichkeit")[5] but also he appeared fundamentally to
reject those concepts, such as "photographic" reproduction or "Nachahmung",[6]
which imply a purely imitative representation of reality. Moreover,
Emrich has argued, such a view reduces Holz's theory purely to the level
of a programmatic demand for Naturalism, whereas Holz was, in fact,
aiming at a totalising conceptualisation of art as such, one which, Emrich
insists, has been of vital relevance to all subsequent developments in
modern art.[7] However, what is normally adduced as the conclusive proof
that Holz's basic intention was never simply a restrictive verism, is the
fact that Holz subsequently reformulated the law[8] given in D i e  K u n s t.
I h r  W e s e n  u n d  I h r e  G e s e t z e as follows: "Die Kunst
hat die Tendenz, die Natur zu sein; sie wird sie nach Maßgabe ihrer
Mittel und deren Handhabung".[9] In this version of the law Holz omitted
the two offending words "wieder" and "Reproduktionsbedingungen" which, it
is claimed, had misled critics into seeing his theory as a demand for the
imitation of empirical reality. This implies a much more expansive
conception of nature such that, in reply to one of his critics' objections
to his "Kunstgesetz", Holz could ask rhetorically: "Ist denn, frage
ich, die Empfindung, die ein Sonnenuntergang in mir wachruft, kein
Naturvorgang?"[10] and insist that by reality he meant "Wirklichkeit unter

selbstverständlichem Einbegriff aller unserer Innenvorgänge".[11] By
nature, therefore, Emrich argues, Holz meant the whole of the spiritual,
social and physical world, including the realm of dreams and imagination,
in so far as it is ever experienced by any single individual or artist;[12]
or, to use Schulz's words, "die Summe alles Äußeren und Inneren, nicht
nur des sinnlich Wahrgenommenen, sondern auch des seelisch Empfundenen,
Erlebten und des Gedachten".[13] Holz himself makes a significant remark
on this subject in response to yet another critic of his "Kunstgesetz":

> Zu jeder Wirkung gehört nun einmal außer dem betreffenden
> O b j e k t  auch noch ein  S u b j e k t...Herr Möller-Bruck
> verschimpfiert meine Formel K=N-x in "K=N+y", indem er "+y" =
> "Vorstellungsbild" setzt, und in seiner Einfalt (...) ahnt er
> nicht einmal, daß dieses "Plus", dieses "Vorstellungsbild",
> mit meinem N einfach identisch ist. Als ob schon je ein
> Mensch irgendein Ding selbst reproduziert hätte und nicht
> bloß immer sein betreffendes Vorstellungbild.[14]

However, by situating the process of artistic creation and reception
concretely in the subject/object relationship, Holz was not only
affirming inner responses as an essential component of the artistic
representation of reality, but also was implicitly posing a fundamental
question about the nature of the human experience of reality. That is
to say, taken to its logical conclusion  the subjectivist view of Holz's
theory argues that his starting-point was not an objective reality,
existing independently of the mediating subject, but a reality that can
only take form as a reflection in the mind. Thus, for John Osborne
it is essentially an epistemological divergency which lies at the heart
of the whole aesthetic debate between Holz and Zola, a divergency,
moreover, which Osborne sees as being causally related to the respective
traditions in which Holz and Zola are located:

> The tradition in which Zola wrote - the tradition of Balzac,
> Stendhal and the French Realists - accepts that there is a
> substantial external reality, as distinct from our subjective
> image of it, and Zola's theory demands that the artist should
> not lose touch with this reality...The impression given by
> Holz's theory is that he is less confident about the existence
> of such a reality; and this is equally characteristic of the
> German tradition in which he stands. As his theory develops
> Holz displays an increasingly monistic tendency to identify
> nature with its reflection in the mind of the individual, or
> with the sensation it arouses in him...[15]

Certainly, some of Holz's theoretical pronouncements, such as "es gibt
für uns Menschen keine K u n s t  an sich wie es für uns Menschen keine
N a t u r an sich gibt",[16] would appear to corroborate this view.
Moreover, such an interpretation would also imbue his "Kunstgesetz"
with a greater subtlety of meaning, at least as regards his primary
concern, literature.  For, as Pascal points out, words can never
"reproduce" reality  if, that is, we understand reality as an objective
situation or event.  Rather words are, in essence, the medium for
expressing and communicating the experience of reality.[17]

The application of these thoughts to Holz's creative writing reveals
a whole new dimension to his imaginative prose.  Or, to be more precise,
the two sketches, "Papa Hamlet" and "Der erste Schultag", possess a
dimension not evident in the sketches of the objectivist category.
That is to say, in "Papa Hamlet" and "Der erste Schultag" the reader is
confronted not primarily with the presentation of a single, objective
reality but rather with a multiplicity of realities, with a reality,
that is, viewed from various perspectives.  Stylistically "Papa Hamlet"
and "Der erste Schultag" still display those features common to the
objectivist sketches and normally associated with the term "Sekundenstil",
i.e. the concreteness and meticulous detail of description etc., although,
as I shall argue later, within a subjectivist interpretation they may take
on a quite radically different function.  What distinguishes the two
types of sketch, however, is the absence in the objectivist type of any
suggestion of multi-perspectivity, for it is only in the subjectivist
sketches that Holz deploys the literary technique responsible for that
effect.  In short, any meaningful analysis of "Papa Hamlet" and "Der
erste Schultag" must start with a re-examination of one of the stylistic
features already discussed in conjunction with the objectivist sketches,
namely  narrative perspective.

Basically, what I am concerned with is the technique which is known in
German as "erlebte Rede".  It is necessary at this point to acknowledge
the debt owed to the work of Roy Pascal, since he has provided both
definitional analysis of the device and close textual examination of
its use, not only in the nineteenth-century European novel but also

specifically in the work of Arno Holz. As will become apparent later, however, the conclusion I draw as regards its ultimate effect in Holz's work differs substantially from that of Pascal and since an important part of his argument revolves around the question of correct terminology, it is first of all necessary to clarify the terms I apply as well as the general problematic to which this discussion addresses itself.

Käte Hamburger expresses the problem in its most generalised form in the following statement: "Die epische Fiktion ist der einzig erkenntnis-theoretische Ort, wo die Ich-Originalität (oder Subjektivität) einer dritten Person als einer dritten dargestellt werden kann".[18] In the traditional narrative mode - and, indeed, in that of Holz's objectivist sketches such as "Die papierne Passion" - the sole perspective is that of the narrator. The narration thus consists of description, possibly including direct authorial comment, punctuated by the statements or views of characters, which are either produced in direct speech with the appropriate punctuation or condensed and presented by the narrator prefaced with such phrases as "he thought" etc. Such a mode, however, does not provide the means with which to present satisfactorily the inner life of fictional characters. This requirement is best fulfilled by another narrative mode[19] of which two aspects can be distinguished. The first is what I wish to call "perspectivised narration", namely where a perspective (in contradistinction to a voice) other than the narrator's is asserted. Here the reader learns how a particular character experiences a thing, but primarily as interpreted and expressed by the narrator: the actual experience is the character's, the interpre-tation and mediation of that experience the narrator's. The second element of this narrative mode is where not merely the experiential level but also the actual voice is that of the character, not the narrator. It is above all this process, in which the thoughts and language of the characters are interwoven without explicit differentiation with those of the narratorial voice, that produces the effect of multi-perspectivity. Moreover, it is this second feature that Pascal is concerned to define in T h e  D u a l  V o i c e.[20] Locating its origin in French and German literary criticism, he contrasts

the two terms, "Le style indirect libre" and "erlebte Rede". The main
difference between the two, he suggests, is that the former describes
the supposed grammatical characteristics of the phenomenon, while the
latter relates to its alleged psychological operation.[21] Pascal himself
adopts the term "free indirect speech", attributing to it two distinctive
features: firstly, it has the syntactical form of a normal narratorial
statement and secondly, it represents the fusion of two voices, that of
a character and the narrator, hence the eponymous "dual voice". It is,
however, precisely this effect that I wish to convey with my term
"perspectivised narration", i.e. the double presence in a statement
of characterial experience and, predominantly, narratorial voice. For
the other aspect I have identified where, I would argue, the interpreting
intermediary is eliminated and the character, as it were, momentarily
deposes the narrator, I will use the term "free indirect style". The
crucial feature I would stress of both "perspectivised narration" and
"free indirect style" is that they communicate experience not objective
information. As such this can have the effect of diluting the narrative's
focal certainty as, for example, in "Papa Hamlet" where it is often
difficult to differentiate between characterial voice and narratorial
irony. The significance of this emphasis, particularly as regards the
conclusions Pascal draws about this narrative mode, will be more apparent
after discussion of the function that the technique fulfils in the
work of Arno Holz.

Before considering Holz's development of this technique in his literary
practice, it is illuminating to return briefly to his theoretical
writings. Although the use of the free indirect style can be found, for
instance, in Goethe and makes a spasmodic appearance in nineteenth-
century, European literature (Jane Austen, Flaubert, Zola), it is only
in the twentieth century that the technique has been consistently
developed both in creative practice and in literary theory. Thus,
Pascal can say of Holz's use of the multiple perspective in "Papa Hamlet"
that "it is one of the most significant German anticipations in the
nineteenth century of a distinguishing peculiarity of modern narrative
fiction".[22] There was, furthermore, at that time no systematic explication

of the principles of narrative perspective which could have provided
Holz with the theoretical basis for his use of the free indirect style.[23]
Nor, it must be added, do Holz's own writings contain any such exposition.
They do, however, reveal certain pertinent generalisations that evince
a degree of awareness as to the question of narrative perspective. The
first occurs in D i e   K u n s t.   I h r   W e s e n   u n d   i h r e
G e s e t z e, where Holz describes how his concern with aesthetic
theory (prior to the composition of the sketches) arose. He relates how
he had been captivated by certain sentences in his autobiographical
novel G o l d e n e   Z e i t e n, an account of his childhood that he
had begun in 1887. One sentence, in particular, affords him great
satisfaction: "In Holland mußten die Paradiesvögel entschieden schöner
pfeifen und die Johannisbrotbäume noch viel, viel wilder wachsen".[24]
The source of the charm, Holz deduces, lies in the fact that there he
was able to reduce to a minimum his **"arrangierendes und Alles umkrempelndes
und zurechtbastelndes Ich".**[25] That is to say, he was able to eliminate
the momentary temperament of himself, the writer, and evoke the actual
response to the world he experienced as the child. This elimination
of the author's consciousness is, in fact, effected by Holz's use of
the free indirect style.

The second reference to this technique is contained in a memorandum
written by Johannes Schlaf which Holz quotes in Vol.10 of D a s   W e r k.
In his account of how the collaboration between the two writers began,
Schlaf observes at one point:

> Holz war damals dahin gekommen, dem Zolaschen Satze 'Un
> chef d'oeuvre est un coin de la nature vu à travers un
> tempérament' den anderen gegenüberzustellen: Ein Kunstwerk
> ist ein Stück Leben, angesehen nicht durch das Temperament
> des Künstlers, sondern aller der Personen, die er geben
> will.[26]

This remark shows that even if Holz was not able to theorise adequately
the problems of narrative perspective, he was at any rate aware of it
and thus that the use of the free indirect style in his prose-writing
was not a fortuitous but a conscious one.

Holz's sketch "Der erste Schultag" is, in fact, the only part of
G o l d e n e   Z e i t e n   that was ever published.  It is an account
of a young boy's first day at school and is divided structurally into
three episodes:  the morning class in which one of his fellow-pupils
is terrorised by the sadistic headmaster, Jonathan's visit to the nearby
fair and finally the discovery on visiting his old friend, the
herbalist, that the latter is sitting dead in his chair.  These experiences are related very much (but not exclusively) from the perspective
of the young boy;  the story's last sentence, for example, "Das war
dem kleinen Jonathan sein erster Schultag",[27] not only sums up the
events described but does so in a manner applicable to that of the
experiencing subject, the young boy himself.  The best example in this
sketch of Holz's use of the free indirect style occurs, however, in the
opening scene.  The young boys in the class, all beginners like
Jonathan, are compelled by Rector Borchert to maintain an absolute
silence, a **feat** rendered impossible not only by the sheer duration of
the demanded passiveness but also by the boys' excitement at the
prospect of visiting the fair in the nearby town.  The strain, caused
by the knowledge that the slightest movement will earn them a beating,
is broken by the nervous laughter of a Jewish boy, Lewin, which,as
Borchert calls the boy to him for punishment, develops into a hysterical
fit:

> Der Herr Rector Borchert hatte sich jetzt aufrecht mitten
> auf sein Podium gestellt.  Seine Lippen waren weiß geworden.
> Seine kleinen, spitzen Zähne knurrschten, als ob er an etwas
> kaute.
> "Herkommen, Knubbel?!"
> Aber der kleine Lewin hörte nichts mehr.  Er lachte nur
> immer und lachte und lachte...Jetzt endlich war der
> Geduldsfaden des Herrn Rector Borchert mitten entzwei
> gerissen!  Mit einem Satz war er auf den wahnsinnigen
> Judenhund zugesprungen, hatte ihn an seinem schmierigen
> Jackenkragen zu packen gekriegt und schleifte ihn nun
> wutschnaubend auf sein Katheder.
> "So ein Hund!!  So ein Hund!!!"
> Die "Knubbels", die wieder ganz mückchenstill geworden waren,
> hatten alle unwillkürlich ihre Augen fest zugemacht.  Die ganze,
> große, rote Stube schwamm jetzt in Blut.  In Blut.  Oh! ...
> Da!!
> Plötzlich, mitten durch all das grausenhafte Schnauben und Gurgeln

vorn, hatte draußen vom Flur her deutlich ein feines, schrilles
Glöckchen angeschlagen. Kein "Knubbel", der nicht jetzt
seine kleinen, rosa Öhrchen spitzte! Das reine Christglöckchen!
Es klingelte jetzt, daß er nur so eine Art hatte. Ja! Ja! Das
war der Herr Spaarmann, der liebe, gute Herr Spaarman!
Jetzt brauchten sie nicht mehr zu sterben. Jetzt war die
schreckliche, schreckliche Stunde aus. Jetzt...Oh! Der
Herr Spaarmann![28]

At first sight this appears a straightforward piece of narratorial
description, marked only by the odd hint of omniscience such as when we
are told that the pupils all shut their eyes "involuntarily". A closer
inspection, however, reveals that the passage is not just objective
information given from a narratorial position. The very formal "Der
Herr Rektor Borchert" may seem rather wooden and conspicuous until we
remember that it would be precisely that form with which the boys would
be required to address him and to refer to him. More unmistakably "den
wahrsinnigen Judenhund" cannot possibly derive from the narratorial
vocabulary but is part of Borchert's language, as surely as is the
explicitly accredited "So ein Hund". Similarly, the "jetzt endlich" is
not just a purely temporal reference but expresses Borchert's felt
exasperation as his patience runs out. The "unwillkürlich" signals
the return of the narrator in his omniscient guise, but the following
line marks a further shift in perspective: "Die ganze, große, rote
Stube schwamm jetzt in Blut". Literally, of course, this cannot be
true, nor even if it were, would the narrator be likely to communicate
it to the reader in this manner. It works equally badly if understood
as an image, for not only would it be totally incongruous with the
detached tone of observation the narrator adopts elsewhere but we have,
in any case, already been informed earlier that the colour of the
schoolroom is blue. The only possible explanation, therefore, is that
the perspective is now that of the boys and, as Pascal explains, what
we have in this sentence is the effect of their fright and terror,
when they squeeze their eyelids together so hard that their vision
floods with red.[29] This is an excellent example of what I termed
"perspectivised narration", for clearly these particular words are
neither said nor even thought by the boys. Rather it is their experience of the moment, but filtered through the mediating voice of the

narrator. Moreover, this perspective is not just a momentary one for the "Oh" and "Da" clearly convey their feelings of terror and subsequent relief as they hear the schoolbell. The "grausenhafte Schnauben und Gurgeln" cannot, therefore, be taken as objective description but as their subjective experience of the noises in the room. In their predicament the ringing of the bell does for them literally mean salvation. Thus, whether the porter, Herr Spaarmann, is in fact "good" and "kind" is uncertain; to the boys he can appear so since it is he who brings the "terrible hour" to its official end. This passage as a whole, therefore, provides a good illustration of the technique of perspectivised narration.[30]

This constant shift of perspective, it must be added, is not merely an artistic refinement but is central to the substance of the narration. Failure to perceive it may have interpretational consequences. Thus, Borcherdt can write of the "Totprüglung"[31] and Osborne of the "violent assault"[32] of the Jewish boy by the schoolmaster whereas, in fact, the boy is not beaten at all, for his fit saves him.[33] Thus, when we read in the text "Jetzt schlug er ihn tot",[34] this is not narratorial comment but, as the preceding word "Gewiß!" emphasises, Jonathan's horrified thought, given in the form of the free indirect style, that the boy will be beaten to death. Elsewhere in the sketch Holz's use of the technique is much more spasmodic and, perhaps, the fact that even here he still felt the need to put certain words in inverted commas is evidence that he was as yet only tentatively applying the style. In "Papa Hamlet" it is more consistently used and ultimately more effective.

Significantly, the sketch even opens in the following manner: "Was? Das war Niels Thienwiebel? Niels Thienwiebel, der große,unübertroffene Hamlet aus Trondhjem? Ich esse Luft und werde mit Versprechungen gestopft? Mann kann Kapaunen nicht besser mästen?..."[35] So even in the first sentence the reader finds not, as he perhaps might expect, a simple introductory remark by the narrator, nor even a piece of dialogue between the characters  but, as the "Ich" reveals, the words in free indirect style of the eponymous main character. Thienwiebel's perspective is, in fact, constantly in evidence throughout the story, both in relation to other characters and objects: we read, for instance, that Thienwiebel closes not a particular Shakespeare volume but "seinen William",[36] while his son is referred to not as the young child but as "der kleine Krebsrote"[37] or "dem kleinen zappelnden Wurm".[38] Often, too, characters are enveloped in the illusion of Thienwiebel's Shakespearean make-believe world so that in the middle of one of his soliloquies, for example, we read: "Der kleine Fortinbras war jetzt ganz ernsthaft geworden. Er hatte seinen großen Papa noch nie so menschlich mit ihm reden hören."[39] This could be narratorial irony. Equally it could be the product of Thienwiebel's imagination, since, so convinced is he by his own imaginings, that he tries to teach the child to talk, despite the fact that it is only three months old. The location of the perspective in a character, however, is by no means limited to Thienwiebel, although since he is the main figure and only rarely out of focus, his is the one which, with the exception of the narrator's, predominates. Often, however, the perspective shifts to his wife, Amalie, or to lesser characters such as Ole Nissen and Frau Wachtel. On some occasions one could even say that the perspective is entrusted to characters that do not actually appear in the story, as in the following description of Amalie:

> Ihre dünnen lehmfarbenen Haare waren noch nicht gemacht, ihre
> Nachtjacke schien heute noch schmutziger als sonst und stand
> vorn natürlich wieder offen; der kleine kirschrote
> Spießbürger, den sie, auf ihr Fußbänkchen gekauert, nachlässig
> aus einem Gummischlauch saugte, sah auf einmal häßlich aus
> wie ein kleiner Frosch.[40]

Undoubtedly, the description of the child, with its peculiar analogy with a frog and its characteristic language, belongs to Thienwiebel; but the slightly moralising irony of the "natürlich wieder" and the "noch schmutziger als sonst" is surely not part of Thienwiebel's response, for he would be hardly likely to notice or care about the untidiness of Amalie's appearance. More probably, therefore, this is the impression of a neighbour or frequent visitor to the Thienwiebel's household. The uncertainty as on this occasion as to who is the author of a

particular statement is not, however, a weakness of the style; rather
it is an enrichment of the text, a constant reminder of the complexity
of subjective experience. Indeed, one might say that the use of the
free indirect style is all the more effective precisely when the perspective is not lodged firmly in one character. Section IV of "Papa
Hamlet" provides good examples of this "shifting perspective":

> Der alten, lieben, guten Frau Wachtel aber war damit ein
> sehr großer Stein vom Herzen gefallen. Sie hatte nämlich
> die niedliche kleine Mieze einmal dabei ertappt, als sie
> dem abscheulichen Ole grade Modell stand, und da sie
> hierfür wirklich auch nicht das mindeste Verständnis besaß,
> ein gewisses, kleines Vorurteil gegen sie gefaßt. Ihr
> gutes Herz zu betätigen hatte sie in letzter Zeit leider
> nur zu wenig Gelegenheit gehabt. Am unzufriedensten aber
> war sie jedenfalls mit den dummen Thienwiebels. Was bei der
> alten Schlamperei dort schließlich rauskommen mußte, konnte
> man sich ja an den Fingern abzählen. Der alte, alberne Kerl
> flözte sich den ganzen Tag auf dem Sofa rum und trieb Faxen, das
> faule, schwindsüchtige Frauenzimmer hatte nicht einmal Zeit,
> seinem Schreisack das bißchen blaue Milch zu geben, zu fressen
> hatten sie alle drei nichts, und die Miete – ach, du lieber
> Gott! Wenn man nicht wenigstens noch die paar Sparkreeten
> gehabt hätte...[41]

In the first paragraph we are introduced to Frau Wachtel, but very much
as a projection of the narrator's attitude to her, as evidenced by the
obvious sarcasm of the "liebe, gute Frau Wachtel" and the stressing of
her philistinism as the reason for her dislike of the Thienwiebels. Even
here, however, Frau Wachtel's own perspective asserts itself momentarily
for the "abscheulich" represents her opinion of Ole and not the
narrator's. In the second paragraph the irony is continued but once
again the "leider" and "dummen" signal the presence of the landlady's
own voice so that gradually she herself takes over the perspective
altogether. The slangy level of speech, the dialect and, above
all, the vehement indignation at the Thienwiebel's behaviour reveals
the rest of the passage as free indirect style that is in no way qualified
by any narratorial presence.

In fact, in passages such as this, where it is not just a case of other
characters' thoughts and views merely mingling with those of the

narrator but actually of the narratorial voice being totally suppressed
in favour of the consciousness of one of the characters, the question
arises as to whether, in this context, free indirect style is a
sufficiently differentiated term and whether this quantitative change
does not, in fact, require a separate term to denote a qualitative
distinction. Pascal addresses himself to this question in his
discussion of the following passage from "Papa Hamlet" that illustrates
this very tendency:

> Seit ihr zweiter, unliebenswürdiger Gatte ihr vor ungefähr
> fünf Jahren auf der "Dicken Selma" treulos nach Kanada
> ausgerückt war, hatte die liebe, gute, alte Frau Wachtel
> keinen solchen Ärger mehr auszustehen gehabt.
>
> Nicht bloß,daß seine Stiefelabsätze noch überall auf dem
> Sofa deutlich zu sehen waren, nicht bloß, daß das Fensterkreuz
> von den dämlichen Leiterstücken, die jetzt natürlich zerbrochen
> unten auf dem Pappdach lagen, total ruiniert war, bewahre:
> auch die ganze Tapete war von oben bis unten mit Ölfarben
> bekleckst! Der vermaledeite knirpsige Schmierpeter schien
> sich die ganze Zeit dran seine schwein' schen Pinsel
> ausgequetscht zu haben. Pfui Deibel ja!
>
> Aber, das war ihr ganz recht! Warum hatte sie das ganze Pack
> nicht schon längst an die Luft gesetzt! Wenn's wenigstens noch
> die verrückten Thienwiebels gewesen wären. Aber die holte
> ja der Satan nicht! Die hakten fest wie Kletten an ihr![42]

The first paragraph is similar to that of the earlier passage concerning
Frau Wachtel: amid the narratorial irony, of which she is once again
the object, her own voice can occasionally be distinguished before the
perspective is totally appropriated in the second and third paragraphs
by her consciousness. The stylistic peculiarity about this passage
that Pascal alerts us to is the fact that we are not told the identity
of the "er" to whom she refers at the beginning of the second paragraph
(the passage comes at the beginning of Section VI, so there is nothing
before the quoted part that might indicate of whom she is thinking).
"Der vermaledeite knirpsige Schmierpeter" is clearly Ole Nissen, but
the earlier "er" is in actual fact Thienwebel, as her later cursing
of "die verrückten Thienwiebels" confirms. The reason why it is at
first unclear who "er" is, can, as Pascal points out,[43] only be

explained if we recognise the passage as free indirect style, as an
excursion, as it were, into the landlady's mind where it is not
necessary to name the object of her fury;  so preoccupied is she with
the hated man that "er" suffices.

Pascal draws attention to this passage for two reasons:  firstly, because this ambiguity he recognises as a stylistic feature of many modern
novels, where the reader may be uncertain for many pages as to who is
thinking about whom;  secondly, because when the free indirect style
is extended in this way, such passages, he claims, can only be called
inner monologues.  In the older narrative monologue, as in the
theatrical monologue, the character speaks without intermediary in the
present tense.  The older convention, as in Walter Scott, Stendhal or
Fontane, for example, was to present such a soliloquy in inverted
commas, as if it were a speech, whereas in the modern convention the
use of free indirect style enables the author to come closer to the
peculiar nature of thought as opposed to speech.  The passages in "Papa
Hamlet", like those already discussed, are thus more typical of the
narrative form of inner monologue, not only because they share the
grammatical form of authorial narrative and are, in this case, related
in the past but also because mostly the content and language of the
passages tell us they convey the thoughts of a character.  As such
they must in fact be termed inner mologues.[44]  Paradoxically, in "Papa
Hamlet" Holz succeeds at one and the same time in both blurring and
heightening the difference between the two forms of monologue.  For,
on the one hand, by working the use of actual Shakespearean soliloquies
organically into the story, he emphasises the sharp contrast in style
between the dramatic and the inner monologue;  while, on the other
hand, by occasionally weaving into Thienwiebel's inner monologues
fragments or stylistic features of Shakespeare's passages, he actually
fuses the two forms and produces, in effect, a monologue within a monologue, as in the following example at the beginning of section III:

> Er hatte seit kurzen - er wußte nicht wodurch? - all seine
> Munterkeit eingebüßt, seine gewohnten Übungen aufgegeben, und
> es stand in der Tat so übel um seine Gemütslage, daß die Erde,

dieser treffliche Bau, ihm nur ein kahles Vorgebirge schien.
Dieser herrliche Baldachin, die Luft, dieses majestätische
Dach mit goldnem Feuer ausgelegt: kam es ihm doch nicht
anders vor als ein fauler, verpesteter Haufe von Dünsten.

Welch ein Meisterwerk war der Mensch! Wie edel durch
Vernunft! Wie unbegrenzt an Fähigeiten! In Gestalt und
Bewegung wie bedeutend und wunderwürdig im Handeln, wie
ähnlich einem Engel; im Begreifen, wie ähnlich einem
Gotte; die Zierde der Welt! Das Vorbild des Lebendigen!
Und doch: was war ihm diese Quintessenz von Staube?
Er hatte keine Lust am Manne – und am Weibe auch nicht.
Die Zeit war aus den Fugen! War es zu glauben? Aber – e –
man hatte ihm noch immer nicht geschrieben. Man war
undankbar in Christiania. Armer Yorick![45]

The real stylistic advance that derives from Holz's use of free

indirect style, however, lies in a quite different area. In summing

up the difference between the two types of monologue, the inner and

the dramatic, Pascal points to the way in which the style of Holz's

consequential Naturalism could be effectively combined with the form

of the free indirect style such that the resulting inner monologue

expressed, in a hitherto unknown way, the complexities of the psyche

and the subconscious:

> inner monologues (are) proper to the narrative form, while
> the older type is proper to the drama. They have one great
> advantage over the older, dramatic type. The latter must
> confine itself to articulate thoughts, that indicate a high
> degree of consciousness, of intellectual awareness and
> literacy. The inner monologue in the form of free indirect
> speech can express more readily subconscious, preconscious
> psychic layers, nervous reactions, that resist conscious
> verbalisation by the characters.[46]

Similarly, Walter Sokel has argued that the stream-of-consciousness

technique – the next stage in the subjectivist scale, as it were –

ultimately derives from the structural principle of "Sekundenstil".[47]

Such views merely indicate the subjectivising tendencies inherent in

Holz's consequential Naturalism.

I have dwelt at some length on Holz's use of the free indirect style,

firstly, because I wish to give some idea of the extent to which it

informs the structure of, in particular, "Papa Hamlet" and secondly,

because I regard it as the crucial (but not the only) stylistic feature that separates the two types of sketch I have identified in Holz's imaginative prose. Above all, it is the prerequisite for the multi-perspectivity so evident in "Papa Hamlet". And yet merely to establish the existence of a plurality of perspectives does not, in itself, tell us what the interpretational consequences of that multiple perspective are. Furthermore, much though my observations on the free indirect style are indebted to Roy Pascal's excellent analysis of that feature of Holz's prose-writing, nevertheless the conclusion I reach regarding the consequences of the multiple perspective in Holz's work is the very converse of that which Pascal proposes. And since I believe that the conclusion he draws plays a definite role both in his analysis of other stylistic elements in "Papa Hamlet" and in his interpretation of the sketch as a whole, then clearly it is appropriate to provide, first of all, a brief exposition of his argumentation. Essentially, however, we are concerned with the question of to what extent the use of free indirect style affects the status of objective reality in Holz's prose.

Pascal begins by asserting the essential difference between two types of prose-fiction, namely the novel of nineteenth-century realism and what he calls "the modern, post-Joycean novel".[48] In the former the position of the narrator is absolute, since the subjective world of the characters can always be clearly differentiated from the authoritative, authorial truth and consequently their views are always "explicitly partial, subordinate to the understanding wisdom of the narrator";[49] in the latter, however, the status of the narrator is undermined and, in some cases, to so great a degree as to present reality as a complex configuration of subjective consciousnesses that ultimately denies the possibility of an objective view of reality. Relating Holz's prose-style (in "Papa Hamlet" and "Der erste Schultag") to these two types, Pascal argues that although the multi-perspectivity deriving from his use of free indirect style shows a richer understanding of the complexity of human beings and is, therefore, truer to reality than the presenta-tion possible within the single perspective of the fictitious onlooker, the resulting complexity neither relativises the position of the

narrator nor shakes in any way the essential objectivity of the narrative.
That is to say, Holz's prose is still basically within the realist
tradition in the sense that "his method as a whole rather tends to
reinforce the idea of a possible objective truth, just as it does
that of an authoritative moral judgement".[50] In other words, while
acknowledging that Holz's use of free indirect style is an enrichment
of realism - one could almost say, paradoxically, it is more objective
in that it is more subjective! - Pascal does not regard this overall
as a subjectivising tendency and this for two reasons: firstly, because
its use does not by and large engender ambiguity and secondly, because
of what he describes as the inherent "authority" of the narrator in
Holz's prose. I hope to show that both these assertions are more
problematical than Pascal would allow for and that, consequently, the
idea of an unchallengeable, objective truth is in "Papa Hamlet"
considerably relativised.

Ambiguity is, in fact, quite common in "Papa Hamlet". Throughout the
sketch, for example, the Thienwiebels are referred to as "der große
Thienwiebel" - which, while clearly a narratorial ironisation of
Thienwiebel's sense of self-importance, may or may not represent an
objective statement on the character's physical appearance - and "die
reizende Ophelia". The latter is not problematical,because once
alerted to the function of the free indirect style we can recognise how
Thienwiebel constantly subsumes other characters into his Shakespearean
world. However, a statement such as "Ihre alten Opheliajahre waren
wieder lebendig in ihr geworden"[51] does raise certain doubts. For as
a narratorial comment it could be taken to mean that formerly Amalie
did actually play on stage the role of Ophelia to Thienwiebel's Hamlet.
Alternatively, it could denote a momentary change in Thienwiebel's
response to his wife, a re-awakening of the feelings he presumably once
had for her and as such this would be a significant qualification of
Thienwiebel's character. Uncertainty can be found, too, at a much
simpler level. A sentence such as "Total vernichtet hatte er sich jetzt
wieder auf das Sofa zurückgeschleudert"[52] appears straightforward enough;
and yet, is the slightly colloquial "total vernichtet" the narrator's
observation or is it Thienwiebel's own evocation of his sense of fatigue,

real or imagined?  Similarly, when we read of Amalie, "Sie sah jetzt
ordentlich wie eine kleine Hausmutter aus",[53] does this represent a brief
effort on her part to try and break out of her own apathy or is it
merely how she appears to the slightly infatuated Ole?  Once suggested
the uncertainty, arising from the constant switch in perspective, can
lead us to question the apparently most trivial aspect of the text,
as in the following example where even the status of the dots is
ambiguous(!):

> "Allerdings, Amalie! Ich behaupte..."
> Amalie war jetzt ein wenig ungeduldig geworden.
> "Ach was! Laß lieber das Kind nicht so schrein!"
> "Auch d a s ist wieder nur so ein Vorurteil von dir,
> Amalie! Was schadet das! Ich habe gelesen, es ist nichts
> gesünder! Die Lungen weiten sich dabei! Aber – e ... wie
> gesagt! Du solltest das Kind selbst tränken! Die heutige
> Kultur freilich, die Kultur der europäischen Welt..."
>
> Die Kultur überging Amalie.  Sie hielt sich nur an die
> Ermahnungen, die sie nur schon so oft zu hören bekommen
> hatte.[54]

In the first instance the dots indicate that Thienwiebel has been
interrupted in mid-sentence by Amalie's impatient "Ach was!". The third
time, however, it could show that Thienwiebel, in switching to his
higher quasi-Shakespearean level of articulation, is stumbling over his
words as in the case of the second example ("Aber -e ... wie gesagt!");
he has, as it were, forgotten his lines.  Alternatively, the following
narratorial passage appears to shift the perspective to Amalie and to
the thought that she has heard this all before.  The narrator's explanation, "Die Kultur überging Amalie", could thus be his ironic way of
telling us that Amalie had, as it were, mentally switched off and thus
the dots represent Amalie's reception of the rest of Thienwiebel's
homily, i.e. objectively he continues speaking, she merely shuts her
mind to it in her fury  at his continued carping.

Similarly, the function of the much discussed episode at the end of the
sketch, where Holz actually represents in the text the dripping of the
melting snow, could be seen to differ according to the perspective from
which it is viewed.  Pascal cites with approval Martini's view of this

scene as an exemplary "still-life", representing, that is to say,
a lyrical moment that reflects the response of the observing artist and
that in no sense interprets the experience or perception of the
fictional characters.[55] And yet, could not this be precisely the
case, namely that this is indeed Thienwiebel's actual experience,
his mind a blank with the realisation of what he has done such that
his now distorted awareness of reality perceives only the rhythmic but
disproportionately prominent sound of the thawing snow?

These may all appear very minor subtleties. There are, however, many
other such examples in "Papa Hamlet" and in their combined effect they
cannot but weaken the narratorial standpoint. There are, in any case,
at least two occasions where the perspectival ambiguity is of major
importance. Mention has already been made of the manner in which the
sketch begins, of how the usual reassuring narratorial introduction is
foresaken in favour of a disconcerting passage in free indirect style.
The disorienting effect of this as regards the narratorial standpoint is
paralleled by the uncertainty surrounding the end of the sketch, for
there we find once again not an authoritative statement from the
narrator but a series of apparently disparate quotations. I shall
return later to this concluding passage; for the moment suffice it to
say that some indication of its ambiguity can be gained from the fact
that in their respective interpretation of this "epilogue", Pascal and
Martini arrive at totally opposite conclusions concerning its meaning for
the rest of the story and its relationship to the position of the
narrator. The second instance of substantial ambiguity concerns the
concluding lines of Section VI where we read: "Der große Thienwiebel
hatte nicht so ganz unrecht: Die ganze Wirtschaft bei ihm zu Hause
war der Spiegel und die abgekürzte Chronik des Zeitalters".[56] The
question here is: whose words are these, Thienwiebel's or the narrator's?
If the latter, then this must be seen as an unambivalent statement by
the narrator - untypically foresaking his ironical stance - which
identifies the disarray of the Thienwiebel household as a symptom and
microcosmic reflection of an entire age in disintegration, with the first
part of the sentence alluding to a remark made earlier by Thienwiebel

himself. If, however, what we find here is Thienwiebel's perspective
transposed once again via his Shakespearean register of articulation
on to the quasi-philosphical level of his monologues  - and the
particular use of a colon does prompt the impression of quotation - then
the first part of the sentence represents not so much an unequivocal
affirmation as an intentional qualification of his view, the narrator's
grudging admission that there might be a grain of truth in what he
says but that his words are not to be taken too literally.

For Pascal, however, this particular problem would not arise;  for him
there is no question of relativism since, he argues, the narrator is still
accorded the inviolable authority of the realist tradition.  However,
while it is true that there are residual traces of this form of narration in "Papa Hamlet", I would argue that this is not the position of
omniscience associated with the traditional narrator.  An episode in
section III illustrates this point.  Here Frau Wachtel has brought
some milk for the baby and bending over the child in its cot starts
affectionately to play with it.  Suddenly for some reason she hurriedly
leaves and the narrator proffers the explanation that this is probably
because she has heard someone coming up the stairs.  At the end of the
scene Thienwiebel, in a rare show of affection, bends over to kiss his
son but he too is repelled by something.  The narrator now reveals the
real cause of Frau Wachtel's exit: "Sei's Farbe der Natur, sei's Fleck
des Zufalls, kurz und gut, aber der kleine Prinz von Norwegen lag wieder
seelenvergnügt mitten in seinen weitläufigen Besitzungen da".[57]  In
other words, the narrator is still very much in the role of onlooker,
experiencing events, like the characters themselves, as they happen.  And
yet he differs in one very important aspect from the impartial observer
we identified in, for example, "Die papierne Passion".  For "Papa
Hamlet" is marked by a pervasive irony and it is through this clearly
identifiable narratorial perspective that the characters and events
are filtered.  The narrator, then, may be anonymous but he is not, as
Pascal would have it, without characteristics.  For his prevailing
sense of doubt, his caustic sarcasm and unrelenting cynicism imbue him
with a moral, if not an actual physical presence, an attribute, moreover,
that situates him not outside but firmly within the context of the

reality depicted. That is to say, far from reinforcing the narrator's
authority, as Pascal claims, the sharp ironic tone of his comments
actually diminishes that authority. The irony creates a double distance:
on the one hand, between the narrator and the characters and, on the
other hand, between the narrator and the reader. Of course, this is
not to say that we accept nothing of what the narrator relates for our
acknowledging the validity of factual items, passages of description
etc. is, as Pascal stresses, the condition for the existence of the
story.[58] Equally, however, this does not mean that we are obliged to
accept as absolute those statements which may or may not purport to be
factual but which actually evince the value-judgements of the narrator.
The intimacy between narrator and reader, as Martini puts it, is broken;
events are related from a perspective which is, ultimately, unambiguously
personal and with which we are not necessarily being invited to identify.
The irony directed against Thienwiebel is a good example. The narrator's
sarcasm has the function of puncturing for the reader the carapace of
illusion with which Thienwiebel coats his relationship to reality. But
what the narrator's "harsh lack of sympathy"[59] does not let him see is
that, as Osborne points out, Thienwiebel's escapism is understandable
since it is only by adopting a role that he is able to attain any sort
of mastery, albeit an illusory one, over the world in which he lives.[60]
That this is the type of conclusion that Holz himself might wish us to
draw is indicated by a statement he made at the time of composing
"Papa Hamlet", one which, moreover, is surely at variance with the
attitude of his narrator:

> Mein Standpunkt, der nicht der 'idealistische' ist, verbietet
> es mir, von ihm aus, 'Verdammungsurteile' zu fällen, Ich fälle
> überhaupt keine 'Verdammungsurteile'. Ich suche in erster Linie
> zu 'verstehen'. 'Non ridere, non lugere, neque detestari, sed
> intelligere'. Das ist meine Devise.[61]

Nor is the narratorial standpoint fully grasped if seen merely as a
residual effect of the bourgeois distaste for the bohemian so evident in
Schlaf's "Ein Dachstubenidyll". For the narrator's sarcasm is pointed
not only at the Thienwiebels but also at decidedly non-bohemian
characters such as Frau Wachtel or the policeman who finds Thienwiebel's
body. Martini is thus surely correct in characterising the narrator's

position, particularly as expressed in the "epilogue", as one of doubt and cynicism. To be sure, one must speak of the dominance of the narrator's perspective, but it is not an insidious but a perfectly transparent form of dominance. Since it is all too evident how the narrator continually tries to put forward his own point of view, his perspective can thus be seen as just one view of reality among many, which is in itself no more valid, exemplary or authoritative than that of, say, Thienwiebel and which certainly does not emanate, therefore, from what Pascal calls an "unchallengeable deity".[62]

The use of the free indirect style and perspectivised narrative is thus an important subjectivising tendency. There are, however, others which likewise can only be found in "Papa Hamlet" and "Der erste Schultag". One such tendency is Holz's use of the symbol of which three types can be differentiated. The first may be termed the "inorganic" symbol, namely those items of the story which possess no inherent narrative function and which merely serve to reflect at a different level of significance the reality depicted. Pascal has provided an excellent example of this type of symbol in his analysis of "Der erste Schultag". In the classroom scene when Borchert is left alone with the hysterical Jewish boy, the narrator describes at some length the girations of a large bluebottle that has fallen on its back and is struggling to right itself. Its effect is clearly to symbolise the writhings of the boy that are then described a little later in the passage.

Just before the incident and following directly on the boys' joyous exit from Borchert's classroom, the narrator switches focus once more to describe the end of the tight-rope walker's act in the nearby town square and the applause from the watching crowd. Here again the release from the tension engendered by the artist's act, which is manifested in their rapturous reception of its end, parallels the sense of relief felt by the boys on hearing the schoolbell and expressed in their adulation of the porter. The difference between the description of the tight-rope walker and that of the bluebottle, however, is that the former, unlike the latter, is organically integrated into the story and

and has an autonomous, narrative significance. "Papa Hamlet", too, has examples of this type, chief among which being the continual evoking of Hamlet, the disillusioned idealist, through the Shakespeare quotations. Indeed, the very incongruity of the two words in the sketch's title symbolises the uneasy fusion of the two spheres of Thienwiebel's existence and the way his private persona is gradually engulfed by the illusion of his public role.

There is still another type of symbolic element in "Papa Hamlet" that occurs when an amorphous collection of things come together in momentary harmony and thereby transcend their significance as mere objects. Such examples can be found quite early in the sketch:

> Mit einem Ruck war jetzt der Shakespeare, den er sich eben aus seiner Schlafrocktasche gerissen, auf den Tisch geflogen, wo er die Gesellschaft einer Spirituskochmaschine, eines braunirdenen Milchtopfs ohne Henkel, eines alten, berußten Handtuchs, einer Glaslampe und einer Photographie des großen Thienwiebel in Morarahmen vorfand.[63]

Such moments occur throughout the sketch and culminate in the typographical representation of the thawing snow. They may, as in the above example, constitute a visionary moment of contrast to the surrounding chaos and disintegration of the Thienwiebel household; alternatively, they may represent a form of poetic anthropmorphism as objects seemingly spring to life in order to participate directly in the unfolding drama. Thus, in the final episode Thienwiebel's drunken homecoming is accompanied by a whole orchestra of objects:

> Die Schere, die ihr vorhin vom Tisch runtergekippt war, lag unten vor ihr auf den grauen Dielen. Sie flinkerte.
> Das Lämpchen auf dem Tisch hatte jetzt leise zu zittern angefangen, die hellen, langgezogenen Kringel, die sein Wasser oben quer über die Decke und ein Stück Tapete weg gelegt hatte, schaukelten. Das Geschirr um das Glas hob sich schwarz aus ihnen ab. Die Kaffekanne reichte bis über die Decke.
> "Brrr...Ae!"
> Ihre Pantoffeln waren jetzt unter den Tisch geflogen, sie hatte sich hastig unter das Deckbett gekuschelt.
> Die weißen Lichtringe fluteten und fluteten, das Öl auf dem Tisch knatterte leise, ein kleines Fünkchen war eben von seinem Docht abgespritzt und schwamm nun schwarz in der dicken, goldgelben Masse.[64]

Martini, since he argues the objectivist case for Holz's sketches, finds
these lyrical moments incongruous with the objectivity that, he argues,
prevails elsewhere in the narrative.  Consequently, he calls them "eine
Inkonsequenz des konsequenten Naturalisten"[65] of which he believes
Holz could not have been aware.  Martini himself, however, seems in turn
unaware that this subjectivising tendency is latent in the very method of
the "Sekundenstil", for the meticulous description of minute detail can
have two possible effects.  On the one hand, it may reproduce reality in
the objectivist sense that it allows the reader to form an imaginary
picture of, say, a particular milieu by piecing together the various
depicted elements into a complete mental image;  on the other hand,
by isolating or emphasising particular objects or details which the
reader, were he actually present in and himself surveying the milieu, would
not consciously register, the style of consequential Naturalism may, in
fact, depict the concrete in such a way as to deprive it of its
reassuring familiarity and imbue it with a sort of magic autonomy
transcending its contextual significance, a process one could perhaps
term the "estrangement effect" of the "Sekundenstil".  Whether one calls
these lyrical images "Stimmungsträger" or "still lifes" (Martini),
"epiphanies" (James Joyce) or simply symbols, is of less relevance than
the fact that as such they clearly constitute a subjectivising tendency,
a stylisation which, significantly, is peculiar to "Papa Hamlet" and
does not appear in those sketches of the objectivist type.

In my discussion of Holz's use of irony and the symbol, reference has
been made to one particular element common to both, namely the integration into the text of quotations from H a m l e t.  These appear in three
distinct forms:  as dramatic lines actually recited by Thienwiebel, as
part of his speech or thought as it occurs in either conversation or
inner monologue and as part of the direct, narratorial comment used for
obvious ironic effect.  All three forms serve to parody and relativise
both Thienwiebel's reality and his view of reality.  However, these
quotations can, I would suggest, also fulfil another function in that
they constitute an important component of the formal structure of
"Papa Hamlet".  This becomes clearer when analysing the manner in which
Holz incorporates the quotations into the text.  Whereas on some

occasions, such as when Thienwiebel is actually rehearsing the
lines, Holz merely transposes without intervention certain parts
of Shakespeare's text, very often his technique of interweaving
quotation is much more complex and abstruse as the following
example from Section IV illustrates:

> --Ja! Es war Wermut! Sein Verstand war krank! Es
> fehlte ihm an Beförderung! Im Schoße des Glückes?
> Oh, sehr wahr! Sie ist eine Metze! Was gibt es
> Neues? Als Roscius noch ein Schauspieler zu Rom
> war ... Geharnischt, sagt Ihr? Sehr glaublich!
> Sehr glaublich! - Ein Mann, der Stoß und Gaben mit gleichem
> Dank genommen, der zur Pfeife nicht Fortunen diente,
> den Ton zu spielen, den ihr Finger griff, ein Bettler,
> wie er ... Nichts mehr davon!! Sprich weiter, komm
> auf Hekuba!
> In der Tat, es ließ sich nicht mehr leugnen:  er
> war jetzt wirklich zu bedauern, der große Thienwiebel!
> Oh, Welch ein Schurk' und niedrer Sklav' er war!! War's
> nicht erstaunlich? War's zu glauben? War's möglich?
> War's nur durch Angewohnheit, die den Schein gefäll'ger
> Sitten überrostet, war's Übermaß in seines Blutes
> Mischung:  kurz und gut, aber er kam jetzt immer wieder
> auf sie zurück:  auf nichts, auf Hekuba!
> Wozu sollten Gesellen wie er zwischen Himmel und Erde
> herumkriechen? Dem Staub gepaart, dem er verwandt, so
> rings umstrickt mit Bübereien ... nicht doch, mein
> Fürst!! Die Mausefalle? Und wie das? Metaphorisch!
> Ich bitte, spotte meiner nicht, mein Schulfreund;  Du kamst
> gewiß zu meiner Mutter Hochzeit!
> Armer Yorick! Denn wenn die Sonne Maden aus einem toten
> Hunde ausbrütet, eine Gottheit, die Aas küßt ... Armer Yorick!
> Sein Wahnsinn war des armen Hamlet Feind. - [66]

This passage is preceded by the inner monologue, previously quoted,
in which Frau Wachtel directs her fury, at the Thienwiebels and is
followed by two further paragraphs, in which Amalie and Ole Nissen,
respectively, are the locus of narration. These various passages
thus blend together into a form of montage. A closer inspection
of the passage itself, however, reveals it to be not an integral
unit but a collage of some twenty-one quotations that are in fact
scattered throughout the five acts of Shakespeare's play.[67]
Furthermore, in being wrenched from their original context the
meaning of some of the quotations is changed, if not lost altogether.
This de-contextualisation thus effects what Martini terms a

"Sinnentleerung"[68] in which the intrinsic meaning of the quotations is subordinate to their function as collage material, a technique modern in concept which, as I shall illustrate later, prefigures its usage in the epic fiction of the twentieth century. In a sense, Holz himself alerts us to the possibilities of this technique for the introduction of the 1889 edition of "Papa Hamlet" closes with a lengthy montage,[69] constructed by the authors, of the various newspaper reviews of the sketches, which covers every shade of opinion from derisive dismissal to unqualified acclamation. When, in his discussion of the montage-effect in "Papa Hamlet", Martini speaks of the "Sprachspiel"[70] that Holz develops, then this could easily serve his argument that Holz is a pioneer of the modern trend towards the "technicisation" of literature.[71] And while it is, indeed, an index of Holz's finely developed formal sense, I believe, however, it also sheds further light on the overall meaning of "Papa Hamlet" in that it perhaps illuminates one of the most problematic aspects of the sketch, namely the so-called epilogue.

The story concludes with the discovery of Thienwiebel's frozen corpse by a hunchback errand boy, prompting his schocked response "Jesus! Jesus!!", and with the arrival of the policeman to deliver the official, legal verdict on Thienwiebel's demise, "Erfroren durch Suff!" The sketch then closes with the following passage:

> Wohlan, eine pathetische Rede!
> Es war der große Thienwiebel.
> Und seine Seele? Seine Seele, die ein unsterblich Ding war?
> Lirum, Larum! Das Leben ist brutal, Amalie! Verlaß dich drauf!
> Aber - es war ja alles egal! So oder so![72]

This passage evokes antithetical responses from Martini and Pascal. The epilogue leads Martini to see the sketch not as the study of a particular "case" but the intensive reflection of a world in disintegration. That is to say, it presents what he terms a "Weltdeutung",[73] a comment on the human condition as such. Roy Pascal, on the other hand, rejects this conclusion seeing this passage only as the re-assertion of the narratorial irony.[74] While I think Pascal is correct to see "Papa Hamlet" as a study of a particular case that may have a more general, symptomatic social relevance, I nevertheless regard the sketch as more open-ended

than he would allow. The final passage consists, in fact, of three
"Hamlet" quotations ("Wohlan! Eine pathetische Rede!"; "Und seine
Seele? Seine Seele, die ein unsterblich Ding war?"; "Lirum, Larum")[75]
and three phrases with which we have become familiar during the course
of the story. "Es war der große Thienwiebel" (a paraphrase of the
sketch's opening) is the narrator's voice, his irony and sarcasm even
at this pathetic end still unrelenting; while the final phrases are,
respectively, Thienwiebel's and Amalie's philosophy of life, the clichéd
expression of their felt helplessness. Holz thus presents us here with
a montage, a distillation of the various perspectives on the reality
presented, that encompasses at one extreme the scepticism of the
narratorial position, at the other the optimism of the Christian viewpoint and, in between, the Thienwiebels' sense of bewilderment. It
represents, therefore, not moralistic condemnation but recognition of
the complexity of reality that makes such confident moralising untenable.

In my discussion of consequential Naturalism as an objectivist literary
mode, I argued that subsequent German developments have thrown up
strikingly few parallels. If, as I believe it does, the real resonance
of Holz's style lies in the possibility of its adaptation for a markedly
subjective kind of writing, then this can be at least partially explained
by considering German Naturalism as a whole in its historical context and,
in particular, in its character as the first literary response to a
period of unparalleled social change. That is to say, German Naturalism
is of great significance, if for no other reason than that it was the
first literary movement in Germany to be confronted with the qualitatively
new reality of advanced industrial society. The belated but rapid and
extremely thorough transition to advanced industrialisation in Germany
appeared less as a stage in the evolutionary process than as a form of
historical rupture so pervasive and dramatic in its effects as to
transform the very nature of social experience. Indeed, it is this
transformation, manifested primarily in a new degree of alienation in
man's relationship to his environment and to other human beings, in a
word, in man's relationship to reality, that so preoccupied the
Naturalists and which,broadly speaking, has continued to preoccupy
subsequent writers.

Richard Hinton Thomas has identified three specific aspects which
reflect this sense of alienation:  firstly, the concern with milieu
as something confronting man now as a bewildering reality and thus all
the more deserving of analytical scrutiny;  secondly, the breakdown of
the belief that the individual can at least to some significant degree
embrace in his experience totality and unity;  thirdly, the questioning
and ultimate rejection of the notion of the unified and unifying
experience of reality and the concomitant recognition of the problematical
nature of identity in a complex industrial society.[76]  If, as Hinton
Thomas argues, it is this third aspect, the question of identity, which,
of all the problems occupying German writers from towards the end of the
nineteenth century, is the most central and the most significant,[77] then
Holz's literary contribution to that continuity is surely not insubstantial.
Thematically, of course, Holz shared the Naturalists' preoccupation
with milieu and in so far as his primary concern in the sketches was not
the "plot" but characterisation, it is possible to argue that he was
thus inevitably confronting the problem of identity.  After all, "Papa
Hamlet" is, at one level, a study of Thienwiebel's relationship to
reality and of the breakdown of his relationship with Amalie.

It is, however, primarily in the realm of form that Holz's real contribution is to be located as regards the literary depiction of the problem
of identity.  Indeed, the "Sekundenstil" itself, replacing the principle
of unified and unifying narrative with that of a second-by-second
succession of detail and denying the narrator the traditional supremacy
of omniscience, expresses in its very essence the felt impossibility of
experiencing unity and totality, emanating, as it does, from a narrator
rooted in the present, a self without continuity.  As Osborne puts it,
the "Sekundenstil" deprives us of the possibility of a panoramic view;
it conveys, without stating explicitly, a sense of loss and anxiety
in a fragmented world.[78]  Indeed, according to Martini, the language of
the "Sekundenstil" reflects and expresses the "atomisation of existence"
itself:

    ... die gesamte Durchformung dieser Prosa ist auf die
    Zertrümmerung der Sprache ins Momentan-Zusammenhanglose,

äußerlich und innerlich Abgerissene und Zerfetzte gerichtet. Und was der Sprache zugemutet wird, wird noch durch die reich besetzte Partitur der Satzzeichen unterstützt, deren Funktion nicht nur im Mimisch-Gebärdenhaften der emotionalen Rhythmisierung, sondern auch im Auseinanderreißen und Atomisieren des Sprachgefüges liegt. Man darf darin nicht nur die technische Analytik einer nuancierten Wirklichkeits-beobachtung ... sehen, sondern muß erkennen, wie diese sprachliche Struktur als Weltdeutung gemeint ist.[79]

He adds that "diese Auflösung im Sprachlichen entspricht ... der Auflösung der Verhältnisse der Menschen untereinander"[80] and defines the outstanding quality of Holz's language, when used in the dialogue-form, as what he terms its "analytischer Psychologismus",[81] its facility for directly expressing the pre- and subconscious layers of the psyche. It is in all these ways, says Martini, that Holz's narrative prose marks such a crucial break with the style of nineteenth-century realism and, we would wish to add, establishes at the same time an essential strand of continuity with certain forms of prose-writing in the twentieth century. In the following analysis of two contemporary works which deal, respectively, with the problem of the self and reality and the breakdown of social relationships between human beings - themes which, as I have suggested, can also be identified in "Papa Hamlet" - I hope to illustrate that in consequential Naturalism, as we find it in the subjectivist type, Holz developed a style which, even if not consciously appropriated by the authors in question, nevertheless constituted a form of literary prototype for this subjective mode of writing. The two works are D e r  S c h a t t e n  d e s  K ö r p e r s  d e s  K u t s c h e r s[82] by Peter Weiss and E i n  s c h ö n e r  T a g[83] by Dieter Wellershoff.

Even the most cursory reading of Peter Weiss's short prose-work  D e r S c h a t t e n  d e s  K ö r p e r s  d e s  K u t s c h e r s  would reveal those stylistic features which are most immediately suggested by the term "consequential Naturalism". The book has no "plot" to speak of but comprises a set of sketches, "Aufzeichnungen", which record certain experiences of an anonymous individual. This series of episodes, the subject matter of which encompasses such largely banal eventualities as the narrator's walk through the kitchen, his reflections and observations while sitting on the earth-closet, the description of the

111

evening meal in the boarding-house etc., do not therefore constitute a
meaningful whole, having nothing in common beyond their authorship and
the fact of their occurrence within a particular time-span and geographi-
can location (the latter characteristics of an unchanging milieu and a
concentrated time-scale are, of course, also typical of the "Sekundenstil").
That these episodes should be called sketches is in itself significant
for the reason stated by Elias Canetti when differentiating between
sketches ("Aufzeichnungen") and diaries ("Tagebücher"): the latter, he
says, serve to demonstrate the continuity of a life but in the former
nothing is anticipated, nothing expected and the aim is not to complete
or to round off.[84] They represent, that is to say, fragments of
experience whose shape is determined solely by the passage of time and
which are capable, therefore, of endless continuation, a fact
symbolised perhaps by the deliberate omission of the full stop at
the end of the final sentence of Weiss's book.

The most obvious similarity with Holz's style, however, lies in the
familiar richness and concreteness of the description, in the typical
concentration on the directly perceivable material world, in a
language more or less devoid of striking analogy, image or metaphor in
which interpretative comment is rare and, above all, in the immense
detail and precision accorded even the most mundane of events. For
Holz the description of a falling leaf may have warranted a passage,
not a mere sentence; but even that pales beside the detail which
Weiss's narrator devotes to the act of lighting a cigarette:

> auch der Hauptmann greift in eine Tasche, in die Brusttasche
> seiner Weste, nimmt ein silbernes Etui hervor, klopft auf
> den Deckel, läßt den Deckel aufschnappen, wendet sich über
> die Rückenlehne des Sessels, reicht das Etui über Schnees
> Schulter, Schnee wendet sich ihm entgegen, läßt seine
> knöcherne Hand in großen Bogen in das Etui hineinstoßen, hebt
> eine Zigarette heraus, worauf der Hauptmann das Etui
> zurückführt, selbst eine Zigarette dem Etui entnimmt, das
> Etui zuklappen läßt und in die Brusttasche zurücksteckt.
> Dann greift der Hauptmann in seine Hosentasche und läßt
> die Hand mit einem Feuerzeug hervortreten; die Hand mit
> dem Feuerzeug schwingt sich über die Sessellehne, Schnee
> wendet sein Gesicht dem Feuerzeug entgegen, die Finger des
> Hauptmanns schlagen Feuer und Schnee saugt, mit der

Zigarette in Mund, an der Flamme.  Das über
die Rückenlehne gewendete Gesicht des Hauptmanns liegt
nahe an Schnees Gesicht, beider Augen sind seitwärts
auf das Feuerzeug gerichtet und die Flamme spiegelt sich
in ihren Pupillen;  nachdem die Glut an der Spitze von
Schnees Zigarette leuchtet und dieser eine Wolke blauen
Rauches zwischen den Lippen hervorstößt führt der
Hauptmann die Flamme an die eigene Zigarette, und Schnee
sieht ihm zu, wie er an der Zigarette saugt und wie auch
diese Zigarette zu glühen beginnt und der Rauch aus dem
Mund des Hauptmanns quillt.[85]

In short, we can recognise here the same striving for objectivity and
totality that underpins the style of consequential Naturalism.  And yet,
the most obvious difference between the two styles illustrates all
the more forcefully the basic paradox which Günther Mahal saw at the
heart of the "Sekundenstil".  For D e r  S c h a t t e n  d e s
K ö r p e r s  d e s  K u t s c h e r s  is a first person narrative,
its narrator is not anonymous and impersonal as in Holz's objectivist
prose but an actual fictional character, who is thus both subject and
object of the sketches.  Consequently, much though the massive detail
is undoubtedly motivated by the narrator's desire for total objectivity,
by his determination that no element of the reality he experiences shall
elude verbalisation, it is in precisely that very detail that what he
writes reveals itself to be the product of a uniquely subjective mode
of perception.  It is interesting  at this point  to recall the manner
in which John Osborne defines the effect of Holz's style:

> Holz and Schlaf do not tell us what any chance observer would
> see, but they describe with a more than ordinary precision;
> ... (they) present their story through the eyes of a narrator
> who is, it seems, u n a b l e  to put things in their places,
> or to differentiate between the significant and the
> insignificant. All he can do is register everything he sees
> and in so doing register his own incomprehension ... the price
> of over-close scrutiny is a frightening loss of grasp.[86]

One could hardly wish for a more cogent summary of D e r  S c h a t t e n
d e s  K ö r p e r s  d e s  K u t s c h e r s!  In fact, the narrator
admits at one point that the effort of ordering his experience is
beyond his endurance such that he is overcome by a feeling of

"extensive boredom". Clearly, we encounter here a self so diminished as to possess no more than a fragmented and discontinuous consciousness. As such his narration represents an intensification of the subjectivist characteristics of Holz's narrator and this, in turn, leads to certain differences: these, however, are differences in degree, not in kind.

Discussing the principle of artistic selectivity in Holz's prose, Roy Pascal writes: "Reality" – even the room of a boarding–house, we might add, à propos of D e r  S c h a t t e n  d e s  K ö r p e r s  d e s K u t s c h e r s  – "is infinite, and narrative art has to select and arrange ... concrete description is not applied as an abstract general principle, but as a function of the story, required here and there, now and then."[87] The impression given by Weiss's narrator is of someone unwilling, or unable, to accept this proposition. No detail is too trivial or self-evident to warrant reference, nothing is pre-supposed. On entering the doctor's room, for example, the narrator's first impression is of "sein von vier Wänden, einem Fußboden und einer Decke gebildetes Zimmer."[88] Osborne also points to the often confusing effect of detail in Holz's work, saying, for example, of one of his descriptions of a room:

> The objects in this room are seen only in their immediate
> context ... and we need to read very attentively, or to
> keep looking back in the text, if we are to understand the
> disposition of objects about the room as a whole.[89]

The indiscriminate detail of Weiss's narrator, however, is so physically disorientating as to make it almost impossible for the reader to produce a mental picture of what is being depicted. On entering the landlady's room, for example, he describes the scene as follows:

> ... indem man zunächst zur Rechten einen ovalen, mit einer
> Spitzendecke gedeckten und mit einer großen violetten
> Glasvase versehenen Tisch, und zur Linken eine Kommode mit
> Fotographen von älteren und jüngeren Frauen, jungen Mädchen,
> einem mit einem Reifen spielenden Kinde, einem auf dem Bauch
> liegenden Wickelkind, älteren und jüngeren Männern, teils
> bartlos, teils mit Schnurrbärten und Kinnbärten, passierte...[90]

Such myriad detail is disorientating and pre-empts any overall perspective on the scene because the narrator accords the same status of

significance to the furniture as to the type of moustaches the men
in the photographs were wearing. The structuring principle is not so
much selectivity as that of pure itemisation and a sentence like the
following is quite common: "Dies sind die Geräusche; das Schmatzen
und Grunzen des Schweinerüssels, das Schwappen und Klatschen des
Schlammes, das borstige Schmieren des Schweinerückens an den Brettern,
das Quietschen und Knarren der Bretter ..." etc.[91] This itemising
process does not require the establishing of any causal connection
between the various phenomena and, indeed, the narrator does not
attempt to interrelate the different visual and audible experiences,
for in his mind they all enjoy an autonomy of significance. And yet,
curiously, certain phenomena do have primacy over others but
characteristically this merely testifies to the unique mode of perception that apprehends them. For example, on one occasion when passing
the family's room he looks through the open window and amongst other
things describes the father as follows:

> der Vater am Tisch in der Mitte des Raums stehend, die
> Hände zu Fäusten geballt, vor sich auf die Tischplatte
> gestützt, das Licht des Fensters voll auf ihn fallend
> und das vorgestreckte Gesicht mit dem weit aufgerissenen
> Mund beleuchtend; und ihm gegenüber, nicht sitzend,
> sondern in der Kniebeuge hockend der Sohn,[92]

This description is peculiarly incomplete, for since it is restricted
purely to the visible reality, it does not indicate whether the father
was merely yawning, talking or shouting at his son. Moreover, since
the narrator does remark on the open window, we must deduce that the
acoustic effects were perceptible. This is significant for, unlike
Holz's narrator, he appears to record his experiences and sensations in
accordance with a definite hierarchy of the senses, in which sight is
primary, hearing secondary and the other three equally subordinate.
That touch, smell and taste should only play a minor role in his
recording of experience is perhaps to be expected, but the impression
arises that the narrator regards hearing as a less differentiating,
less sensitive and more inaccurate organ of perception than sight, as if
he distrusts it for somehow being intrinsically more subjective. Thus,
when in the utter confusion of the landlady's room the curtains crash

down, it is not so much this inescapable audible reality that attracts
his attention as the relatively insignificant but nevertheless visible
fact of the captain twiddling his thumbs under his coat-tails. The
uncertainty as to the objective status of audible reality, however, is
reflected above all in his recording of human speech. For dialogue,
in so far as it is recorded at all in these sketches, is nearly always
presented in fragmentary form. This is not, however, as is mostly the
case with Holz, how it actually occurs but the narrator's consciously
subjective and ambiguous reception of it. He makes no attempt to
distil the perceived fragments of speech into a meaningful conversation
and on occasions even offers possible alternative versions:

> Von den Worten die die Haushälterin ... äußerte, verstand
> ich folgende Bruchstücke ... gestocktes Fett, Schmalz, Gans
> (ganz); worauf ich die Mutter ... sagen hörte, wohl schläft
> losstrampeln, Decke (Deckel) fallen ...[93]

The fact that on another occasion he is uncertain whether the house-
servant is saying "Wasser sucht", "Wassersucht" or "was er sucht"[94]
indicates that speech has only a phonetic existence for the narrator
and that its semantic qualities elude his grasp. His solution is thus
to present as fully as possible what he actually hears, as, for
example, in his characteristically Holzian, typographical representation
of an echo ("... noch viel viel zu früh früh, lange noch lange noch
nicht zurück zurück")[95] and to compensate for this acknowledged subjectivity of the audial faculty by relying increasingly on his powers
of observation. The primacy of visual response is clear from the way
he defines the aim of his act of perception, for he consciously takes
up positions at certain "observation posts", such as on the earth-
closet and at his bedroom window, "um damit dem Gesehenen eine Kontur
zu geben, und das Gesehene zu verdeutlichen, also das Sehen zu einer
Beschäftigung machend, ..."[96] That he should describe this activity
as an "occupation" is significant for, indeed, he is not so much an
observer as a voyeur, who prefers to view events rather than participate
in them.

This total immersion in the act of observation, however, has certain
consequences for the quality and nature of his perception. Firstly,

his descriptions often evince a loss of proportion.  When, for example,
in examining his own excreta in the earth-closet, he talks of a
"lavaartiger Wall, in dem der Eimer halb vergraben steht ...",[97] at
the moment of viewing this phenomenon, as Rose Zeller points out, the
narrator has no point of comparison with other objects that would put
its dimensions into perspective.[98]  His involvement leads him to view
things in such minute close-up that more or less anything would
assume similarly immense proportions.  The episode on the earth-closet
also illustrates the second effect of his immersion in the process of
perception, for he remarks that while sitting there he falls into a
state of "Selbstvergessenheit".[99]  The extreme passivity induced by
the concentration of observing seems to sever his mind from his body
and it is only the cold of the exposed parts of the body that eventually
reminds him of his physical state and breaks the sense of distance from
the self.

The narrator's total passiveness is also mirrored in the dispassionate
nature of his depiction of events.  He is not so much detached - the
word would imply the act of distancing himself, of suppressing feelings
- as actually incapable of experiencing emotions.  Thus, the description
of the doctor, whose wounds might be expected to evoke sympathy, is
intended merely to capture the actual condition of the wounds and is
concerned only with the sight itself, not with feelings of sympathy.
The almost unnatural restraint of this description, like that of the
sexual act at the end of the book, on the one hand underlines the
degree to which the narrator denies himself the use of any senses other
than seeing and hearing but, on the other hand, makes the description
distinctly surreal.

This surreal quality is further compounded by the prominence of a
technique similar to that which earlier I termed the "estrangement
effect" of Holz's "Sekundenstil", namely the emphasising or isolating
of objects in such a way as to imbue them with a magic autonomy.  The
evening meal in the boarding-house, for example, is described in the
following way:

> Die Löffel senken sich in die Schüsseln und steigen, beladen
> mit Kartoffeln und Rüben, wieder daraus empor, laden die Last
> auf dem Teller ab und schwingen sich zurück in die Töpfe,
> füllen sich, leeren sich wieder über den Tellern, wandern
> weiter hin and her bis jeder auf seinem Teller einen Haufen
> Kartoffeln und Rüben gesammelt hat der seinem Hunger entspricht
> ... Die Löffel heben sich jetzt, gefüllt mit Kartoffelbrocken
> und Rübenstücken, zu den Mündern empor, die Münder öffnen
> sich, ... Die Becher werden an den Mund geführt und die
> Flüssigkeit dringt in den Mund ein, füllt den Mund aus und
> gleitet durch die Kehle hinab, ...[100]

Moreover, not only objects but even the bodies and limbs of people

appear to take on a life of their own, moving, as it were, of their own

volition, independently of human control. So in the landlady's room,

when glasses are being passed round, the narrator notes: "hierbei

entstand ein vielfältiges Vorbeugen und Zurseitebeugen der Oberkörper der

Anwesenden, ein Kreisen, Auslangen und Einziehen von Armen ..."[101]

This de-personalisation culminates in his description of the act of

intercourse which is perceived purely in terms of limbs and movements.

On other occasions it can produce an effect remarkably akin to that

of the "still lifes" Martini identified in "Papa Hamlet". One such

occasion is the example mentioned earlier when the narrator catches

a glimpse of the family, on passing an open window in their room. The

full description reads as follows:

> Vorübergehend an dem offenen Fenster zu ebener Erde
> erhielt ich einen kurzen Einblick in das Zimmer der
> Familie, ich nahm den Vater, die Mutter, den Säugling und
> den Sohn wahr, in folgender Verteilung und gegenseitiger
> Beziehung: die Mutter sitzend auf dem Rand des Bettes in
> der Tiefe des Zimmers, halb ins Dunkel gehüllt, mit
> entblößter Brust und an der Brust den Säugling; der Vater
> am Tisch in der Mitte des Raumes stehend, die Hände zu
> Fäusten geballt, vor sich auf die Tischplatte gestützt,
> das Licht des Fensters voll auf ihn fallend und das
> vorgestreckte Gesicht mit dem weit aufgerissenen Mund
> beleuchtend; und ihm gegenüber, nicht sitzend, sondern
> in der Kniebeuge hockend, der Sohn, das Kinn auf die
> Tischkante gepreßt die Schultern bis zu den Ohren
> hinaufgezogen, in den Mund des Vaters hineinstarrend.[102]

This is truly "photographic depiction". For it is not only that the

family is de-personalised by the "in folgender Verteilung", a term one

would normally use of furniture or inanimate objects, nor simply the
fact that the father's mouth is open without apparently emitting any
sound - as, of course, would be the case in a photograph - rather it is
the great disjunction between actual experienced time, a mere fraction
of a second, and narrative time, a lengthy passage, which creates the
impression of time standing still  in the same way as a still from a
film, for example, has the effect of freezing one particular moment in
time.  Such static moments symbolise a whole style of perception as
do Weiss's collages, which not only reinforce by their very nature the
idea of photographic representation but also mirror at the same time
the narrator's mode of perception in the sense that they itemise and
isolate particular details without interrelating or fusing them into a
harmonious or significant whole.

This symbolic function is even clearer in the narrator's description
of the sexual act that gives the story its title.  Here the participants
are not even the impersonal, disembodied figures who live in the house;
these are mere shadows, lacking any physical substance.  Despite the
meticulous, anatomical details this sexual act remains devoid of
reality, it is shadow-play only.  It is a poor imitation that cannot
be true-to-life since the vital ingredient, "life" itself, is missing.
As such it symbolises the way in which the narrator perceives reality,
a way Karl Krolow has likened to the pinning of a butterfly under glass
for inspection.[103]  The fact, the object, is there, is tangible and can
be examined, but the essential quality of life is missing and thus it is
no longer a completely real butterfly.  Similarly, in spite of all his
efforts, it is only the "shadow" of reality that the narrator ever
attains.  He hopes by capturing in prose the transient detail of life to
be able to reorientate himself in reality.  The result, however, far from
helping him grasp and comprehend reality, merely expresses and thus
intensifies his inability to do precisely that.  His prose-style, to
repeat once more Osborne's description of the "Sekundenstil", can convey
only his sense of loss and anxiety in a fragmented world.

This is equally true of the imaginative work of Dieter Wellershoff whose
similiarities with Arno Holz extend well beyond the coincidental claim

to have founded a new form of realism.[104]  In  D e r  S c h a t t e n
d e s  K ö r p e r s  d e s  K u t s c h e r s  Weiss was still working
very much within the original territory of consequential Naturalism,
namely the short prose-form, and so far that particular work has marked
his sole exploration of the possibilities of the style.  The interesting
thing about Wellershoff is not only that his writing evidences the
transportation of certain of Holz's stylistic features on to the novel-
form but also that he has consistently, though not exclusively, attempted
to develop the possibilities of one particular style.[105]  Consequently,
although we are concerned here primarily with analysis of Wellershoff's
first novel  E i n  s c h ö n e r  T a g, the relationship to Holz is not
restricted solely to this work.  Indeed, Wellershoff's very conceptualisation of literature as "ein der Lebenspraxis beigeordneter Simulationsraum"[106]
evokes the familiar idea of the reproduction of reality;  and even if
Wellershoff's ultimate aim is not merely the reproduction but the
illumination of reality, then this, as the following quotation indicates,
by no means in itself transcends the critical potential of Holz's
style:

> (während) die eigentliche Literatur ... vor allem die gewohnten
> Schemata angreift und verändert.  Sie versucht den Leser zu
> irritieren, ihm die Sicherheit seiner Vorurteile und gewohnten
> Handlungsweisen zu nehmen, sie macht ihm das scheinbar
> Bekannte unvertraut, das Eindeutige vieldeutig...und öffnet
> ihm so neue Erfahrungsmöglichkeiten, die...die Enge und
> Abstraktheit der Routine durchbrechen, auf die er in seiner
> alltäglichen Praxis angewiesen bleibt.[107]

This fundamental statement on the function of literature suggests two
immediate similarities with Holz's prose.  The effect of divesting the
familiar of its familiarity is not, of course, a quality peculiar to
consequential Naturalism but, in fact, as a consideration of  E i n
s c h ö n e r  T a g  will reveal, the manner in which Wellershoff seeks
to achieve it  is very much related to the "estrangement effect" of
Holz's "Sekundenstil".  Moreover, the emphasis Wellershoff lays on the
idea of routine and "everyday" reality suggests that his fiction will
focus on the banal and evince the same lack of incident and drama
that is so characteristic of Holz's subject matter.  This is particularly

true of **E i n  s c h ö n e r  T a g,** for what we encounter in this study of an ordinary small family living a typically petty-bourgeois existence in Cologne, is the very epitome of "Alltäglichkeit". Indeed, it is the very banality and tedium of their existence that Wellershoff wishes to dissect, for what the novel shows is not a living family relationship but, on the contrary, the breakdown of personal relationships conveyed above all in the total absence of real communication between the three members of the family, a condition which, as we have already noted with Martini, the Naturalist dialogue deployed here is eminently suited to express. Similarly, Wellershoff like Holz evokes mental states by portraying gestures and physical reactions, such as Carla's nervous shrugging of the shoulders or the continual perspiring of all three characters. Above all, it is the sense of existential inertia that the novel conveys:

> Ihre persönliche Erlebniswelt beschränkt sich auf die
> Monotonie ihres Alltags und die Banalität ihrer Lebensum-
> stände. Sie befinden sich in einer monolithischen
> Dauergegenwart eingekerkert, deren feste Erlebnis- und
> Denkschablonen weder Vergangenheit noch Zukunft als
> mögliche Erfahrungsbereiche gelten lassen. Ihr Leben
> spielt sich in einem unentrinnbaren, hermetischen Jetzt
> ab,...[108]

This corresponds to the static temporal quality of the "Sekundenstil", intensified here by the continuous use of the present tense and further reinforced by the geographical concentration on the family flat to suggest the same sense of physical imprisonment that Holz achieved by focusing uninterruptedly on the Thienwiebels' household in "Papa Hamlet". In fact, Martini's view of "Papa Hamlet", namely that "das Thema dieser Skizze sind psychische Vorgänge im individuellen Menschen",[109] is equally applicable to **E i n  s c h ö n e r  T a g,** for essentially what Wellershoff presents are three differentiated, individual psychologies that, in turn, represent three specific stages in the breakdown of identity. Analysis of this particular problematic I have provided elsewhere.[110] For the purposes of the present discussion I must restrict myself to a consideration of the formal aspect of Wellershoff's work and, in particular, its affinities with Holz's style.

Essentially, what underpins Wellershoff's concept of "Neuer Realismus"
and distinguishes it from conventional realism is the rejection of the
notion of totality. That is to say, "Neuer Realismus" shares with
Naturalism the recognition of the panoramic perspective - what Wellershoff
terms "die große Attitüde der Deutung des Ganzen"[111] - as a narrative
position that is unsuited to embracing and comprehending the multiple
relationships and complexities of the many disparate elements that
comprise reality. His intention is to present instead "eine unüberschaubare,
in ihre Einzelteile zerfallene Welt"[112] and it is from this basic premise
that many of Wellershoff's stylistic features derive. His primary aim,
therefore, is to avoid all simplification of reality since this ignores
both its inherent variety ("die Mannigfaltigkeit der Welt")[113] and the
necessarily fragmentary nature of the experience of reality. As with
Holz, Wellershoff substitutes for a totalising perspective one which
focuses on detail and its attendant effects, concreteness and precision.
Thus, for example, the simple sentence "alles ist verdreckt, die ganze
Wohnung hat sie verkommen lassen" presents for Wellershoff an inadequately
differentiated picture and is supplemented by details of the following
type:

> Im Waschbecken liegen ihre Haare, verfilzt und halb in den
> Abfluß gerutscht, und in dem angetrockneten Seifenschaum
> kleben seine Barthaare, das pulvrige graue Gehäcksel aus
> dem Rasierapparat, kleine Punkte in den Schmutzringen.[114]

Similarly, it does not suffice simply to state that Günther takes off his
clothes; rather the process must be broken down, after the fashion of
Holz's falling leaf, into the various individual moments and stages in
the act of undressing:

> Er bückt sich und knüpft die Schuhe auf, lehnt sich aufatmend
> wieder zurück. Im Sitzen bindet er die Krawatte ab und
> öffnet den Hemdkragen, bleibt so eine Weile, die Arme neben
> sich auf den Sessellehnen, mit gespreizten Fingern fühlt
> er die Polsternägel vorne am Wulst. Nacheinander hebt er die
> Finger und setzt sie wieder auf. Er blickt auf seine
> aufgeknüpften Schuhe und legt den Kopf zurück.[115]

Wellershoff calls this inventory-style "die Technik der Häufung der
Realitätselemente"[116] but in its stark details and flat narratorial

language, with the repeated basic syntactical formation of subject-predicate-object, the almost intentionally monotonous succession of similarly structured sentences without either conjunctions or subordinate clauses and with the exclusion of figurative or metaphorical phrases, Wellershoff's prose is highly redolent of Holz's narrative style.

The fragmentation of reality that Wellershoff chooses as his perspective also has the consequences for narrative structure that were identified in Holz's sketches, namely the eschewing of a precisely structured "plot". In E i n   s c h ö n e r   T a g the reader is confronted not so much with a story in the conventional sense as with a series of detailed episodes, "Wirklichkeitsbilder", which could just as easily be given titles such as "Nachts nicht einschlafen können", "In der Stadt", "Anzug kaufen" etc. Failure to recognise this narrative principle can lead to a misinterpretation of the conclusion of E i n   s c h ö n e r T a g,  for the birthday at the end of the novel is not, as Gunther Zehm proposes, [117] an artificial happy ending but rather the converse: it is neither happy, nor in reality an ending, but rather the ironisation of a self-perpetuating condition. The father's sense of happiness is merely a willing self-deception at the restoration of the family circle. No special significance is to be attached to these particular events in the novel. The implication is that Wellershoff could just as easily have portrayed the situation of this family at an earlier or later point in time.

All these features of Wellershoff's writing suggest unmistakable affinities with consequential Naturalism. However, undoubtedly the most crucial aspect of Wellershoff's work is the problem of perspective and in this respect the most interesting thing is that, despite widely differing theoretical statements, in their prose-style Holz and Wellershoff nevertheless achieve a remarkably similar perspectival effect. The narrative focus which Wellershoff selects is the opposite to that of objectivity, distance and detachment. His "Neuer Realismus" is characterised above all by a total subjectivisation of perspective that he describes as follows:

> Realistisch...wäre eine bewegte, subjektive Optik, die
> durch Zeitdehnung und Zeitraffung und den Wechsel zwischen
> Totale und Detail, Nähe und Ferne, Schärfe und Verschwommenheit
> des Blickfeldes, Bewegung und Stillstand, langer und kurzer
> Einstellung und den Wechsel von Innen-und Außenwelt die
> konventionelle Ansicht eines bekannten Vorgangs und einer bekannten
> Situation so auflöst und verändert, daß eine neue Erfahrung
> entsteht. Die subjektive Blickführung, verwandt den
> Kamerabewegungen des Films, demontiert die konventionellen
> Sinneinheiten, zerlegt und verzerrt sie, isoliert Einzelheiten,
> macht sie auffällig, zeigt das Fremde, Ungesehene im scheinbar
> Bekannten und fügt neue ungewöhnliche Komplexe zusammen.[118]

The reader is thus denied the secure position of observer that traditional
realism affords him; rather "er wird...hineingestoßen in einen
Fiktionsraum, der sich erst allmählich und vielleicht nie richtig, nie
endgültig erschließt, der aber auch keine Fenster, keine Tür in ein
sicheres Außerhalb hat."[119] In Wellershoff's novels, therefore,
reality is presented only as it is experienced by particular individuals
and events are related only when and in so far as those individuals
experience them. Furthermore, this process of subjectivisation also
encompasses dialogue so that the reader hears conversation not as an
objective reality but as the experience of one of its participants.
In Ein schöner Tag the subjective narrative position is, in fact, divided
into the three separate perspectives of the members of the family and
the narration alternates, chapter by chapter, from one to the other.

Wellershoff's concept of the subjectivised perspective is not, however,
unproblematical. Clearly, what he intends is the elimination of the
narrator, of a consciousness, that is, independent of the character(s)
in whom the perspective is located; and yet this is not the equivalent
of the traditional first person narrative. Rather the effect he achieves
can be described as follows:

> Es wird in der Er-Form erzählt, aber dennoch zugleich in der
> subjektiven Perspektive. Das Er ist nicht Er, aber auch nicht
> einfach Ich. Das hat zur Folge, daß die Grenzen zwischen dem
> Menschen als Subjekt und dem Menschen als Objekt der Erzählung
> sich verwischen, aber nicht gänzlich verschwinden.[120]

The fact thus remains that Wellershoff does not wholly succeed in eliminating the narrator as a mediating consciousness, since certain elements of the text evidence an independently registering presence and thus puncture the intended total subjectivisation. To take one particular example: when, in E i n   s c h ö n e r   T a g, it is said of Carla's classroom at school "der Raum ist mit Gesichten gefleckt", then clearly this remark reflects Carla's inner state as she watches the class, but when we read a few lines earlier the sentence "sie geht auf die Tür zu",[121] then equally clearly this statement emanates from a consciousness that is in no sense identical with the "sie", i.e. with Carla. The following examples illustrate similar tendencies:

1. Ich will es nicht, d e n k t   e r, es deprimiert mich nur, ich muß an eine Frau denken...[122]

2. Erst als er an seinem kleinen Sekretär unter dem Seestück und den gerahmten Fotografien sitzt, g e s t e h t   e r   s i c h   e i n, daß er wartet.[123]

3. "Warum essen Sie nicht?" fragt sein Nachbar, d e r   S i e m s   h e i ß t, den er auf dem Friedhof getroffen hat, nach Jahren, nach zwanzig Jahren...[124]

4. Sie lächeln sich an, und gleichzeitig wenden sie sich zum Gehen, immer noch lächelnd und für einen Augenblick i n   p u p p e n h a f t e r   H a r m o n i e.[125]

In the first two examples we find instances of what Käte Hamburger calls "inner verbs", i.e. verbs which denote inner processess.[126] The words "denkt er" are superfluous since they merely interrupt the flow of consciousness and actually create a distance between the character and the reader. Similarly, the interjected "gesteht er sich ein" does not belong directly to the thought-process related, but constitutes an interpretative comment on the thought itself. In the third example  the words "der Siems heißt  are only provided as information for the reader, since the name would have occurred to the subject of this passage much earlier in the encounter. Finally, the metaphor in the last quotation clearly belongs not to Carla's but to the narrator's vocabulary.

This irrepressible narratorial presence has the further consequence of counteracting the desired effect of destroying the objectivity of the

the dialogue. In E i n  s c h ö n e r  T a g  the reader is aware that
in the various chapters of the novel the perspective alternates between
the figures, but there is nothing further to make him doubt the objective
validity of the dialogue. On one occasion, however, in a conversation
between Carla and Fräulein Stefany, Wellershoff does succeed in arousing
precisely that impression:

> Draußen sagt die Stefany, das sei jedesmal so, sie solle sich
> nicht beeindrucken lassen, das Weinen gehöre bei ihrer Mutter
> zum Zeremoniell. Während der Rückfahrt sprechen sie über die
> Schule. ... Sie unterhalten sich noch weiter im Auto, als sie
> vor dem Haus stehen...sie will sich beim Vorstand des Heims
> für sie einsetzen, damit sie einen Platz für den Vater bekommt
> und nicht auf die Warteliste muß, aber auch jetzt könnten sie
> doch öfter treffen und einen Ausflug machen, sie könnten es
> dabei weiter besprechen, es sei sicher jetzt schwierig für sie,
> das könne man verstehen. Sie widerspricht nicht.[127]

In this instance the impression suggested earlier that Carla's attention
is occupied by thoughts other than this particular topic, is combined
with a stylistic device in order to evoke in the reader the feeling that
he or she is experiencing the conversation very much from the position
of one of the participants, whose mind is, as it were, elsewhere. And
yet, it is this very exception which proves the rule, for basically the
reader only interprets this conversation as a subjective experience and
not an objective event because the passage is written at the relevant
points in the subjunctive. Needless to say, however, it would be
stylistically intolerable to present all dialogue in the novel in this
form.

I have been at some pains to demonstrate that Wellershoff does not
succeed in translating his idea of the absolute subjectivisation of
perspective into actual literary practice, since I believe that what he
does  in fact  produce is an effect with which we are already familiar
from our discussion of Holz's prose. The following passage from  E i n
s c h ö n e r  T a g  illustrates the technique to which I refer:

> Er hat die Arme auf dem Rücken und kreuzt sie jetzt über
> der Brust. Genau gegenüber sitzt eine Gruppe von jungen
> Mädchen, die ihre Beine ins Wasser hängen lassen, eine
> streckt beide Beine über das Wasser und schaukelt auf der

Kante, als wollte sie gleich vornüberkippen, dabei
spricht sie weiter zu den anderen neben sich, es
sind sicher Schülerinnen, die jeden Nachmittag hier
im Schwimmbad sind. Und das sind Jungen aus ihrer Schule,
die spritzend durch die Fußrinne laufen und sie ins Becken
stoßen. Er sieht, wie die Mädchen schreien, kann nicht
viel hören, weil um ihn herum Geschrei ist und der Lärm
des Nichtschwimmerbeckens...128

Despite Wellershoff's intention there are two distinct perspectives
here: that of a detached observing narrator, recording the exact details
of the swimming-pool setting and that of Günther, reflecting on the scene
he surveys. In the phrase "es sind sicher Schülerinnen" it is the word
"sicher" which signals the transition from narratorial perspective to
Günther's perceptions and thoughts. This interaction of objective and
subjective response, the subtle interpenetration of character's thoughts
and narratorial voice is clearly recognisable as the shifting perspective
identified in Holz's prose. There are, however, three minor ways in
which Wellershoff's usage of free indirect style differs from Holz's.
Firstly, since in each chapter one particular character provides the
focal point, the shift in perspective is restricted to that character
and the narrator and does not develop into the truly multiple perspective
that prevails, for example, in "Papa Hamlet". Correlatively, Wellershoff's
conscious subjectivisation facilitates the tendency for the free indirect
style to develop into inner monologue. Thirdly, Wellershoff is less
consistent than Holz in the differentiation between language-registers
that is so crucial to the effectiveness of the free indirect style.
Whereas in Holz's sketches it is nearly always possible to distinguish
the educated, literary language of the narrator (if not his irony) from
that of the characters, in E i n  s c h ö n e r  T a g this distinction
is often blurred. When, for example, Carla's father thinks about his
daughter "sie ist ein Fleck dort in der Tür",129 or Günther reacts to the
heat as "ein Glänzen, das die Gegenstände vermummt, das auf ihnen klebt
als ein Belag, ein heller düngestrichener Schleim",130 then this
intellectualised language makes it exceedingly difficult for the reader
to identify the experiences these words represent as those of the actual
characters. In a sense, therefore, the individual perspectives are
insufficiently subjectivised. The curious thing about both

writers' use of the free indirect style, however, is the paradoxical
effect it has within their respective styles. With Holz, who was,
according to one point of view, supposedly aiming at absolute objectivity,
it constitutes a subjectivising tendency; while in Wellershoff, whose
intention is total subjectivisation, it reasserts the presence of the
narrator and thus represents to a certain extent an objectivising
tendency.

This paradox, however, in no sense invalidates the clear relationship
between Wellershoff's "Neuer Realismus" and Holz's consequential
Naturalism, an affinity which, as his response to the above analysis
shows, Wellershoff himself readily acknowledges:

> Es ist richtig, wenn Burns in seiner...Analyse des
> "Schönen Tages" die Verwandtschaft zu naturalistischen
> Schreibweisen nachweist und die Gefahr, daß der Text
> in Faktographie abrutscht. Ich habe das für mich immer
> so rationalisiert, daß das Zerfallen der Welt in
> Einzelfakten eben die Struktur der Zukunftslosigkeit des
> Lebens ausdrückt. Aber ich sehe jetzt doch, daß der
> Text stellenweise in der Gefahr ist, in die Nähe der
> Aufzählung zu geraten.[131]

It is, however, an indication of the disrepute in which Naturalism as
a whole is held that Wellershoff should consider this affinity as a
weakness. This is undoubtedly because, concerned as he is primarily
to illuminate reality, Wellershoff can only equate consequential
Naturalism with an essentially positivistic reproduction of
reality. Ironically, much though he himself has done to extend the
critical possibilities of Holz's prose-style, he fails to appreciate,
unlike Martini or Schulz, that Holz's literary aim was not dissimilar to
his own, namely: "Dichtung zum Erkenntnismittel selbst zu machen."[132]

(iii)    O b j e c t i v i s t   a n d   S u b j e c t i v i s t
         N a r r a t i o n   i n   B e r l i n   A l e x a n d e r p l a t z

The work of Alfred Döblin merits special attention here for two reasons.
Firstly, his most successful literary achievement, B e r l i n
A l e x a n d e r p l a t z,  actually draws on not one but b o t h
of the tendencies in Holz's prose-work, for as Herbert Scherer has
observed, at one level the novel can be seen as the formal representation
of "the conflict between objectivity and subjectivity".[1] That is to say,
Döblin actually fuses within the context of a single literary work –
and, in my opinion, in a hitherto unique manner – the objectivist
and subjectivist modes of consequential Naturalism. Furthermore,
Döblin's work is also of special significance in that it contains not
only a positive appraisal of Naturalism in general but also an
acknowledged debt to the work of Arno Holz in particular.[2].

The very title of the essay "Der Geist des naturalistischen Zeitalters",
for example, indicates what the essay itself makes clear, namely that
Döblin rejected the common but restrictive identification of Naturalism
with a scientistic materialism[3] and regarded it much more in terms akin
to those of Jost Hermand's broader conception (quoted above). Moreover,
when in another context he speaks of "Naturalismus im echten und
vorbildlichen Sinn von Arno Holz",[4] it is thus clear with which German
writer Döblin primarily identifies such a conception of Naturalism. He
points to the enduring relevance of Holz's theoretical writings
expressing, for example, Holz's idea of the social determinacy of
literature in the recognition: "daß jede poetische Technik eng mit den
Lebensverhältnissen der Nation verflochten ist;  diese aber ändern sich
und mit ihnen unterliegt die Technik dem historischen Wechsel der Dinge".[5]
Similarly, Döblin finds Holz's discussion of language, in particular his
problematisation of its relationship to reality, a fruitful one. Not
surprisingly, perhaps, Döblin therefore regards Holz's "Kunstgesetz" as
a significant stage in both Holz's and Naturalism's development. What
is surprising, however, is just how unproblematical Döblin considers
this law to be, for having quoted Holz's original formulation he
continues:

Ich drücke das einfach so aus:  Holz will einen Ausschnitt
Proletarierexistenz geben, diese Proletarierexistenz ist
Natur, Reproduktionsbedingungen sind die derzeitigen
Theater- und Bühnenverhältnisse, die Regietechnik, die
literarischen Ausdrucksmittel des Autors.[6]

The political concreteness of this statement, markedly incongruous with
the abstractness of Holz's own formulation, presumably derives from
Döblin's view that underpinning Holz's Naturalism there was to be found
what he terms a "materialist Socialism".[7] Arguably, however, such an
interpretation reveals more about the assumptions underlying Döblin's own
writing at the time than Holz's.[8] Returning to this problem in a later
essay, however, he argues more modestly that what Holz in fact meant
by "Natur" was "die unentstellte Wahrheit und ihre Fülle".[9] The
significant thing about the two interpretations is that the first defines
"Natur" above all in terms of a particularised c o n t e n t
("Proletarierexistenz") whereas the second relates primarily to the
m o d e  of literary representation ("unentstellte/Fülle").  There is no
reason to believe, however, that in proffering the narrower definition
Döblin was thus oblivious to the formal considerations he expressed
in his later formulation.  Indeed, I believe consideration of two
crucial works  both published in 1929, the year before the first Holz
essay appeared, demonstrates that precisely the opposite was the case.
The two works are Döblin's essay "Der Bau des epischen Werks" and his
novel  B e r l i n  A l e x a n d e r p l a t z.[10]  It is common
practice to see in the latter the transformation into fiction of the
principles explicated in the former.  The task here, however, is not to
explore in detail that particular relationship, nor can it be to offer
a complete reading of Döblin's novel.  Rather I wish to look at  B e r l i n
A l e x a n d e r p l a t z  in a different light, namely as a work
which has, more successfully than any before or since, at once both
appropriated and transcended and, as will be shown, thus intensified
those stylistic elements I have identified as constituting the two
separate modes of consequential Naturalism.

One of the primary concerns of "Der Bau des epischen Werks" is to
demonstrate the validity of the following two assertions:  "Die Kunstwerke

haben es mit der Wahrheit zu tun. Der epische Künstler kann auch heute
noch in vollem Ernst die Berichtform gebrauchen."[11] In other words,
Döblin here addresses himself to the problem with which Holz was
primarily concerned, namely the aim and the mode of the literary
reproduction of reality, and in Döblin's view a central category for
the epic artist must be that of "proximity": "er muß ganz nahe an die
Realität heran, an ihre Sachlichkeit, ihr Blut, ihren Geruch...[12]
Was macht das epische Werk aus? Das Vermögen seines Herstellers, dicht
an die Realität zu dringen..."[13] As a literary technique proximity
involves, on the one hand, a concern with detail and a striving towards
totality (exemplified in Döblin's use of such words as "Fülle",
"Reichtum",[14]"ihr unbeschreiblich großes Inventar"[15] to qualify the notion
of reality) and, on the other hand, a commitment to empiricism as the
ideal starting-point for epic narration. Describing the origin and
style of B e r l i n  A l e x a n d e r p l a t z, for instance,
Döblin explains:

> Ich kenne den Berliner Osten seit Jahrzehnten...Hier sah ich
> nun einen interessanten und so überaus wahren und noch nicht
> ausgeschriebenen Schlag von Menschen. Ich habe diesen
> Menschenschlag zu den verschiedensten Zeiten und in den
> verschiedensten Lagen beobachten können, und zwar beobachten
> in der Weise, die die einzig wahre ist, nämlich indem man
> mitlebt, mithandelt, mitleidet.[16]

Clearly, the concept of proximity would apply equally well to the method
of consequential Naturalism and it is hardly surprising, therefore, that
its literary realisation in B e r l i n  A l e x a n d e r p l a t z
has stylistic consequences similar to that of Holz's prose. The first
of these is what Döblin has termed above "Sachlichkeit", a stylistic
and syntactical characteristic with which we are well acquainted through
analysis of Holz's creative writing. The following is a typical example
of how such a style is deployed by Döblin:

> Am Alexanderplatz reißen  sie den Damm auf für die Untergrundbahn.
> Man geht auf Brettern. Die Elektrischen fahren über den Platz
> die Alexanderstraße herauf durch die Münzstraße zum Rosenthaler
> Tor. Rechts und links sind Straßen. In den Straßen steht Haus
> bei Haus. Die sind vom Keller bis zum Boden mit Menschen voll.
> Unten sind die Laden.

Destillen, Restaurationen, Obst- und Gemüsehandel,
Kolonialwaren und Feinkost, Fuhrgeschäft, Dekorations-
malerei, Anfertigung von Damenkonfektion, Mehl und
Mühlenfabrikate, Autogarage, Feuersozietät...[17]

The first paragraph reveals the familiar, short sentence-structure and
syntactical simplicity of Holz's narration, while the second utilises
the process of itemisation which, as was noted earlier, forms the underlying structuring principle of the "Sekundenstil". Elsewhere, however,
Döblin develops this technique into a major component of the novel,
one which Erich Hülse has termed "Tatsachenreportage".[18] By this is
meant the direct incorporation into the text of elements such as newspaper cuttings, weather reports, statistics, advertisements etc. but,
significantly, in explaining his predeliction for the factual in this
particular form, Döblin still remains firmly within Holz's frame of
reference: "Ich gebe zu, daß mich noch heute Mitteilungen von Fakta,
Dokumente beglücken, aber Dokumente, Fakta, wissen Sie, **warum?** Da
spricht der große Epiker, die Natur, zu mir. ..."[19]

The second manifestation of the idea of proximity is the language Döblin
considers essential to epic narration. This, he argues, cannot be the
language of abstraction but, on the contrary, must be "(der) lebende(n)
Sprache...ein blühendes, konkretes Phänomen".[20] Such language, Döblin
insists, is a "Produktivkraft",[21] particularly, he remarks à propos of
B e r l i n  A l e x a n d e r p l a t z, the language of Berlin: "die
gesprochene Berliner Sprache; aus ihr konnte ich schöpfen..."[22] Thus
the dialogue, with its rich Berlin dialect and jargon, is a vital part
of the novel's texture, constituting as in consequential Naturalism
an important element of characterisation. So, for example, the two
moods in Franz Biberkopf of frivolity and shocked disbelief are effectively
conveyed in the following by the use of naturalistic dialogue:

"Cilly, uffn Schoße setzen, jetzt nich. Und hau mir man nich
gleich. Bist mein Pusselken. Nu rat mal, mit wem daß ich
zusammen war." "Will ich gar nicht wissen". "Schnutekan,
Killikilliken, also mit wem? Mit - Rheinhold".[23]

"Um Gotteswillen, wat wollen wir machen, Eva, wat wolln wir
machen"..."Wat is det, Eva, wat is mit unser Miezeken los, wat

is denn passiert, die is tot, mit der is wat passiert, jetzt
is es raus, die is nich weg von mir, die hat einer umgebracht,
Eva, unser Miezeken hat eener umgebracht, mein Miezeken,
wat is denn los, is denn det wahr, sag mir, det is nich wahr."[24]

The impetus for this use of language is not difficult to ascertain, for
Döblin counts it as one of Holz's major achievements that "er ist gegen
die Kunstsprache...aufgetreten und hat zur natürlichen Sprache des
Volkes und seiner Melodie gedrängt."[25]

The third and most important aspect of proximity, however, is what we can
call the "immediacy" of depiction. Döblin emphasises this point by
entitling one of the sections of the essay "Die Epik erzählt nicht
Vergangenes, sondern stellt dar" and by insisting that "alle Darstellung
ist gegenwärtig".[26] Later in the essay he elaborates on what this notion
of literary immediacy entails:

> Der Leser macht also den Produktionsprozeß mit dem Autor mit.
> Alle epischen Werke haben es mit dem Werden und Geschehen,
> zu tun, und so, möchte ich sagen, ist es auch in der Ordnung,
> daß der epische Bericht nicht fertig vorgelegt wird und
> angeschwirrt kommt aus der Pistole geschossen, sondern der
> Leser erlebt ihn in statu nascendi.[27]

Moreover, he adds, this effect can never be reduced to the simple level
of a technical problem and is in no sense contingent on the narrative
being in the present tense, a fact aptly demonstrated by the tense-scheme
of B e r l i n   A l e x a n d e r p l a t z, in which Döblin alternates
in apparently arbitrary fashion between the present, perfect and imperfect
tense. In the novel as a whole the effect of immediacy, while a dominant
one particularly in the "Großstadt" sections, is not, however, mono-
lithic since there are certain narrative elements which manifestly and
quite intentionally puncture the immediacy. I shall return to this
later when discussing the problem of narrative perspective in B e r l i n
A l e x a n d e r p l a t z. As far as the relationship to Holz is
concerned, hopefully this is self-evident since, in my analysis of Holz's
sketches, I sought to demonstrate to what degree the idea of immediacy
is an intrinsic characteristic of consequential Naturalism.

One of the best examples of proximity in Döblin's work - and one which
offers at the same time the most striking and direct parallel to the
style of consequential Naturalism - is the extended passage in B e r l i n
A l e x a n d e r p l a t z describing the Berlin abattoir. The episode
begins in typically laconic fashion, "Der Schlachthof in Berlin",[28]
describing the geographical location of the establishment before focusing in minute detail on the animals and the process of slaughter:

> Über die Viehrampen mähen, blöken sie herunter. Die
> Schweine grunzen und schnüffeln am Boden, sie sehen
> nicht, wo es hingeht, die Treiber mit den Stecken laufen
> hinterher. In die Ställe, da legen sie sich hin, liegen
> weiß, feist beieinander, schnarchen, schlafen. Sie sind
> lange getrieben worden, dann gerüttelt in den Wagen, jetzt
> vibriert nichts unter ihnen, nur kalt sind die Fliesen,
> sie wachen auf, drängen an andere. Sie liegen übereinander-
> geschoben. Da kämpfen zwei, in der Bucht ist Platz, sie
> wühlen Kopf gegen Kopf, schnappen sich gegen die Hälse,
> die Ohren, drehen sich im Kreis, röcheln, manchmal sind
> sie ganz still, beißen bloß. In Furcht klettert eins
> über die Leiber der andern, das andere klettert hinterher,
> schnappt, die unten wühlen sich auf, die beiden plumpen
> herunter, suchen sich.[29]

The description continues for several pages - almost a little Naturalist
sketch in itself - but the detached tone of the experiencing observer
never gives way to sensationalism or over-dramatisation despite the
evident brutality of the scene. Another example, this time of linguistic
"Sekundenstil", occurs when Döblin reproduces at length the sales-
patter of a salesman at a local market.[30]

Where Döblin transcends and thus develops the function of consequential
Naturalism is in his technique of combining various disparate fragments
of such closely viewed reality to form a collage that in their overall
combined effect evoke not so much the experience of proximity as the
distance of a panorama. The first chapter of Book Two, entitled
"Franz Biberkopf betritt Berlin", provides an excellent example. The
first part focuses on the Rosenthaler Platz, creating a general picture
of the everyday activity taking place there and is followed by a collage,
consisting of official notices from a newspaper, a weather-report, various
details of the Berlin public transport system and of the general milieu

of the Rosenthaler Platz such as street-names, advertisements etc. In
the middle of this collage - with what must be the literary equivalent of
the film camera's "zoom-in" technique - we suddenly read the stark phrase
"Kleine Kneipe am Rosenthaler Platz"[31] and there follows the strictly
naturalistic episode of a dialogue between two men in a public house
with the camera then, as it were, panning out again at the end of the
chapter. With this technique Döblin succeeds in throwing into relief
the various episodes while at the same time, by doing precisely that,
in fact emphasising the effect of proximity in the individual scene.
The rapid change of perspective thus never allows the reader to become
totally immersed in, and so possibly inured to, one particular effect.
In transcending the specific effect, Döblin here actually intensifies
it.

The idea of proximity, important though it is for the present discussion,
constitutes for Döblin, it must be emphasised, merely one element of
epic narration. Allied to that must always be what he terms "das
Exemplarische".[32] That is to say, the epic writer can never be content
merely to imitate and reproduce surface reality; rather he must penetrate
beyond that reality "um zu gelangen zu den einfachen großen elementaren
Grundsituationen und Figuren des menschlichen Daseins".[33] I have already
pointed out how the Naturalists' concern with the specificity of the
particular militates against the notion of typicality and in so far as
Döblin deploys in his fiction certain similar methods of depiction he is
thus, to a certain extent, confronted with the same problem. Certainly
Holz, since he operated exclusively within the confines of the short prose-
form, was with one significant exception never able to transcend the
particularising tendency inherent in his literary method. That exception,
I have suggested, is "Papa Hamlet" and it is this which provides the most
interesting similarity between Holz's work and Döblin's. That is to say,
those tendencies which, I argued, imported to Holz's sketch a dimension
over and above the significance of the particular, are even more fully
developed in B e r l i n   A l e x a n d e r p l a t z.

Especially important in this regard is Döblin's usage of quotation. In
the analysis of "Papa Hamlet" I showed how Holz employed the quotations

from Shakespeare partly in order to counterpose another level of
existence to the banality and decadence of the Thienwiebels' household.
Similarly, the effect of the passages from the Bible that are quoted
in B e r l i n  A l e x a n d e r p l a t z  is to relativise both the
novel's concern with the purely individual fate of Franz Biberkopf as well
as its pre-occupation with one particular realm of existence, namely the
everyday reality of the "Großstadt". Erich Hülse describes this process
as follows:

> ... mit der Tatsachenreportage bleibt Döblin auf dem Boden
> der überschaubaren Wirlichkeit; die Bibelzitate dagegen
> eröffnen einen neuen Raum, sie übersteigen die Ebene des
> Alltäglichen, in dem der Roman mit seiner vordergründigen
> Handlung spielt. Die Realität wird durchstoßen ... und
> erreicht eine "Überreale Sphäre",das ist die Sphäre einer
> neuen Wahrheit und einer ganz besonderen Realität. Erst
> das Durchstoßen der Realität erhebt die Geschichte von
> Franz Biberkopf in den Rang des Exemplarischen. Indem
> durch die Bibelzitate und freie Variationen über
> Bibeltexte die Fäden zum Mythischen geknüpft werden, wird
> die Geschichte zum Beispiel schlechthin, zum
> "Enthüllungsprozeß besonderer Art", zur Geschichte vom
> wahren und aufhellenden Dasein.[34]

This defines the collective significance of the biblical passages but
individually the quotations have the further function of symbolising
either the course of events or a character's inner state. At the
beginning of Book Two, for example,there appears for the first time the
Garden-of-Eden motif, an image of happiness and harmony that clearly
relates to Biberkopf's psychological condition of contentment at the
prospect of beginning a new life in Berlin. The second appearance of
this Paradise motif is in the description of a pub brawl symbolising,
perhaps, Biberkopf's ideal, his desire for peace and order. The theme's
third occurrence, however, brings an important change with the arrival
of the serpent: "Da raschelte es in einem Baum; eine Schlange,
Schlange, Schlange streckte den Kopf vor, eine Schlange lebte im
Paradies, und die war listiger als alle Tiere des Feldes und fing an
zu sprechen, zu Adam und Eva zu sprechen".[35] The image of peace and
harmony is thereby destroyed and this anticipation of evil is reflected
in the action of the novel immediately after in the deception of

Biberkopf by his friend, Lüders. Shortly afterwards the serpent warns Adam and Eve that bad times are approaching, which once again is really a disguised warning for Biberkopf. This biblical symbol, in fact only one of many in the novel, thus appears four times and with a different function on each occasion. Where such quotations fulfil a symbolic function, they correspond to what I earlier termed an inorganic symbol. In my discussion of "Papa Hamlet" I pointed to another type of symbolic element, namely the "Stimmungsträger". This, too, is deployed by Döblin as, for example, in the abattoir episode in which, due to the impact and intensity of the description, the scene would appear to reflect the brutality not just of the slaughter-house but of life itself. Significantly, in his discussion of this technique in B e r l i n  A l e x a n d e r p l a t z Martini expressly relates it to the work of Arno Holz.[36]

The biblical passages in B e r l i n  A l e x a n d e r p l a t z, however, do not exhaust Döblin's use of quotation. On other occasions he combines fragments of classical literature with other material such as popular songs, children's nursery rhymes, advertisements etc. For example, Biberkopf recites at one point a poem he has learnt from a fellow-prisoner:

> Willst du, o Mensch, auf dieser Erden ein männliches
> Subjekte werden, dann überleg es dir genau, eh du dich
> von der weisen Frau ans Taglicht befördern läßt! Die
> Erde ist ein Jammernest! Glaub es dem Dichter dieser
> Strophen, der oft an dieser dofen, an dieser harten
> Speise kaut! Zitat aus Goethes Faust geklaut: Der
> Mensch ist seines Lebens froh gewöhnlich nur als
> Embryo! ... Nun frag ich dich, o Freund, mit Beben, was
> ist der Mensch, was ist das Leben? Schon unser großer
> Schiller spricht: "Der Güter höchstes ist es nicht".
> Ich aber sag: es gleicht ner Hühnerleiter, von oben
> bis unten und so weiter.[37]

This is the same process of de-contextualisation and "Sinnentleerung" that Holz also uses with some of the quotations from H a m l e t and, as Martini rightly argues, Holz can thus be seen to have anticipated the technique of "epic quotation" developed by Döblin in B e r l i n  A l e x a n d e r p l a t z.[38]

In D a s   Z i t a t   i n   d e r   E r z ä h l k u n s t   Hermann Meyer
proposes the following idea as the central premise of his study of
quotation:

> (es) fällt immer wieder auf, daß sich die Leistung der
> verwendeten Zitate nicht auf deren gehältliche Aussage
> beschränkt, sondern daß sie in übergreifende Zusammenhänge
> gestalthafter Art hineingestellt werden und in diesen eine
> wesentliche Aufgabe erfüllen.[39]

This is certainly true of both "Papa Hamlet" and  B e r l i n
A l e x a n d e r p l a t z  and although Meyer does not, in fact,
analyse the use of quotation in Holz's sketch, the similarity between
the two is nevertheless clear.  Meyer's reference to the idea of
"gestalten", however, indicates another area of even more substantial
affinity, namely the problem of narrative perspective.

In an essay on the historical novel Döblin discusses the status of
the author in terms which suggest an obvious relationship to
Naturalism:

> Im Augenblick, wo der Roman die genannte neue Funktion
> einer speziellen Wirklichkeitsentdeckung und -darstellung
> erlangt hat, ist der Autor schwer Dichter oder Schrift-
> steller zu nennen, sondern e r   i s t   e i n e
> b e s o n d e r e   A r t   W i s s e n s c h a f t l e r.
> Er ist in spezieller Legierung Psychologe, Philosoph,
> Gesellschaftsbeobachter.[40]

These three roles which Döblin ascribes to the author correspond,
roughly speaking, to the three different functions that the narrator
fulfils in  B e r l i n   A l e x a n d e r p l a t z.  That of the
"Gesellschaftsbeobachter" and its similarity, as regards technique,
to consequential Naturalism have been discussed earlier.  In this
guise the narrator appears primarily in the form of a reporter of
events, who restricts his task to that of registering the reality that
confronts him and who is concerned above all to convey the immediacy
of the experience.  Moreover, as with consequential Naturalism  this
leads certain critics to speak of the "disappearance" of the narrator:

138

"Über weite Strecken hin will es scheinen, als erzähle die große Stadt sich selbst, als träten die Texte in den Roman, ohne daß sie noch des aufnehmenden und erzählend wiedergebenden Vermittlers bedürften."[41] Indeed, Walter Jens expresses the significance of immediacy in even broader terms: "Die klassische Literatur des Ich wandelte sich endgültig zur Literatur des Ist, das Vorgetragene und nicht der Autor bestimmte den Ablauf des Geschehens."[42] As in "Papa Hamlet", however, the narrator in B e r l i n   A l e x a n d e r p l a t z can be said to disappear in another sense, namely in his elimination as a direct presence in favour of the fictional characters he presents. It is this concern with the consciousness of characters that might allow us to speak, with Döblin, of the role of the narrator as psychologist.

Moreover, Döblin follows the methods for achieving this effect which were identified in "Papa Hamlet", namely those of perspektivised narration, free indirect style and inner monologue. Thus, when at the beginning of the novel the narrator repeatedly refers to Biberkopf as "der Entlassene" or "der Strafentlassene",[43] then this designation, while lacking the element of irony in Holz's "der große Thienwiebel", nevertheless fulfils the similar function of evoking the subjectivised perspective of the character's own self-awareness. Similarly, when in the description of Minna's rape by Biberkopf we read "Sie läßt läßt läßt ihm ihren Mund, sie erweicht wie im Bad", we can see in this the narrator's attempt to translate into his own (on this occasion) almost lyrical language the physical sensations which Minna is experiencing. However, when the passage continues "sie zerfließt wie Wasser, es ist schon gut",[44] it is clear that Döblin wishes to convey the experiential level more directly than with only perspektivised narration. In "Papa Hamlet" Holz achieved this through the use of free indirect style and this technique is also used by Döblin in B e r l i n   A l e x a n d e r p l a t z as in the following example:

> Franz handelt nun völkische Zeitungen. Er hat nichts gegen
> die Juden, aber er ist für Ordnung. Denn Ordnung muß im

Paradiese sein, das sieht ja wohl ein jeder ein. Und
der Stahlhelm, die Jungens hat er gesehen, und ihre
Führer auch, das ist was.[45]

Although syntactically the passage appears to have the status of
narratorial statement, in fact it consists, apart from the first sentence,
of Biberkopf's thoughts presented in the free indirect style. However,
whereas in "Papa Hamlet" Holz's tendency was to expand such passages of
free indirect style into indirect inner monologues, Döblin prefers to
convey characterial consciousness even more directly either through the
stream-of-consciousness-technique or the inner monologue proper, as
in the following example:

> Er hat Lina an Arm, blickt sich auf der finsteren Straße um.
> Könnten auch mehr Laternen anstecken. Was wollen die Leute
> von einem, erst die Schwulen, die einen nichts angehen, jetzt die
> Roten. Was geht mich das alles an, sollen ihren Mist alleene fahren.
> Sollen einen sitzen lassen, wo man sitzt; nicht mal sein Bier kann
> man ruhig austrinken. Am liebsten geh ich zurück und hau den Henschke
> seinen ganzen Laden in Klump. Es flackert wieder und pulsiert in
> Franzens Augen; seine Stirn und Nase wird dick.[46]

Where Döblin particularly refines the technique that Holz was beginning
to develop in his subjectivist prose is in the intensification of the
element of ambiguity that, I argued, constituted one characteristic
of the narrative perspective of "Papa Hamlet". One way in which this
arises is that Döblin increasingly tends to elide the distinction between
the language of the narrator and that **of the characters.** Whereas in
"Papa Hamlet" the narrator can usually be distinguished by his articulate
educated style, in B e r l i n   A l e x a n d e r p l a t z   this
separate linguistic identity is gradually dissolved as the narrator
tends more and more towards the colloquial Berlin jargon of his
characters. More crucially, however, Döblin often combines all the
various possibilities of narrative perspective in such a way as
to collapse more or less totally any immediately discernible distinction
between narratorial and characterial perspective. The result, as the
following lengthy passage illustrates, is not just the weakening but
rather the total loss of any fixed narrative centre:

Sie unterhalten sich weiter, Franz ißt und trinkt gemütlich,
denkt an Lina und daß das Vögelchen im Schlaf nicht abkippt
und sieht rüber, wer da eigentlich Pfeife raucht. Kasse
hat er heute ganz schön gemacht, aber kalt wars. Von drüben
verfolgen immer welche, wie er ißt. Die haben wohl Furcht,
ich werd mir verschluckern. Es hat mal einen gegeben, der
hat eine Wurststulle gegessen, und wie sie im Magen war, hat
sie sich besonnen und ist nochmal raufgekommen in den Hals
und gesagt: war kein Mostrich bei! und dann ist sie erst
richtig runtergegangen. Das macht die richtig Wurststulle,
die wo von guten Eltern ist. Und wie Franz fertig ist und
sein Bier hintergießt, richtig ruft der schon rüber:
"Nu, wie ist, Kollege, willst du uns nu was vorsingen?"
Die bilden wohl einen Gesangverein, können wir Eintritt nehmen,
wenn sie singen, rauchen sie nicht. Bei mir brennts nicht.
Was ich verspreche, wird gehalten. Und Franz denkt nach,
indem er sich die Nase wischt, das tropft, wenn man ins
Warme kommt, ziehen hilft nicht, er denkt, wo Lina bleibt, und
soll ich mir noch ein Paar Würstchen genehmigen, ich nehme
aber zu sehr zu, was soll man denen denn vorsingen, die
verstehen ja doch nichts vom Leben, aber versprochen ist
versprochen. Und plötzlich irrt durch seinen Kopf ein Satz,
eine Zeile, das ist ein Gedicht, das hat er im Gefängnis
gelernt, die haben es öfter aufgesagt, es lief durch alle
Zellen. Er ist gebannt im Augenblick, sein Kopf ist von der
Hitze warm und rot und hat sich gesenkt, er ist ernst und
gedankenvoll. Er sagt, die Hand am Seidel: "Ein Gedicht
wees ich, aus dem Gefängnis, ist von einem Sträfling, der
heiß, wart mal, wie der hieß, das war Dohms".

Das war er. Ist schon raus, ist aber ein schönes Gedicht.
Und er sitzt allein am Tisch, Henschke hinter seinem
Spülbecken und die andern hören zu, es kommt keiner rein,
der Kanonenofen kracht. Franz, den Kopf aufgestemmt,
sagt ein Gedicht auf, das Dohms gemacht hat, und die Zelle
ist da, der Spazierhof, er kann sie ruhig ertragen, was
mögen jetzt für Jungens drinstecken; er geht jetzt selbst
auf dem Spazierhof, das ist mehr als die hier können,
was wissen die vom Leben.[47]

This passage, which is immediately followed by the poem quoted above,

given in direct speech, reveals an almost bewildering shift in linguistic

levels and perspectives. The narrator, for example, is represented by

three different levels: the matter-of-fact, straightforward reporter

(as in the opening sentence), the colloquial tone of the more directly

experiencing participant ("richtig ruft der schon rüber", "es

kommt keiner rein") and the more elevated, lyrical style of perspectivised

narration ("Er ist gebannt im Augenblick"). Biberkopf's voice, on the other hand, appears in four forms: direct speech, indirect speech, free indirect style and inner monologue. None of these levels is allowed to assert itself over and above the others and at one point two levels are even fused within the context of the single sentence ("ziehen hilft nicht, e r denkt, wo Lina bleibt, und soll i c h mir noch ein Paar Würstchen genehmigen"). For this intentional blurring of narrative focus Martini has devised the term "Stil der parallelen Simultanität",[48] but although the complexity of this example clearly surpasses anything that Holz achieved, we can nevertheless recognise the underlying principle as the technique of "multiple" or "shifting perspective" that was identified as a main characteristic of Holz's subjectivist prose-style.

The authority of the narrator, however, is by no means always diminished in this way in B e r l i n  A l e x a n d e r p l a t z, for this reticent presence is complemented elsewhere by the traditional status of omniscience;  or, to use Döblin's own categories once again, by the position of the narrator as philosopher. Döblin sees this not as a contradiction but as an essential authorial attribute:  "Darf der Autor im epischen Werk mitsprechen, darf er in diese Welt hineinspringen? Antwort:  Ja, er darf, er soll und muß".[49]  This omniscience is reflected in the conventional manner:  by supplying information which the chance observer could not possibly know, by explaining or recapitulating situations that have already been described and by doing so in a tone that invites familiarity with the reader or the characters ("Da steht unser Franz Biberkopf anders da").[50]  In addition, however, there is one particular device that more than any other attests to the position of omniscience, namely Döblin's use of chapter headings and content-summaries. The novel opens, in fact, with a preface which not only prepares the reader for what is to take place but also points towards a possible interpretation of Biberkopf's fate:

> Das furchtbare Ding, das sein Leben war, bekommt einen
> Sinn.  Es ist eine Gewaltkur mit Franz Biberkopf vollzogen.
> ... Dies zu betrachten und zu hören wird sich für viele
> lohnen, die wie Franz Biberkopf in einer Menschenhaut

wohnen und denen es passiert wir diesem Franz Biberkopf, nämlich vom Leben mehr zu verlangen als das Butterbrot.[51]

Similarly, the individual books are prefaced by a short prologue summarising the action and each book is subdivided into sections with interpretative headings.[52] In this guise, therefore, the narrator appears as a didactic figure, concerned to explain to the reader the significance of the story he presents. His moralising tone is particularly prominent towards the end of the novel, since not only does he decide at what point the story should end but he also points to its moral: "Da werde ich nicht mehr schreien wie früher: das Schicksal, das Schicksal. Das muß man nicht als Schicksal verehren, man muß es ansehen, anfassen und zerstören."[53]

It is important to emphasise the contrast between the two sides of the narrator in B e r l i n  A l e x a n d e r p l a t z, for when assessing his role as a whole in the novel, critics have tended to take into account only one of his functions. Thus, whereas Martini and Muschg[54] still accord him the authority of the traditional narrator, Albrecht Schöne ascribes a quite different status to him:

> Der Erzähler ist eine Figur, die allein durch ihr
> Erzählen sich aufbaut, kraft ihrer Sprache persönliche
> Kontur gewinnt. Wenn man daraufhin ihn beobachtet,
> so zeigt sich doch, daß er vor dem Gegenstande
> seines Erzählens, vor der herandrängenden Fülle von
> Figuren und Geschehnissen eine Abschweifungsbereitschaft
> erweist, in der nicht mehr die Souveränität des alten
> Epikers, sondern Nachgiebgkeit und Schwäche sich
> äußern. So zeigt sich, daß er auch auf die Sprache
> des Kollektivwesens Großstadt in einer Weise sich
> einläßt, die seinen Eigencharakter, seine Überlegen-
> heit sehr in Frage stellt.[55]

In my opinion, however, Volker Klotz proposes the most satisfactory definition when he speaks of "the dual role" of the narrator, since this conception seeks not to ignore but to express his dichotomous nature. Moreover, as I attempted to indicate in the discussion of narrative perspective in Holz's work, this dual role of omniscient moralist or " souveräner Veranstalter", on the one hand, and self-effacing recorder or "situationsnaher Vermittler",[56]

on the other, is not dissimilar to that played by the narrator in
"Papa Hamlet".

At the end of "Der Bau des epischen Werks" Döblin summarises the
argument he has presented in the essay:

> Was macht das epische Werk aus? Das Vermögen seines
> Herstellers, dicht an die Realität zu dringen und
> sie zu durchstoßen, um zu gelangen zu den einfachen
> großen elementaren Grundsituationen und Figuren des
> menschlichen Daseins. Hinzu kommt, um das lebende
> Wortkunstwerk zu machen, die springende Fabulierkunst
> des Autors. Und drittens ergießt sich alles im Strom
> der lebenden Sprache, der der Autor folgt.[57]

In my analysis of B e r l i n  A l e x a n d e r p l a t z  I have
tried to show that the translation of this prescription into literary
form produces a style which, in many significant aspects, is close
to that of consequential Naturalism. One of several terms Martini
devises to define the style of the novel is "expressiver Naturalismus".[58]
Essentially, however, Martini intends this to denote a contrast to the
style of consequential Naturalism, whereas my analysis wishes to show
that, on the contrary, Döblin in fact developed and intensified (and
added to) certain effects inherent in the two modes of Holz's prose.

This relationship between "Papa Hamlet" and B e r l i n
A l e x a n d e r p l a t z  and, more generally, between Holz and
Döblin is, I believe, of great importance in that it helps us to
locate the achievement of Holz's prose-work historically. For the
tendency is to stress Holz's scientistic fascination with empiricism
and thus view his writing solely in terms of representing the culmina-
tion of realism in its traditional form; whereas the affinities
between his work and B e r l i n  A l e x a n d e r p l a t z,
which is commonly regarded as historically marking a radical
literary departure, show that Holz stands at the same time at the
beginning of another tradition. Indeed, Döblin himself was fully
aware that it was the initiation of this break with tradition that
constituted Holz's major achievement:

> seine Rolle war, ist und wird sein: in Deutschland
> den Bruch mit einer faulen und unechten Überlieferung
> einzuleiten und vollziehen zu helfen. [59]

PHANTASUS

(i)  T h e  R e v o l u t i o n i s a t i o n  o f  P o e t i c
F o r m

Although, after the publication of  N e u e  G l e i s e  in 1892,
Holz was also responsible for the authorship or co-authorship of
several dramas, the genre which increasingly dominated the last
thirty years of his creative writing was that of poetry, as
represented by the various volumes which appeared during that time
under the title of  P h a n t a s u s.  Indeed, thematically at least,
Holz's concern with the idea of "Phantasus" can be said to span
almost his entire literary output for, as noted earlier, B u c h  d e r
Z e i t too contains a cycle of poems bearing that name.  However,
the three most significant developments of the "Phantasus" poetry
to appear during Holz's life-time were, respectively, the two
small volumes published by Saßenbach in 1898/99, the enormous Insel
edition of 1916 and the three volumes published as part of Holz's
collected work by Dietz in 1924/25.  These have been supplemented
by the recent Luchterhand edition of Holz's work[1] which contains
three further volumes from Holz's "Nachlaß" and which, it has been
assumed, represents Holz's P h a n t a s u s  in its definitive
form.[2]  Each succeeding version marked not only a quantitative but
also a qualitative development of the previous one, for as well as
adding to the number of poems already composed Holz was constantly
involved in a meticulous process of revision and elaboration of his
existing material.  Just how painstaking that revision became at
times is evidenced by the fact that even such an apparently simple
line as "Plitsch!-? Ein Frosch" in the 1916 version was altered
in the "Nachlaß" edition of the poem "Verglastende Dämmerung" to
read "Plitzsch...?! Ein ... Frosch".[3]  However, while I do not
wish to present P h a n t a s u s  as an undifferentiated whole, a
detailed discussion of the exact genesis and chronological development
of the work clearly lies beyond the scope of this study.[4]  Moreover,
since my ultimate purpose in this chapter is to evaluate the
significance for the twentieth century of Holz's development of
poetic form, I will draw mainly on the later versions for examples
as, in my opinion, these illustrate most clearly the manner and extent
of that development.

As was the case with his prose-works Holz's creative writing was accompanied by a number of theoretical excursions into the nature of poetry which have been brought together in Vol.10 of D a s  W e r k under the title "Evolution der Lyrik". Although much of these writings is consumed by some rather trivial polemics against certain critics of the earliest version of P h a n t a s u s, they nevertheless indicate the premises and principles of construction on which the creative writing was based and so provide a convenient starting-point for analysis. Moreover, as at least one contemporary critic regards P h a n t a s u s (and not, that is to say, the prose-works) as the true realisation of Holz's theory of art[5], it is also necessary to reconsider briefly some of Holz's earlier propositions in the light of his subsequent poetic writing.

In his assessment of Holz's contribution to aesthetics, Emrich defines the underlying aim of Holz's theorising as the desire to discover not only the essence of art but also those factors which prevent the practical realisation of that essence. These, Emrich suggests, are to be found for Holz, on the one hand, in the artist's inherent subjectivity and, on the other, in the external limitations imposed on the writer by his chosen medium, namely conventional language.[6] Leaving the idea of artistic subjectivity aside for the moment, I would argue that the real problem Holz was attempting to confront was not simply that of language but rather the much wider question of the artist's relationship to form as such. Significantly, Holz emphasises at one point in his reflections on poetic form: "Gerade die p e r m a n e n t e Kongruenz dieser beiden (i.e. form and content, R.B.) ist aber der Kern dessen, was ich predige!"[7] Above all Holz was aware that one particular disjunction between form and content could place the artist in the position of the epigone, a fate which, after the experience of B u c h  d e r  Z e i t, he was intent on avoiding. Reviewing this earlier work Holz writes self-critically that "Epigonentum beginnt für mich erst dort, wo Stillstand eintritt. Mein B u c h d e r  Z e i t ... war bereits Stillstand."[8] Indeed, he re-asserts this idea elsewhere when he argues that poetry must from now on

eschew traditional artistic means, not simply because they are
traditional but because in the main they have ceased to be what he
terms "Entwicklungswerte".[9] This idea of development, that is to
say, the process of change but within a framework of continuity, was
crucial to Holz, so much so, in fact, that he altered the title of
his script of 1899 from "Revolution der Lyrik" to "Evolution der
Lyrik" in order to emphasise that he was concerned not so much to
make a radical break with tradition as to develop usefully what
was rooted in it. Moreover, in his insistence that poetry must adapt
to a changed situation by developing its own form, it is clear that
Holz was articulating not simply his own problems as a poet but
rather what he felt to be those of his generation, "einer Jahrhunderte
langen Epigonenzeit".[10]

The danger of "Epigonentum" for Holz derived principally from the
writer's attitude to form, and of central importance to his own
aesthetics was the view that: "Man revolutioniert eine Kunst also
nur, indem man ihre Mittel revolutioniert".[11] Holz, then, not only
rejected the uncritical acceptance and appropriation of traditional
forms but in effect was alluding to the historical specificity of
literary form:

> Alle bisherigen Formen der Wortkunst, gleichgültig
> welcher Zeit, gleichgültig welchen Volks, ohne Ausnahme,
> beruhten auf W i l l k ü r. Diese Willkür, als solche
> erkannt, hatte ihre geschichtliche Rolle im Entwicklungssinne
> damit ausgespielt und ergab zwingend den Begriff und die
> Forderung: Notwendigkeit! .. Jeder Wortkünstler bisher
> fand zwischen sich und dem, was er ausdrücken wollte,
> bereits immer etwas vor...In eine ihm überlieferte Form
> preßte er willkürlich seinen Inhalt, statt umgekehrt,
> wie ich dieses verlange, die erst gesuchte, noch gar nicht
> vorhandene Form aus seinem Inhalt unwillkürlich, dafür
> aber um so notwendiger erst wachsen zu lassen.[12]

This somewhat abstract dichotomy - "Form-Willkür" and "Form-
Notwendigkeit"[13] - Holz then attempts to concretise through various
examples:

> Lese ich z.B. bei Heine: "Glücklich der Mann, der den
> Hafen erreicht hat und hinter sich ließ das Meer und
> die Stürme", so habe ich die Empfindung, als ob die

Steine auf diesem Knüppeldamm auch anders liegen
könnten. Der Rhythmus ist hier bei Licht besehn
nichts weiter als ein Konglomerat von metrischen
Reminszensen. Er hat mit der Sache, die er eigentlich
ausdrücken sollte, nichts zu tun. Seine ausschließliche
Sorge, der alles übrige sich unterordnen muß, ist, daß
er "klingt"...der heimliche Leierkasten. Daß er
gerade d e s w e g e n  n i c h t  mehr klingt,
sondern nur noch eine Art sich fortwälzendes übeles
Geräusch verursacht, das als "Musik" eigentlich
nur noch für Jahrmärkte paßt...,ist von einer Komik,
die es heute, nachträglich, zwar gratis gibt, die aber
darum doch für die Kernfrage hier natürlich nicht in
Betracht kommt. Die Beispiele, die Mehring anführt,
"Bedecke deinen Himmel, Zeus mit Wolkendunst",
das Heinesche "Friede": "Hoch am Himmel stand die
Sonne"...,sind zwar nicht ganz so schlimm, aber ihre
Struktur is die gleiche. Trifft der Rhythmus in
ihnen an einigen Stellen mit dem Inhalt zusammen,
so ist dies nicht Absicht, sondern Zufall. Letzte
formale Absicht...bleibt stets das Tetterettetätä.
Ihm zuliebe mauschellierte Goethe unsere arme Sprache,
indem er statt unter der Sonne "unter der Sonn"
schrieb, und Heine genierte sich nicht das gleiche
zu tun, indem er das schöne Imperfektum 'wandelte
er' in 'wandelt' er' korrumpierte, wodurch es für
unser Ohr selbstverständlich zum Präsens wird. Und
von solchen Ungeheuerlichkeiten wimmelt es nur so,
wimmelt die ganze gepriesene Technik unserer 'Klassik.''[14]

The arbitrary nature of poetic form would thus appear to be
represented for Holz by all those elements normally associated
with traditional poetics: metre, assonance, alliteration,
versification and, above all, rhyme. Such things, says Holz,
merely conspire in their artificiality against the poetic word,
whereas what he seeks is its direct expression. That is to say,
he aims to reveal and develop what he calls its "innerste
Immanenz"[15] by restoring to words their "natürlichen" or "ursprünglichen Werte".[16] Holz's proposed rejuvenation of poetry can thus
be seen to be located at one level in a return to a natural
simplicity of expression: "letzte Einfachheit (ist) das höchste
Gesetz,...möglichste Natürlichkeit die intensivste Kunstform".[17]
At a theoretical level, however, possibly what he was attempting
to do with his concept of "immanence" - although, characteristically,
Holz does not spell it out - was to define the specificity of the
work of art. At any rate, as far as poetry is concerned, it is

clear that what Holz considers immanent to lyric poetry is rhythm:
"Ich würde also für eine Lyrik ohne Sprache plädiert haben, wenn ich
für eine Lyrik ohne Rhythmen plädiert hätte!....Du greifst ihn, wenn
du die Dinge greifst. Er ist allen immanent".[18] According to Holz
everything has its own rhythm and the task of poetry is to express those
inner rhythms through language.[19] Rhythm is thus the only valid form
since it changes according to what is expressed - "Dieser Rhythmus
wächst, als wäre vor ihm irgend etwas anderes noch nie geschrieben
worden, jedesmal neu aus dem Inhalt"[20] - hence Holz calls it "notwendigen Rhythmus".

Holz tries to clarify what he means by necessary rhythm by making two
particular distinctions. Firstly, he rejects the equation of "necessary"
with "free" rhythms since free rhythms, he argues, are not necessarily
"natural" ones.[21] He dismisses Goethe's free rhythms, for example,
since "sie mögen...von allem frei sein, von dem man wünscht, daß sie's
sein sollen; nur nicht von jenem falschen Pathos, das die Werte um ihre
ursprünglichen Werte bringt".[22] Furthermore, it is precisely the existence of this necessary rhythm, Holz claims, that distinguishes poetry
from prose:

> Ich schreibe als Prosaiker einen ausgezeicheten Satz nieder,
> wenn ich schreibe: "Der Mond steigt hinter blühenden
> Apfelbaumzweigen auf". Aber ich würde über ihn stolpern,
> wenn man ihn mir für den Anfang eines Gedichts ausgäbe. Er
> wird zu einem solchen erst, wenn ich ihn forme: "Hinter
> blühenden Apfelbaumzweigen steigt der Mond auf". Der erste
> Satz referiert nur, der zweite stellt dar. Erst jetzt, fühle
> ich, ist der Klang eins mit dem Inhalt. Und um diese Einheit
> bereits deutlich auch nach außen zu geben, schreibe ich:
> "Hinter blühenden Apfelbaumzweigen
> steigt
> der Mond auf."[23]

Certainly, there is much in this statement - and in the cited examples
- which is problematical and I shall discuss later the validity of the
distinction Holz proposes. For the moment, however, it is only necessary
to note the primacy of the rhythmic component of poetry for Holz and
the fact that it is this which, Holz claims, distinguishes his new
conception of poetic form from previous models. Holz thus defines his
own model as follows: "eine Lyrik, die auf jede Musik durch Worte als
Selbstzweck verzichtet und die, rein formal, lediglich durch einen

Rhythmus getragen wird, der nur noch durch das lebt, was durch ihn zum Ausdruck ringt".[24] If we now relate Holz's particular prescription for poetic form to his more general definition of art ("K = N - X": "Die Kunst hat die Tendenz, die Natur zu sein. Sie wird sie nach Maßgabe ihrer Mittel und deren Handhabung"), it is clear that the importance of rhythm for Holz lies in the fact that potentially it enables the artist to reduce one of the "x" factors (namely the handling of the artistic means) to the process of divesting language of the weight of conventional usage in order to reveal its intrinsic significance, or what Holz calls, alternately, its "natürlichen", "notwendigen" or "ursprünglichen Werte".

This reference to the nature of language, however, reminds us of what, at least in the view of Emrich quoted earlier, constituted for Holz the major cause of literary "Epigonentum", namely the inherent limitations of language. Indeed, in one sense this is implicit in Holz's law of art itself since it defines the "x" factor not only as the deployment of the artistic means but also as the artistic means themselves. As language undoubtedly constitutes the primary artistic means of literature,[25] it is thus possible to interpret Holz's "Kunstgesetz" as implying that language will always represent an impediment in the process of literary production. Various critics have pointed out that Holz was not alone in his feeling of what is now commonly known as "Sprachskepsis".[26] Moreover, as Ingrid Strohschneider-Kohrs observes, it was an experience that remained with Holz from the completion of B u c h   d e r   Z e i t   onwards.[27] Looking back on his collaboration with Johannes Schlaf, for example, Holz himself expressed quite vividly to what extent the process of literary creation had become for him a question of wrestling with language:

> Bei jedem Satz, den ich niederschrieb, gähnten um mich Abgründe, jede Wendung, die ich aus mir riß, schien mir ein Ungeheuer, jedes Wort hatte die Niedertracht, in hundert Bedeutungen zu schillern, jede Silbe gab mir Probleme auf.[28]

Moreover, in view of the almost fanatical linguistic revision to which Holz subjected the various versions of his P h a n t a s u s, there seems little reason to believe that these doubts in the efficacy and immediacy of language ever totally abated.

As regards the relevance of these thoughts to poetry, Holz gives perhaps the most concrete example of what he means when discussing rhyme,
for it is clear that underlying his analysis there is something much
more important than simply the rejection of one particular poetic device:

> Wozu noch der Reim? Der erste, der - vor Jahrhunderten! -
> auf Sonne Wonne reimte, auf Herz Schmerz und auf Brust Lust,
> war ein Genie; der tausendste,...ein Kretin. Brauche ich
> den selben Reim,den vor mir schon ein anderer gebraucht
> hat, so streife ich in neun Fällen von zehn den selben
> Gedanken. Oder, um dies bescheidener auszudrücken, doch
> wenigstens einen ähnlichen. Und man soll mir die Reime
> nennen, die in unserer Sprache noch nicht gebraucht sind!
> Gerade die unentbehrlichsten sind es in einer Weise, daß die
> Bezeichnung "abgegriffen" auf sie wie auf die kostbarsten
> Seltenheiten klänge. Es gehört wirklich kaum "übung" dazu:
> hört man heute ein erstes Reimwort, so weiß man in den weitaus
> meisten Fällen mit tödlicher Sicherheit auch bereits das
> zweite. Wir vom Publikum haben dann schon immer antizipiert,
> womit...der "Tichter" nun erst hinterdreinhinkt...So arm ist
> unsere Sprache an gleichauslautenden Worten, so wenig liegt
> dies "Mittel" in ihr ursprünglich, daß man sicher nicht allzu
> sehr übertreibt, wenn man blind behauptet, fünfundsiebzig
> Prozent ihrer sämtlichen Vokabeln wären für diese Technik von
> vorneherein unverwendbar, existierten für sie gar nicht. Ist
> mir aber ein Ausdruck verwehrt,so ist es mir in der Kunst
> gleichzeitig mit ihm auch sein reales Äquivalent. Kann es
> also wundern, daß uns heute der gesamte Horizont unserer
> Lyrik um folgegerecht fünfundsiebzig Prozent enger erscheint
> als der unserer Wirklichkeit? Die alte Form nagelt die Welt
> an einer bestimmten Stelle mit Brettern zu, die neue reißt den
> Zaun nieder und zeigt, daß die Welt auch noch hinter diese
> Bretter reicht.[29]

What concerns Holz here basically, therefore, is the relationship between language and reality. For if it is true that, as Schulz puts
it, Holz had perceived the changed relationship of men to themselves
and to their reality and thus saw the task of art as being to convey
the changed nature of that relationship,[30] it is equally true that he
was also aware of the paradox that language was at once both the means
with which to attain that aim and at the same time the greatest barrier
to its achievement. An awareness of the key role of language was thus a
precondition for any attempt to transform the nature of literature:"Eine
Erneuerung unserer Literatur...kann nur erfolgen aus einer Erneuerung

ihres Sprachbluts. Sie bleibt ohne eine solche...Utopie".[31] In what
way Holz sought concretely to effect the renewal of literary language
will hopefully emerge from an analysis of P h a n t a s u s  itself.
But for the moment I would like to return briefly to the other
"minus-factor" that Emrich identifies in Holz's equation,namely the
question of the subjectivity of the artist, since this illuminates
not only the form but also to a certain extent the basic theme of the
"Phantasus" poetry.

In a previous chapter I pointed to the divergent interpretations of
Holz's "Kunstgesetz" and to the implications of that divergence for
an analysis of consequential Naturalism.  With regard to Holz's
P h a n t a s u s, however, I would argue that a similar divergence
is untenable and the main evidence for this assertion is a document
that Holz appended to his script of 1899, "Revolution der Lyrik",
in which he reconsidered the law he had formulated in 1891.  Although
it adds nothing new to our understanding of the "Kunstgesetz" as
such, it does, I think, define quite clearly the relationship between
Holz's own then understanding of his law and the literary work on
which he had just embarked.  That is to say, the ambiguity which
surrounds the relationship between subject and object in Holz's
prose-work is not apparent in the "Phantasus" poetry, which admits
of only a subjectivist interpretation.  In the appended article Holz's
main aim was to refute the accusation that what he was, in effect,
advocating in D i e  K u n s t.  I h r  W e s e n  u n d  i h r e
G e s e t z e  was the total elimination of the subjective
individuality of the artist and, significantly, it is in this later
reassessment of 1899 that he reformulates his law in the way I
referred to earlier, so as to omit the offending words
"Reproduktionsbedingungen" and "wieder".[32]  This then prompts him to
assert quite explicitly the relativity of all art:

> Alle bisherigen Sätze liefen darauf hinaus, die Kunst ist
> ein Absolutum;  dieser Satz, zum ersten Mal von einer
> anderen Weltanschauung her, behauptet, sie ist ein
> Relativum.  Er sagt:  es gibt für uns Menschen keine
> K u n s t  an sich, wie es für uns Menschen keine N a t u r
> an sich gibt.  Es existieren genau so viele K u n s t
> auffassungen, als entsprechende N a t u r  auffassungen

existieren. Zwei sich völlig deckende sind unmöglich.[33]

Moreover, as regards the process of artistic representation Holz
remarks: "Als ob schon je ein Mensch irgendein Ding selbst
reproduziert hätte und nicht bloß immer sein betreffendes
Vorstellungsbild!"[34] This dissolution of the boundary between
subject and object leads to the conclusion that, for Holz, the
artistic representation of reality can only ever be understood as
the specific mediation of the perceiving subject, what Emrich calls
the "Selbstpreisgabe des Subjekts an den Gegenstand seiner
Gestaltung".[35] Although, in my opinion,he falls into the trap of
appearing to conflate Holz's various theoretical pronouncements
into one historical moment, I would argue nevertheless that
Hans-Georg Rappl's interpretation of Holz's theory defines precisely
the position which he had adopted by the time he began work on his
"Phantasus" project and for this reason I quote at length Rappl's
summary of his own analysis:

> Es wurde gezeigt, daß der Natur als erfaßbarem Gegenstand
> keine außerhalb der Subjektivität bestehende Existenz
> zukommt und ihr Sein an sich niemals zum Gegenstand
> einer Aussage gemacht werden kann. Die Existenz ihrer
> verfügbaren Gegebenheit erklärte sich allein aus dem
> Subjekt, dessen Empfindungen den Inhalt und dessen
> Kategorien die Formen der Natur ausmachten. In diesem
> Rückgang auf das Subjekt stellt sich sein Gegenstand,
> die Natur, als Inbegriff der inhaltlichen und formalen
> Immanenz des Subjekts dar, so daß die Darstellung von
> Natur identisch wird mit der Darstellung dieser
> Immanenz selbst. Das Subjekt ist in seinen Akten, die
> Natur erfassen und darstellen, notwendig auf sich
> selbst gerichtet und erschöpft sich in der Betrachtung
> seiner Zustände, durch deren Ausdruck Natur gestaltet
> wird. Dieser Bezogenheit des Subjekts auf sich selbst
> entspricht konsequent die Gleichsetzung von Natur und
> Immanenz des Subjekts. Im Satz der Theorie: "alle
> Kunst ist im letzten Grunde Selbstdarstellung" hat
> dieser Sachverhalt seinen endültigen Ausdruck
> gefunden. Natur und Selbst sind damit der Theorie
> identischer Gegenstand des künstlerischen Aktes.[36]

Moreover, it is precisely because, in his view, P h a n t a s u s
constitutes the best literary representation of the subject/object
relationship explicated in the theory that Rappl, like Emrich

("in seinem..."Phantasus" hat Arno Holz die letzte künstlerische
Konsequenz aus seiner Dichtungstheorie gezogen"),[37] considers
Holz's later poetic work to be the true realisation of his
aesthetic theory.

Certainly, Holz embodies in his own conception of the work the two
poles of this relationship when he states that his intention in
P h a n t a s u s  was to present the "Gestaltung eines Weltbildes",[38]
on the one hand, and the "Autobiographie einer Seele",[39] on the
other. Expressed in terms of the subject/object relationship this
can only be understood to mean that the "Ich" is the subject, the
"Welt" the object (in **the** sense of everything that confronts the
"Ich") and the "Gestaltung"represents the projection of the "Welt"
through the perceiving "Ich". Demler expresses it as follows:

> Um der Welt habhaft zu werden, muß ich sie also durch den
> Erlebnisakt in Besitz nehmen...Zur Kunst als Mittel der
> Weltverbesserung tritt so die Kunst als eine Form der
> Welterfassung; als Mittel einer scheinbaren Auflösung
> des Ich ins All, die aber in Wahrheit eine Einbeziehung
> des Alls in das Ich bedeutet.[40]

Holz, too, defines the relationship between "Weltbild" and "Ich"
when explaining why  P h a n t a s u s   assumed the particular form
it did:

> Ein "Weltbild" heute noch in den Rahmen irgend einer
> "Fabel" oder "Handlung" spannen zu wollen, hätte mir
> kindlichstes Vermessen geschienen! Was zu einem
> Weltbild heute "gehört", ist in seinen einzelnen
> Bestandteilen zu weit auseinanderliegend, in seinen
> Elementen zu buntwimmelnd kaleidoskopisch, als
> daß auch die komplizierteste, raffinierteste
> "Legende" imstande wäre, für einen solchen "Inhalt"
> den dazu nötigen Untergrund zu schaffen! Ich
> gestalte und forme die "Welt", sagte ich mir, wenn
> es mir gelingt, den Abglanz zu spiegeln, den sie mir
> in die "Seele" geworfen! Und je reicher, je
> mannigfaltiger je vielfarbiger ich das tue, um so
> treuer, um so tiefer, um so machtvoller wird mein
> Werk![41]

This view of  P h a n t a s u s   - fully consistent with the claim
he makes elsewhere that "Wortlyrik ist sprachliche Wiedergabe von

Empfindungen"[42] – defines quite clearly the subjectivist nature of
the "Weltbild" presented in this work. More problematical, however,
is the identity of the "Ich" who confronts that reality, for Holz's
statement quoted above, to the effect that "alle Kunst ist im
Grunde Selbstdarstellung"[43] might lead one to identify the auto-
biography in question with that of Holz himself. That some of the
experiences described in the course of the work – the basic situation
of the poet in his garret, for example – were also Holz's own,
is undeniable but, as a letter he wrote in 1900 makes quite explicit,
the "Seele" we encounter in P h a n t a s u s is meant only in the
very broadest and mystical of senses to be equated with the
historical figure of Arno Holz:

> Das letzte "Geheimnis" der von mir in ihrem untersten
> Fundament bereits angedeuteten Phantasuskomposition
> besteht im wesentlichen darin, daß ich mich unaufhörlich
> in die heterogensten Dinge und Gestalten zerlege. Wie
> ich v o r meiner Geburt die ganze p h y s i s c h e
> Entwicklung meiner Spezies durchgemacht habe, wenigstens
> in ihren Hauptstadien, so s e i t meiner Geburt ihre
> p s y c h i s c h e. Ich war "alles", und die Relikte
> davon liegen ebenso zahlreich wie kunterbunt in mir
> aufgespeichert. Ein Zufall, und ich bin nicht Arno Holz,
> "der formale Erneuerer der modernen deutschen Poesie",
> dessen mißglückte Zinkotypie der letzte Literaturkalender
> brachte, sondern ein beliebiges Etwas aus jenem Komplex.
> Das mag meinetwegen wunderlich ausgedrückt sein, aber
> was dahintersteckt, wird mir ermöglichen, aus tausend
> Einzelorganismen nach und nach einen riesigen
> Gesamtorganismus zu bilden, der lebendig aus ein und
> der selben Wurzel wächst.[44]

This description points to one of the main themes of the work,
what Jost Hermand terms its "lyrischen Darwinismus",[45] namely
the idea of metamorphosis and reincarnation contained in the very
first poem of the cycle:

> Sieben Billionen ... Jahre ... vor meiner Geburt
>
>    war ich
>
>    eine Schwertlilie.
>
>
>    Meine suchenden Wurzeln
>
>    saugten

sich

um einen Stern. [46]

As Schickling observes,[47] in the ensuing poetic voyage through
history and pre-history not only historical but also ontological
identity is dissolved as the division between the realm of the
human and that of the non-human is suspended. And yet, as Holz
himself insists, it is the artist, man's apotheosis, who is the
real focus of the work since he alone embodies the experiential
extremes of which man is capable:

> als Grundstruktur die in dankbar weitestem Ausmaß
> abgesteckte "Autobiographie einer Seele"! Des
> "Schaffenden", des "Dichtenden", des "K ü n s t l e r s",
> der, wie namentlich aus dem großen, resümierenden
> Schlußstück hervorgeht, als der letzte, gesteigertste
> Menschheitstyp hingestellt wird, durch den, in irgend
> einer "Beziehung", in irgend einem "Betracht", mit
> gleicher Intensität, "alles" geht: Alle Qual, alle
> Angst, alle Not, alle Klage, alle Plage, alle Wonnen,
> alle Verzückheiten, alle Jubel, alle Beglücktheiten,
> alle Seligkeiten, alle Ekstasen, alle Entrücktheiten!
> Nicht nur seine eigenen, sondern die der ganzen
> Menschheit. In allen Formen, unter allen "Verkleidungen",
> durch alle Zonen, aus allen Zeiten![48]

The identity of the "Ich" is thus clear: it is the human
individual as such, in all his historical generality, but
encompassed at the immediate and specific level within the figure
of the artist, Arno Holz.[49]   P h a n t a s u s   can be quite
properly described, therefore, as "eine Art 'Lied der Menschheit',
wie sie sich in ihrem einzelnen Individuum spiegelt".[50]

Moreover, despite all the subsequent and extensive development of
the work, it is true to say that its underlying theme always remains
basically the same (and in addition to the fact that we are primarily
concerned here with an examination of form, this is another reason
why a detailed content-analysis of  P h a n t a s u s  is not
essential). This rests – as, indeed, it did in the very first
"P h a n t a s u s" cycle in  B u c h  d e r  Z e i t  on the
antithesis between dream and reality, on the tension between the

156

grim material world of the poet's existence in his urban garret
and his transcendence of and escape from that reality in the world
of his dreams and imagination.  That is to say, the expansion of
P h a n t a s u s  during the thirty years that Holz worked on it
was not primarily a thematic or ideational one but a formal one.
Indeed, in many ways the real subject of  P h a n t a s u s  is
language itself, for the more static the work's thematic development
became, the greater was Holz's compensation in the form of a
previously unparalleled wealth of formal and linguistic innovation.
Indeed, Holz himself virtually said as much when he wrote of his
first version:

> Ich setzte über diese beabsichtigte Reihe meinen alten
> Titel "Phantasus", weil es mich drängt, eine Idee,
> die ich als junger Mensch nur unvollkommen habe aus-
> drücken können und mit Mitteln, die nicht mir selbst
> gehörten, heute unvollkommener auszudrücken und mit
> Mitteln, die ich nicht mehr meinen Vorgängern
> verdanke.[51]

As stated earlier, what Holz turned against in particular was the
traditional form of metre and in this he could justifiably claim
to be the first modern poet to do so.  "Die letzte "Einheit" der
bisherigen Metrik", he wrote "war der Versfuß.  Die letzte Einheit
"Rhythmik" ist eine ungleich differenziertere: die Zeile".[52]
Moreover, he added, the flexibility of this basic unit was such that
it would vary in length from anything from one to over fifty
syllables.  In his study of rhythm in modern poetry, Hartwig
Schultz demonstrates with the following sentence from  P h a n t a s u s
the precise effect of Holz's rejection of conventional metre:[53]
"Wie leer, wie öd, wie grämlich grau, wie traurig trüb, wie elend
trostlos gestern noch lag mir die Welt".  This sentence can be
constructed, without making any alterations, to form either a
verse in free rhythm or even a more conventional verse with lines
of four stresses;  for, as Schultz points out, the basic rhythm of
the sentence consists of an almost regular alternation of rising and
falling stress.  It could then be written as below, producing the
following metre pattern:

Wie leer, wie öd, wie grämlich grau     x| x́ x| x x| x́ x| x́∧

Wie traurig trüb, wie elend trostlos    x| x́ x| x́ x| x́ x| x́

Gestern noch lag mir die Welt.      x́ u u| x́ u u|   x́∧|∧ ∧

In fact, however, the rhythm which Holz achieves in his
P h a n t a s u s  setting of these lines is totally different
since, if each line-ending is taken as signifying a pause or slight
pause - what Donald Davie has called "typographic breathing spaces"[54]
- the sentence is patterned as follows:

                    Wie                 ́

              leer, wie öd          x́  x|  ́

                    wie

                 grämlich          x́  u

                    grau            ́

        wie traurig trüb, wie      x|  x́  x|  ́|  ́

            elend trostlos,        x́  x| x́  u  ⋏

                 gestern           x́  u ⋏

                    noch            ́

        lag mir ... die Welt!      x́  x| ∧  x|  x́  ∧

Schultz concludes his analysis of these lines with the comment that
"Holz erzeugt durch die Gliederung des Wortmaterials in verschieden
lange, durch kurze Pausen begrenzte Abschnitte einen äußerst
spannungsreichen Rhythmus,der keinen permanenten Wechsel  von Hebung
und Senkung kennt."[55]

The above example also illustrates the basic structuring principle
that Holz deployed in all the versions of his  P h a n t a s u s,
namely the so-called "Mittelachse", the grouping of words or lines
round a central axis.  Crucial though this was to Holz's formal
concept, at the time many critics were reticent in according it any
innovatory significance, seeing it rather as a somewhat superfluous
importation from the Baroque.  Turley, however, attempts to distinguish
it from that period - in terms of which Holz would have undoubtedly
approved - when he argues:

158

Im Barock war, wenn die Form überhaupt einmal gewählt
wurde, zuerst die Figur da (z.B. Szepter-Kelch- oder
Harzform), auf die der Inhalt geformt wurde. Bei Holz
ist das Primäre der Inhalt, aus dem sich dann die Form
ergibt, die außerdem eine Figur im Sinne des carmen
figuratum gar nicht vorstellt.[56]

Views as to the exact purpose and effect of the "Mittelachse" vary,
however, as perhaps can be best demonstrated by considering one of
Holz's poems in its entirety:

Schönes, grünes, weiches

Gras.


Drin

liege ich.

Inmitten goldgelber Butterblumen!


Über mir,

warm,

der Himmel:


Ein

weites, schütteres,

lichtwühlig, lichtwogig,

lichtblendig

zitterndes Weiß,

das mir die Augen, langsam, ganz langsam

schließt.


Wehende ... Luft, kaum ... merklich ein Duft,

ein

Zartes ... Summen


Nun

bin ich fern

von jeder Welt,

ein sanftes Rot erfüllt mich ganz,

                              und

    deutlich ... spüre ich ... wie die Sonne
                              mir
                 durchs Blut rinnt.


                    Minutenlang.

             Versunken alles.  Nur noch ich.

                      Selig!                    57


According to Käthe Lichtenstern, the primary effect of the "Mittelachse"
presentation is a cognitive one in that it reinforces what she calls
the poem's "Tempoplastik",[58] which in turn heightens the suggestive
power of the words.  Thus the isolation of "schließt", for example,
encapsulated as it is by pause and so retarding the rhythmic tempo of
the previous lines, connotes, Lichtenstern suggests, the poet's final
surrender to blissful relaxation in the mid-day warmth.[59]  In contrast,
the extending of the following lines with pause-insertions reduces
the tempo even further to suggest the blurring of sensations that
accompanies the approach of sleep.  Moreover, the isolating process
which is so integral a part of the "Mittelachse" structure can work
in two different ways, either emphasising the significant, as in the
case of the final jubilant "Selig!", or, by inviting the eye to pass
over subsidiary elements such as "und", "mir", "ein", etc., deflecting
attention from the insignificant.  These subtleties would be missed,
Lichtenstern argues, were traditional verse and metre patterns
adopted.

Clearly, however, the "Mittelachse" formation has effects other
than simply aiding comprehension, important though this undoubtedly
is for the enormous sentences of the later versions of P h a n t a s u s.
Holz wrote that he chose this particular form with the intention of
"die jeweilig beabsichtigten Lautbilder möglichst auch schon typographisch zuzudeuten"[60] and goes on to emphasise its distinct visual
value:

> Warum sollte das Auge am Drucksatz eines Gedichts
> n i c h t  seine besondere Freude haben? Jedenfalls
> diese Frage einmal aufgeworfen, ziehe ich eine
> besondere Freude einem besonderen Mißfallen entschieden
> vor ... ein solches Mißfallen würde durch die alte
> Anfangsachse bei meinen 'Kreisgedichten' unbedingt
> erregt werden. Denn wenn vielleicht die eine Zeile
> nur  e i n e  Silbe enthält, enthält vielleicht
> bereits die nächste Zeile  z w a n z i g  Silben und
> m e h r. Ließe ich daher die Achse, statt in die Mitte,
> an den Anfang legen, so würde dadurch das Auge gezwungen
> sein, immer einen genau doppelt so langen Weg
> zurückzulegen. Nach dem unbestreitbaren Prinzip des
> kleinsten Kraftmaßes aber et cetera![61]

As will be shown later when I assess the implications of the
"Phantasus" form for modern literature, this identification of the
optical dimension of poetry as an essential element of the
aesthetic effect was an extremely modern insight. Moreover, when
Holz further describes the "Mittelachse" as "das Ohrbild eines
Gedichtes" and defines its effect as "typographische Musik",[62]
it is clear that he accords equal significance to the acoustic
dimension. Holz, in fact, frequently likened his poetry to music,
seeing the function of the "Mittelachse", for example, as being
to project the verse's "inner melody"[63] and describing P h a n t a s u s
as nothing more or less than a musical score, which is meant,
therefore, to be played not read.[64] It is probably this striving
for musical effect that accounts for Holz's predilection for
alliteration - the following line being a fairly typical example:
"verkoste, verkauserierte, verkaressierte, verfetierte,
vermenuettierte, verflatterierte"[65] - and which ultimately even
induces him to rehabilitate the tabooed device of rhyme:

> urherwärts rollende, urherwärts grollende
> lichtauf, lichtempor, lichthoch tollende
> sich drängen, sich zwängen
> sich
> kunden wollende.[66]

On one occasion Holz even attempts to translate music directly into
words, when he describes an organ improvisation by J. S. Bach in a
passage composed almost exclusively of onomatopoeic verbs and

sustained by a regular rhythm.[67] This analogy with music merely
underlines the extent to which rhythm in all its forms became the
basis of composition, a rhythm that was perceptible to both ear
and eye and of which Holz himself once said: "Grade d e r  scheint
mir oft mehr zu sagen als die Worte selbst."[68]

Ultimately, however, Holz's preoccupation with rhythm extended beyond
his interest in it as a purely aesthetic effect, for his positivistic
proclivities convinced him that rhythm, like all other phenomena,
must be governed by some definable law.  In his essay of 1918,
"Idee und Gestaltung des Phantasus", Holz explains what he thought
that law was:

> Ein Beiwort zu viel, eine Bestimmung zu wenig, kurz ein
> Defekt! ... Dieses bringt mich auf ein Gesetz, dessen
> Vorhandensein ich entdeckte, dessen Gründe sich mir
> entziehen, dessen Vorhandensein mir aber nichtsdestoweniger,
> und zwar mit aller Bestimmtheit, immer wieder und wieder
> mein 'Gefühl' verrat. Nämlich, daß meiner Rhythmik als
> a l l e r l e t z t e s  ein  b e s t i m m t e s
> Z a h l e n v e r h ä l t n i s  zugrunde liegt!
>
>       Schönes, grünes, weiches
>
>         Gras
>
>
>         Drin
>
>        liege ich
>
>    Inmitten goldgelber Butterblumen!
>
> Es ist nicht möglich, daß ich eins der drei 'Eigenschafts-
> oder Beiworte' zu  'Gras' weglassen kann.  Die Zeile
> fiele sofort in sich zusammen und würde tot wirken!
> Und der ganze Gedichteingang, der mich bestrickt in
> seiner Einfachheit, der mich 'gefangen' nimmt durch
> seine 'Stimmung', und von dem ein Empfinden mir sagt,
> er ist 'vollendet', schließt sich abermals in eine
> Dreiheit![69]

This discovery led Holz to subject his entire work to similar
scrutiny in search of a mathematical definition of the dynamics of
rhythm and from this he evolved his "Zahlenarchitektonik",[70] a
complex system of numbers that would regulate its development.
Robert Ress, one of Holz's most ardent disciples, then completed

this analysis in his manuscript entitled  D i e   Z a h l   a l s
f o r m a l e s   W e l t p r i n z i p.[71]  This aspect of Holz's
writing, however, need not detain us, for in truth it marked
a contradiction of all the principles that Holz had previously
expounded.  For despite his attempts to reconcile his new
discovery with his earlier but still central thesis that rhythm
should develop organically from the content,[72] in adopting a
purely mathematical determinant of rhythm Holz was, in effect,
imposing the same kind of extraneous pattern on his material,
albeit one decidely more complex, that he had so roundly condemned
in the case of conventional metre.  Such a process, abstracted
from content, could only produce either results so mechanistic
as to be inimical to the essence of rhythm as Holz conceived
of it, or alternatively the type of poetry which he always claimed
he rejected, namely "eine(r) Musik durch Worte als Selbstzweck".
Far from recognising this contradiction, however, Holz actually
believed that he would revolutionise poetry with his system:

> Diese Zahlenarchitektonik ... drängte sich mir ... als
> eine so notwendige, sich, 'mit den Dingen deckende'
> auf, daß ich mir eine noch tiefere, gewaltigere und
> zwingendere Bindung, da sie jetzt alles umfaßt und
> absolut nichts mehr außerhalb der Grenzen ihrer
> Greifmöglichkeit liegt, nicht mehr vorstellen kann.[73]

The consequences for his own writing, however, were not so beneficial
and for this reason I would agree with Franz Kleitsch that in
P h a n t a s u s   it is necessary to differentiate between two
types of rhythm, namely "eine sich stets aus den Dingen
gebärende oder immanente Rhythmik" and "eine dieser ursprünglich
zugrundeliegende, dann aber sich verselbständigende Zahlenarchitektonik".[74]  In my opinion, it is the first of these which constitute
Holz's real literary achievement in  P h a n t a s u s   and, as I
hope to show, that would also appear to be the verdict of
subsequent creative writers.

If rhythm is one area in which  P h a n t a s u s   can be said to
have made a substantial formal advance, than the other major

achievement of Holz's poetry is his use and development of language
itself in the sense of the individual word. As a comparison of the
final 'Nachlaß' edition (over 1500 pages in all) with the original two
slim volumes of 1898/99 indicates, P h a n t a s u s's main mode
of development was that of word-expansion. The proliferation of
words in which this process resulted has been described variously
as gratuitous ornamentation[75] and as the inevitable product of Holz's
poetic attempt to create a "Weltbild" as an extensive totality.[76]
Holz himself, however, regarded it as an essential process of
differentiation and rejected the criticism that his method of expansion was simply an arbitrary augmentation of vocabulary: "Sie ver-
wechselten Addition and Division, wo Sie mir 'Häufung' vorwarfen,
während Differenzierung vorlag."[77] However, that this process of
differentiation is in theory infinite, with each new qualification
in turn requiring its own further differentiation, can be
illustrated by a simple comparison. Earlier I quoted the first
five lines of the 1898 version of the poem "Sieben Billionen Jahre
vor meiner Geburt". The next lines read as follows:

> Auf seinem dunklen Wasser
> schwamm
> meine blaue Riesenblüte.[78]

In the 'Nachlaß' version these eight words have expanded to eighty-
two and the only element of the sentence to retain its relative
absence of characteristics or, to use Holz's terminology, the only
element to escape complex differentiation, is the "Wasser" which
nevertheless is now plural and no longer "dunkel" but "sich wölbend".
The "Riesenblüte", for example, is not simply blue but is "meine
dunkel-metallische, halkyonisch-phallische, klingend-kristallische
Riesenblüten-Szepterkrone", while the relative passivity of
"schwamm" is replaced by a series of dynamic verbs: "stieg, stieß,
steilte, teilte, speilte, verglühte, zerströmte, versprühte sich".
This dynamic intensification is further effected by a number of
adverbs and present participles describing the volcanic quality of
the flower:

geheimnisträchtigst, geheimnismächtigste

geheimnishehrst

sich selbst begattend, sich selbst befruchtend,   ...   sich selbst

zerzeugend,

Flammenkugelmeteore,

Kometenkaskaden, Planetenbuntkränze

verschwenderisch

um sich regnend, verspenderisch um sich segnend,

vergeuderisch

um sich

schwingschleudernd.

Finally, the effect of the flower on the water (described in the
1916 verson simply as "neue, kreisende Weltenringe")[79] is "neue,
wallende, werdende, wogende, brauende, brodelnde, kreisende
Weltenringe". Whether such "differentiation" is deemed to
heighten or reduce the effect of the original lines, certainly
there seems no logical reason why this version should mark the end
of the process, even though it is at a third stage of differentiation
removed from the original. Moreover, its real significance lies not
so much in the quantity of differentiation – and astonishingly in
"Das Tausendundzweite Märchen" Holz succeeded in constructing a
single sentence of 2516 lines in length – but rather in the quality
of differentiation, that is to say, in the type of language that
this process generated. In this respect Holz himself claimed, with
characteristic immodesty but, on this occasion at least, with
undoubted justification, that P h a n t a s u s was unique:

> Man wird finden: die Zahl der Worte in ihm, die noch nie
> bisher in einem deutschen Verse, geschweige denn gar in
> deutscher "Lyrik", gebracht und gebraucht wurden, ist eine
> so ungeheuere, die Anzahl der Neubildungen, die sich als
> solche erst bei näherem Zusehn entpuppen, so sehr gehen sie
> in den Ton des Übrigen auf, außerdem eine so überraschende,
> daß ich mich nicht scheue hier niederzuschreiben: kein
> Wortkunstwerk unserer Sprache kann nach dieser Richtung ...
> ... mit ihm ... in Vergleich gezogen werden![80]

As this quotation indicates, the aspect of poetic expression that
Holz extended more than any other is that of vocabulary. Alfred Döblin

described this trait of Holz's writing as "der Zug ins Enzyklopä-
dische",[81] an apposite metaphor in more senses than one since Holz
considered the encyclopaedia as "der lebendigste, bewegtste,
reichste Orbis pictus der Welt, ein Verzeichnis ihrer Schätze, die
nur darauf warten, gewürdigt und genossen zu werden."[82] It is
hardly surprising, therefore, that the "Weltbild" of P h a n t a s u s,
corresponding to a reality that Holz perceived as "buntwimmelnd
kaleidoskopisch",[83] should be reflected in a mosaic of words and
references which was,in nature and extent, itself virtually
encyclopaedic. As certain examples from P h a n t a s u s have
already illustrated, one particular lexical element to which Holz
was drawn was the synonym, partly because from the point of view
of content it facilitated the subtlety of differentiation to which
he aspired, and partly because it was conducive to the formal
technique of extended word-chains, as in the following example:

in
den von mir
gewaltheftigst, gewalthitzigst
gewaltätigst
aufgerenkten, aufgerissenen, aufgesprengten
krampfigst
verquollenen, blaurotst verschwollenen,
gaumenbögenzatterigen, zäpfchenzipfelzitterigen,
ruckweis, schluckweis, zuckweis
notgedrungen, notgenötigt, notgezwungen,
klückkluckernd
schlingernden, schluckernden,
zungenschlubbernden, zungenschubbernden,
zungenschlabbernden
Schlundrachen[84]

Another encyclopaedic characteristic of P h a n t a s u s is the
wealth of specialist expressions it contains, drawing on various
branches of science and the arts and referring to a plethora of
names, both geographical and terminological as well as those of

people, real and imaginary.

The "Fremdwort" also plays a substantial role in the vocabulary of
P h a n t a s u s  and Holz drew his material from innumerable
languages including English, French, Italian, Greek, Latin, Dutch,
Spanish and Arabic.  "Das Tausendundzweite Märchen" is particularly
rich in examples, but it is also a characteristic of the earliest
versions, as in this poem of 1898:

> So eine kleine Fin-de-Siècle-Krabbe,  die Lawn tennis schlägt!
>
> Rote, gewellte Madonnenscheitel,
>
> eine lichtblau Blouse aus Merveilleux
>
> und im flohfarbnen Gürtel ein Veilchensträußchen,
>
> das nach amerikanischen Cigaretten duftet.[85]

This was, perhaps, one obvious way Holz saw of effecting the
necessary "Erneuerung ... (des) Sprachbluts", particularly as it
provided a new source of rhyme material, in which he regarded the
German language to be so impoverished.  Schulz attributes an ironic
function to its use, as a means of distanciation from his own
language - not so much a "Fremdwort", then, as a "Verfremdungswort"
- and this is surely correct, for any critical reading of
P h a n t a s u s  must take into account the two crucial
elements of irony and word-play.[86]

Without doubt, however, the most radically innovatory aspect of
Holz's vocabulary is his facility for coining neologisms which, again,
is a constant and increasingly pervasive feature of  P h a n t a s u s's
development.  Sometimes they take the simple form of a new word
derived from an existing one - "sich kilometern",[87] for example -
but much more common is the tendency to combine two or more words
into a single unit as in an adjective like "innenfühlerhohlraumver-
steckt."[88]  Such word-combinations serve two functions.  Firstly,
they enable Holz to compress as much content as possible into one
semantic unit, what Schmidt-Henkel terms "kondensierte(n)
Wirklichkeitsbeschwörungen".[89]  Thus, an extended noun like
"Baumriesenwipfelblütengigantenschmetterlinge"[90] can be broken down
into the phrase "Schmetterlinge, groß wie Giganten in den Blüten

und Wipfeln von Baumriesen". Secondly, the word-combinations
serve as a means of intensification, as in such extremes of
tautology as "bis in meine untersten Grundgrundgründe"[91] or "das
fernstfernst Fernste".[92] This last example illustrates a further
predominant characteristic of P h a n t a s u s, namely Holz's
predilection for superlatives often strung together in an extended
series. This was not just a stylistic device, Holz insisted,
but also a fundamental expression of content:

> Nehmen Sie sich fünf beliebige Seiten vor und streichen
> Sie auf diesen die betreffenden 'Estees', und Sie werden
> a n d e r e r  Meinung werden! Fast der gesamte 'Phantasus'
> entspringt einer beinahe ununterbrochenen 'Ekstatik' und
> dieser 'Seelen'-Zustand g e f o r d e r t  diese Form.
> Sie finden sie, wie ich hoffen mochte, nirgends, wo
> 'Ruhe' und 'Erfüllung' herrscht. Aber sie überstürzt sich
> geradezu selbst, wo das Gegenteil herrscht. Dafür kann
> nicht ich sondern das 'wollen' und 'setzen' durch die
> Dinge![93]

If there was one particular type of neologism that fascinated
Holz, however, it was onomatopaeia. P h a n t a s u s contains
not only all manner of interjections - "Pphh", "Ah-hemm!",[94]
"Wüllenwüschen! Tülltlüllelüdel! Guckeruku! Krillekrällekrolle!
Bridibidibomm"[95] - but also a number of sound-portraits, such as
the following rendition of birds singing in a tree:

Jückjuckjanners! Nu mal wat anners!

Jückjuckjachter! Nu von achter!

Jückjuckjarscher

Jümmer karscher! Jümmer harscher! Jümmer barscher!

Jümmertau!

Jückjuckjör Wedder von vör!

Treck em rut! Schreg de Brut! Greint un Grind! Tgifft n Kind!

Zippzippzenn! Na, un wenn! Schlippschluppschlenn!

Wenn schon, denn!

Deidüdeldomm! Dreih di omm! Quitschquitschquiet! Vun de Sied!

Düwels Dunner! Lat mi drunner!

Widibridibröwer! Legg die dröwer! Widibridibrupp! Leg di drupp!

Hahaha! He lett all na! Hüjüjönn! Fallt em nich ön!
Tscharktscharktschack! Autsch min Sack!
Tscharktscharktschien! Olet Swien! Tscharktscharktscharken! Olet Farken!
Knirreknärreknarr! Uck de Pfarr!
Knörreknärreknöster! Uck de Köster! Knirreknärreknanter! Uck de Kanter!


The passage illustrates another facet of Holz's use of language,
for interspersed between the various bird-sounds is a series of responses reproduced in Prussian dialect. Elsewhere, too, can be
found jargon and everyday language, all of which has rightly been
characterised as the "Sprechton" of  P h a n t a s u s, namely
"der Versuch, abgebrauchte Alltagsworte poesiefähig zu machen".[97]
As with the use of punctuation to indicate a pause in speech, hesi-
tation etc., Kleitsch sees this as a residual effect of consequential
Naturalism,[98] but it is surely most improbable that some thirty-five
years after  N e u e   G l e i s e   Holz would still have asserted
the validity of "Sekundenstil" characterisation. For this reason
and bearing in mind also the way Holz manipulates language generally
in  P h a n t a s u s, I find much more convincing Schulz's view
that this represents another example of Holz's self-irony, that is
to say, a relativisation of his former style.[99]

This argument seems all the more tenable when seen in relation to
the way Holz utilises quotation in  P h a n t a s u s, for a close
study of the text reveals many an ironic self-reference, to his
"Kunstgesetz", for example, the "Sein oder Nichtsein" of  H a m l e t
and, of course, "Papa Hamlet",[100] the deployment for long passages
of the Baroque language of Holz's  D a f n i s   and also actual
quotations from that work.[101]  Holz's own work, however, is only
one source of material for, as Schulz's extensive analysis of
this aspect of  P h a n t a s u s   demonstrates,[102] Holz incorporates
a wealth of quotation in either direct, modified or blatantly
parodied form and ranging from the clichéed familiar to the
abstrusely opaque. For the moment it is sufficient to add that frequently Holz structures such material into a collage, as is the case
with a poem in the 1916 version which takes as its subject a

"Litfaßsäule":

"ACHTUNG ! ACHTUNG !! ACHTUNG !!!

Mit

grellen Farben schreit die
Litfaßsäule:

"Mondamin !"

"Dreißigtausend Menschen waren im Meßpalast !"

"Pst, Sie !
Die geplatzte Emma !"

"Halt !
Mehr Goethe !"

"Papst Cohn !"

"Wilhelm, der Geschmackvolle,

als

Erzieher !"
"Das neue Weib !"

"Abeles,

der
Neo-Romantiker !"

"Das

weltenträtselnde Substanzgesetz !"

"Wie
sag ich's meinem
Kinde ?"

"Nietzsche oder die Philosophie

als

Serpentintänzerin !"


"Wählt Zubeil !"


Ein

Platzregen prasselt,

der ganze Dreck ... hängt in Fetzen.[103]

As can be seen from previous chapters, the use of quotation is a
constant feature of Holz's work. In B u c h  d e r  Z e i t it
was a clumsy, almost obtrusive device, an index in itself of the
lack of formal awareness in Holz at that time; whereas in "Papa
Hamlet", although much more refined in its implementation and beau-
tifully integrated into the body of the story, it was restricted
in the main to one effect and served primarily as a function of
content. In P h a n t a s u s, however, it is developed through
its pervasive and differentiated application into an effect in and
for itself such that ultimately it is reducible primarily to the
dictates of form. As I hope to show in the following analysis, it is
in this fully developed stage as a purely formal technique that
Holz's use of quotation prefigures its appearance in modern
literature.

In conclusion, I would concede that in one sense the assessment of
P h a n t a s u s  I have provided so far is somewhat artificial in
that the analysis has tended to abstract from their overall context
the various literary techniques which Holz developed. To a certain
extent this was determined by the nature and aim of this study having,
as it does, its focus primarily on the formal and the innovatory,
which has the, perhaps, inevitable effect of short-circuiting any
evaluation of P h a n t a s u s  as a whole and eschewing discussion
of its very real weaknesses as a work of literature. In truth, the
relative obscurity of P h a n t a s u s  in its own time was not
coincidental (nor, for that matter, is its subsequent resonance over
the last two decades). Significantly, Holz himself wrote of

171

P h a n t a s u s  in 1919 that he would be happy if people had
even begun to understand it after thirty years[104] and a charitable
interpretation of that statement might take it as indicating at
least a subconscious awareness on Holz's part of the work's defects
(for only rarely did he consciously admit to them!) Identification
of defects does not mean, though, that like Roy Cowen - for whom the
significance of  P h a n t a s u s  lies in the curious proposition
that it supposedly demonstrates the impossibility of a consequential-
Naturalist poetics[105] - we must evaluate the work in purely negative
terms;  but certain weaknesses there are nonetheless.  The most
obvious is that its sheer length and, at times, impenetrability
makes a reading of the entire  P h a n t a s u s  in its later forms
the literary equivalent of at least two of the Herculean labours!
That is to say, my analysis, although it defines the nature of
Holz's formal techniques, can give no proper indication of the extent
of their deployment and it is a sad but inescapable fact that many
become positively tiresome through over-use (the repetition of
superlatives, to give but one example).  Arguably the main failing,
however, is that the dualistic conception on which Holz based the
work (i.e. "Weltbild" and "Autobiographie einer Seele") is not
realised.  As Schulz puts it, Holz forgot the boundaries of
subjectivism, with the result that the claims of the "Weltbild" are
submerged by those of the "Ich".  The intended dialectic between
"Ich" and "Welt" is curtailed by the identity of the work's
experiencing subject and its author and the result, for Schulz, is
solipsism.[106]  Rappl, in fact, goes beyond this and formulates
the problem at the level of an antinomy:

> Die Intention des Theoretikers und Künstlers Arno Holz
> war es, die Unmittelbarkeit der Natur und des Daseins
> zurückzugewinnen;  nur durch die Aufhebung der
> Verfestigungen, in deren Natur und Dasein den Subjekten
> verfügbar waren, vermochte sich diese Intention zu
> verwirklichen.  Aber indem der Künstler die
> Unmittelbarkeit beschwor, entzogen sich die Gegenstände
> ihrer Begrenzung und keine Vermittlung durch Erkenntnis
> und Sprache vermochte die Unmittelbarkeit wieder in
> Bilde zu versöhnen.  Nur in der Zerstörung des Bildes
> bewahrte sich der Anspruch der Kunst, "wieder die
> Natur zu sein."[107]

This seems to me, as far as P h a n t a s u s is concerned at
least, too negative a verdict in that it does not acknowledge
the positive side effects of Holz's attempt at "Unmittelbarkeit".
Döblin, on the other hand, as ever the most perceptive of Holz's
admirers, expressed it more dialectically when he wrote:  "Das
Ganze entglitt ihm.  Aber sein Unbewußtes, gegen sein Gehirn,
befahl ihm zu folgen, und er kam auf ein neues Gebiet."[108]  The
"new realm" that Holz discovered was his formal legacy to modern
literature and the task now is to identify the heirs to that
legacy.

(ii)  T h e  L e g a c y  o f  P h a n t a s u s

In her analysis of Holz's work  Ingrid Strohschneider-Kohrs has
argued that his writing is dominated by one aim, namely that of
developing language as an artistic means into a vehicle of
immediacy, of attaining through language the maximum proximity to
reality.[1] The attempted realisation of this aim in  P h a n t a s u s,
she argues, opened up two different possibilities:  the first is
what she describes as "radikale Steigerung einer Einfühlungskunst...,
die die Identität von lyrischem Ich und erlebtem Gegenstand in
detaillierten Gestalten zu vergegenwärtigen sucht" and the
relationship it defines is that between Holz and Expressionism.
The second possibility which it offers is "eine ästhetische
Totalität, die nicht mehr  S i n n g e s t a l t, sondern nur
artistische Eigenwelt zu bedeuten scheint"[2] and the relationship
which this suggests is one between  P h a n t a s u s  and a
particular type of formalist poetry, which could be subsumed
under a term I deployed in an earlier chapter,namely "the technicisation of literature".  To these I would add one further possibility,
namely a type of prose-writing which is neither Expressionist nor
expressly formalist but of which certain characteristics, it could
be argued, relate it to particular stylistic tendencies in
P h a n t a s u s.  Clearly, however, such parameters of relationship, while useful as guidelines, are broad enough to accommodate
any number of different concrete cases.  In the following, therefore,
I shall restrict myself either to those relationships which have
been most commonly asserted or - which may or may not be the same
thing - those which, in my opinion, allow of the best textual
verification.

Certainly, the affinities with Expressionism fall into the first
category since this is a relationship that has been continually
posited by critics both within and since Holz's life-time.  Fritz
Martini's comments, for example, are fairly typical:

> Erst der geschichtliche Rückblick und eine allmählich
> vertiefte Kenntnis der sogenannten expressionistischen

174

Bewegung lassen begreifen, daß Arno Holz der gesamten
deutschen spätneuzeitlichen 'Moderne' entscheidende
Anregungen gegeben hat; daß der P h a n t a s u s-
Dichter sehr wesentliche Impulse an die ihm meist
nur verschwiegen folgende lyrische Entwicklung von
Alfred Mombert bis zu Herwarth Walden ... mitteilte,
ja, daß diese ohne ihn kaum zu denken ist. Arno
Holz hat die deutsche Moderne bis tief in den
Expressionismus hinein eingeleitet.[3]

In this respect it is instructive - though by no means conclusive,
of course - to turn to Holz's own assessment of the relationship
between his poetry and Expressionism. This was occasioned by an
article written in 1917 by John Schikowski which described Holz
as the "pioneer of Expressionism". The young generation for whom
Holz provided this stimulus was, he argued, one in which "man
verachtet die Welt der Sinne und die Tätigkeit des Intellekts
und sucht durch inneres Schauen die Rätsel zu ergünden, die hinter
dem Diesseits verborgen liegen".[4] Expressionist art, Schikowski
continued, by-passes the circuitous route of reason and appeals
directly to the emotions; it aims not to describe or narrate but
to penetrate with the power of its language directly through into
the soul. Moreover, it was claimed, Holz had provided the means
with which to express this in his discovery of rhythm as the
ultimate determinant of poetry, for the recognition of the primacy
of rhythm released art from the dictates of grammatical coherence,
which the Expressionists saw as the embodiment of reason in
language. Holz's use of language had paved the way, therefore,
for "eine noch radikalere Ausmerzung alles rein Verstandesmäßigen".[5]
Holz's response to Schikowski's argument indicates that it was
above all the conception of literary content that in his view
separated him from the Expressionists, for one or two side-
swipes at their style notwithstanding - "was dadurch entsteht, ist
nicht "Rhythmik", sondern ... plumpste, primitivste ...
"Untermetrik"!"[6] - it was precisely their subordination of reason
to the emotions that Holz rejected most strongly: "durch inneres
Schauen    a l l e i n. ...   o h n e   daß ich "naturalistischer
Beobachter" gewesen wäre, ... hatte ich das "Fundament", auf
dem nun die  j ü n g s t e  G e n e r a t i o n ... "weiterbaute",

n i e m a l s   g e l e g t".[7]  P h a n t a s u s, as an earlier
quotation from Holz showed,[8] may well have in common with
Expressionism an attempted communication of ecstacy but fundamental
to that communication is, to borrow Heinrich Fauteck's phrase,
the distinction between Holz, the  "r a t i o n a l e (n)
Ekstatiker", and the "v i s i o n ä r e n  Ekstatiker" of
Expressionism.[9]

In one sense, of course, the very attempt to establish a
relationship between the style of  P h a n t a s u s  and that of
Expressionism as such is in itself a highly undifferentiating,
not to say hazardous undertaking for as Armin Arnold has
emphasised, it is virtually impossible to identify that heterogeneous movement with any one particular mode of writing, since
the only thing which many of the linguistic experiments of
Expressionism have in common is the desire to break with tradition.[10]
For this reason I shall focus comparative analysis on the writer,
who, of all the Expressionists, is most often singled out in
relation to Holz, August Stramm. Walter Muschg, for example, goes
so far as to refer to Stramm as a "student" of Holz's;[11] nor can
it be without significance that in his work of commemoration to
Holz of 1951, entitled  V e r s c h o l l e n e  u n d
V e r g e s s e n e.   A r n o  H o l z.  D i e  R e v o l u t i o n
d e r  L y r i k, Alfred Döblin includes along with a selection
from Holz's own work two poems by Stramm.[12]  In fact, however, the
relationship of Holz's work to Stramm's is a curiously paradoxical
one in that their surface-similarities often contain many a deeper
divergence. That is not to say that there is no area of genuine
relationship between Holz and Stramm, but only that it is a
different type of relationship to the unproblematical and substantial
one that has been so commonly asserted in recent criticism.

Generally speaking, there are two real areas of similarity and in
view of what we have defined as the primary location of Holz's
"revolutionisation" of poetry, the first of those, not
unnaturally, is that of rhythm. In the study of rhythm referred

176

to earlier, Schultz identifies the same sort of rhythmic
structuring process that he described in Holz's work and illustrates this with a sentence from the poem "Heimlichkeit";
"Die heissen Ströme brennen heiß  zu Meere, und unsere Seelen
rauschen ein in sich".  These words could fit easily into a poem
with regular rhythms and thus produce the following metrical
scheme:

x|  x́ x|  x́ x|  x́ x|   x́ x|   x́ x

x   x́ u u|x x́   x́ x|   x́ x|   x́ ∧

whereas, in fact, Stramm structures the sentence as follows:

Die heissen Ströme

Brennen

Heiß

Zu Meere

Und

Unsere Seelen

Rauschen      x|  x́ x|   x́ u∧|x́ u∧|  ⁻|∧ x|   x́ u∧

Ein           ⁻| x u u|   x́ u∧|x́ x|   ⁻| ⁻ |  ⁻

In

Sich[13]

The effect is thus that of the "gestauter Rhythmus"[14] that Holz
achieved in P h a n t a s u s  and this prompts Schultz to the
view that the technique of employing one to three syllable line-
units in his poetry is one that Stramm directly appropriated from
Holz.[15]  Although he does not substantiate this claim beyond the
textual evidence, there are in fact a number of historical clues
which would support it.  Firstly, Stramm was a member of the so-
called "Sturmkreis".  This was named after the art journal, D e r
S t u r m, which was founded by Herwarth Walden in 1910 and on
which Holz collaborated for the first four years of its publication.[16]
Walden not only determined to a large extent the theoretical and
practical direction of the "Sturmkreis" but was also a major and

177

acknowledged influence in Stramm's own development.[17] To what
degree Walden himself assimilated the main propositions of Holz's
poetics can perhaps be judged by comparing certain of his
statements with others by Holz quoted earlier. In his article of
1921 entitled "Kritik der vorexpressionistischen Dichtung", for
example, Walden wrote the following about Heine's poem, "Der Asra":

> Täglich ging die wunderschöne
> Sultanstochter auf and nieder
> Um die Abendzeit am Springbrunnen
> Wo die weißen Wasser plätschern

> Diese Strophe ist ohne Rhythmus. Die Sultanstochter auf und
> nieder plätschert in demselben Tempo wie die weißen Wasser
> gehen. Sie geht also einen Rhythmus, dem der Begriff gehen
> nicht entspricht. Hören wir dagegen die Verszeile des
> Sturmkünstlers August Stramm: Durch die Büsche winden Sterne.
> Rhythmisch gibt diese Zeile sinnlich die Vorstellung des
> Windens. Durch die Büsche winden Sterne. Keine Senkung
> zum Spaß. Wenn die Sterne sich winden würden, würden
> wir das Winden nicht mehr fühlen. Durch die Büsche
> winden sich Sterne. Hören Sie, wie die Sterne sich
> dagegen auflehnen? Jedes Wort und die Stellung jedes
> Wortes ist k ü n s t l e r i s c h e N o t w e n d i g-
> k e i t. (my italics)[18]

There are also similarly Holzian statements denouncing conventional
metre and rhyme[19] and if Walden's position can be characterised by
the following:

> Das Material der Dichtung ist das Wort
> Die Form der Dichtung ist der Rhythmus[20]

then it is true to say that although the apothegmatic character of
this particular formulation does not derive from Holz, its essence
certainly does! Thus, even had Stramm not been directly acquainted
with Holz's writing, he would nevertheless have encountered its
influence within the "Sturmkreis". In fact, however, an entry from
Stramm's diary informs us that he had read Holz's poetic theory.[21]

As regards Stramm's literary practice, however, three things need
to be mentioned about his use of rhythm. If, as Schultz believes,
the real innovation in Holz's poetry was the use of one-word or

even one-syllable verse-lines,[22] then arguably it is Stramm who,
of all subsequent poets, has most developed that technique, as is
best illustrated by his poem "Urtod" in which each of its forty-
eight lines consists of no more than a single word. Secondly,
although Stramm may have appropriated or adapted Holz's rhythm, he
did not adopt one of Holz's other trademarks, namely the
"Mittelachse" structure, but retained what might on the surface
appear as a more conventional typographical form. Thirdly, it
is surely this, coupled with the recognition of the importance of
rhythm in Stramm's writing, which led F. J. Schneider to describe
Stramm's poetry as "eine Dichtung, die nach Verlebendigung durch
den Vortrag schreit, die nicht mehr gedruckt und gelesen, sondern
g e s p r o c h e n  sein will."[23] This immediately invites
comparison with Holz, for critics have frequently argued that
ideally P h a n t a s u s  should be spoken not read[24] and
indeed, as noted earlier, on one occasion Holz more or less said
as much himself. However, this comparison conceals a very real
difference. For apart from the purely visual effect, which is in
any case common to both Holz's and Stramm's work, it is true to
say that while much would be gained from a spoken reading of
P h a n t a s u s, little would be lost. This is most certainly
not the case with Stramm for as J. J. White has well pointed out,
what Schneider's comments ignore is the element of ambiguity in
Stramm's poetry from which it derives so many of its effects and
which the interpretative act of reading will destroy.[25] I will say
more about this crucial dimension of Stramm's poetry later and
for the moment content myself with the observation that it is
not a comparable feature of Holz's  P h a n t a s u s.

The second area in which it is possible to establish similarities
between Holz and Stramm is in their relationship to language. It
may well appear to be a platitude to say that as poets both
revealed a meticulous concern with language, but Holz's and Stramm's
attention to words, it seems to me, is demonstrably greater than
most. In Stramm's case the existence of numerous versions of the
same poem (twenty-five of the poem "Untreu" and thirteen of "Blüte",

for example)[26] indicates a sense of dissatisfaction with the
finished article similar to that which drove Holz on from one
revision of P h a n t a s u s to the next. Moreover,
their common preoccupation with the myriad nuances of language
was motivated by the same concern, namely the avoidance of
cliché. In this respect the following passage about his poem
"Freudenhaus", taken from a letter that Stramm wrote to Walden
in June 1914, is of particular interest since it illustrates
how scrupulous Stramm was in his choice of words:

> Anbei schicke ich Dir die Korrektur. Es sind einige
> Kleinigkeiten drin. Besonders erwähnenswert erscheint
> mir die vorletzte Zeile, in der das Wort "schamzerpört"
> zu "schamzerstört" geworden ist. Ich weiß nicht, ob
> da nur ein Lesefehler oder eine Regung des
> Sprachgefühls des Druckers vorliegt. Jedenfalls sagt
> mir "schamzerpört" mehr als das andere. Scham und
> Empörung ringen miteinander und die Scham zerdrückt.
> Auch "schamempört" sagt das lange nicht; außerdem
> liegt das Wesen des Wortes "empört" meinem Gefühl nach
> nicht in dem "em", das höchstens für die Wortlehre als
> Erklärung Bedeutung hat, für das Gefühl liegt der
> Begriff des Empörens aber lediglich in dem "pören"
> oder vielmehr einfach vollständig in der einen
> Lautverbindung "pö" . Laß übrigens die beiden Striche
> drüber fort und der ganze Begriff stürzt zusammen!
> Deshalb halte ich "schamzerpört" hier für das enzige
> alles sagende Wort.[27]

This quotation also indicates another aspect of language which
Stramm has in common with Holz, namely his use of neologisms.
Indeed, Stramm's poetry contains many examples reminiscent of Holz;
for instance, words formed from a simple base such as "zermilliont"
or word-combinations like "Richtespurvag".[28] Similarly, Stramm's
poem "Der Marsch" consists mostly of onomatopoeia, highly
redolent of Holz in their effect:

> Rum und Trum
> Rum und Trum
>   "Potz Kerle! hebt die Beine!
> Rum und Trum
> Rum und Trum
>   "Verfluchte Sonne!" ... Schweine!

```
Flüt und Tü
Flüt und Tü
    "Der Brand! ... die heiße Kehle!"
Flüt und Tü
Flüt und Tü
    "Wie lang noch das Gequäle?"

Träterä
Träterä
    "Ei schaut! bläht dort das Röckchen!"
Träterä
Träterä
    "Verteufelt! steht das Böckchen!

Rum und Trum
Rumlidibum
    "Wie blinkt das Dörfchen heiter!"
Flüt und Tü
Träterä
Und "weiter! weiter! weiter!"²⁹
```

This poem - curiously, one of only four in Stramm's work to retain
verse-divisions - also reveals other Holzian traits: the insertion,
emphasised typographically, of the comments of onlookers in
colloquial form - the use of not altogether common dialect words is
a regular feature of Stramm's writing - and the marked use of
punctuation with its numerous exclamation marks, its idiosyncratic
but typically Holzian combination of punctuation elements (?!)
and its use of dots as a notation of silence.

However, the incidental similarities between Holz's and Stramm's
neologisms are less important than the fundamental difference
between them, in the sense that these differences could also be said
to characterise their poetry as a whole. Firstly, the basic
principles of construction are diametrically opposed in nature for
whereas Holz, as we have seen, principally used the technique of
expansion, Stramm's mode was based on the condensation of language.
Consequently, Holz increasingly sought to create neologisms or
experiment with language generally by extending individual words
or syllables into word-chains or combinations, whereas Stramm tended
to the opposite effect of stripping language down, either by condensing
words or returning to their root-form. Indeed, the example cited

earlier typifies this difference for whereas Stramm coins the
evocative neologism "schamzerpört" by compressing three concepts
into one, Holz would undoubtedly have extended the concepts into a
word-chain so as to form a line such as, say: "schamempört,
schamzerstört, schamzerdrückt." One could almost argue that Stramm
was truer to Holz's theory than its author in the sense that in his
concentration of meaning, in his search for an occasional discovery
of "das einzige alles sagende Wort" and in his reduction of poetry
to its essentials Stramm could be said to have implemented what
Holz preached but rarely practised, namely "letzte Einfachheit ...
das höchste Gesetz".[30]

And yet, of course, Stramm's poetry is only "simple" in one sense.
Indeed, one could cite Stramm's work as a paradigmatic realisation
of the following suggestions by Charles Olson in his essay
"Projective Verse":

> It would do no harm ... if both time and meter, and, in
> the quantity of words, both sense and sound, were less
> in the forefront of the mind than the syllable ... With
> this warning, to those who would try: to step back here
> to this place of the elements and minims of language, is
> to engage speech where it is least careless - and least
> logical.[31]

Thus, the second crucial difference between Stramm's neologisms and
those of Holz - and, by extension, between their styles generally
- is that Stramm's are simple in formation but complex in significance,
while Holz's are the reverse of that. That is to say, the language
of Stramm's poetry is very often rich in ambiguity or - to use a
term which J. J. White prefers - in "plurisignificance".[32] Thus,
to give but one example, the title of Stramm's remarkable poem
"Urtod" is, as Jeremy Adler has admirably shown, susceptible to a
whole range of interpretations being "a word, which, when treated
to constituent part analysis, signifies both beginning and end,
the beginning of the end, and the end of the beginning."[33] It is
precisely this multi-dimensionality of meaning to which the quality
of much of Stramm's poetry is attributable and Adler has accurately
described the method from which it derives:"Operating within one

comparatively enclosed semantic field, Stramm nonetheless invokes
a whole world of meanings, exploiting a minimum of means to the
maximum extent."[34] Nothing could contrast more forcibly with Holz's
method, and inventive though his use of language undeniably is at
times, it offers no real equivalent to the subtle "plurisignificance"
of Stramm's poetry.

I suggested earlier that the relationship between Holz's work and
Stramm's is a paradoxical one and by way of conclusion I would like
to compare two poems which illustrate both the similarities and the
differences that are discernible in their poetry as a whole:

(Holz)

> Auf ihr,
> Einsam,
> Ein Haus,
> Draußen Regen,
> Ich am Fenster.
> Hinter mir,
> Tiktak,
> Eine Uhr,
> Meine Stirn
> Gegen die Scheibe
> Nichts.
> Alles vorbei!
> Grau der Himmel,
> Grau die See,
> Und grau
> Das Herz.[35]

(Stramm)

> Lichte dirnen aus den Fenstern
> Die Seuche
> Spreitet an der Tür
> Und bietet Weiberstöhnen aus!

Frauenseelen schämen grelle Lache!

Mutterschöße gähnen Kindestod!

Ungeborenes

Geistet

Dünstelnd

Durch die Räume!

Scheu

Im Winkel

Schamzerpört

Verkriecht sich

Das Geschlecht![36]

The first thing to be noted is the typically staccato rhythm that earned from Holz's contemporaries the pejorative label of "Telegrammlyrik"[37] and which is intensified here by the fact that in this poem Holz eschews the longer sentences so characteristic of the later P h a n t a s u s versions. The concomitant of this rhythm is the equally typical isolation of particular words, the most important example of which is in both cases the final word of the poem. In Holz's poem the effect is to deepen the connotations of "grau" from the purely visual sense it derived from qualifying "Himmel" and "See" to the metaphorical level of "Herz". Just as the final isolation of "das Herz" thus reveals the whole poem as the evocation of a state of mind, so too the concluding "das Geschlecht" of "Freudenhaus" conveys in its pointed isolation the same debasement and impersonal character of prostitutional sex that the poem thematises as a whole. Stramm himself underlines his intention in isolating the words when, in the letter quoted earlier, he points out to Walden a further printing error in the published version of this poem:

> Ebenso könnte in der letzten Zeile zwischen
> "Verkriecht sich" und "Das Geschlecht" eine Lücke
> bleiben, wie das im Manuskript auch stehen wird.
> Hinter "sich" ist die scharfe Senkung und "das
> Geschlecht" ist neue starke Hebung. Ich habe es
> absichtlich nicht in eine neue Zeile gesetzt, weil

durch die Lücke und das Seitwärtsschieben des ganzen
Wortes mir eben das Verkriechen auch äußerlich zum
Ausdruck gebracht schien...[38]

In other words, the final verse-line is to be isolated for
emphasis not only rhythmically but also graphically. This points
to a further similarity between these two poems which, in one sense
at least, is in fact rather untypical, namely their lay-out. For
once Holz does not use the "Mittelachse" structure but the vertical
axis, which was a constant feature of Stramm's poetry, with the
result that the poems appear visually more similar than any other
examples. This should not be taken to mean, however, that Stramm
was typographically more conservative than Holz, for both were
keenly aware of the visual element of poetry. The two basic
structures most commonly deployed in Stramm's poems could be seen
as the pillar and the triangle. In his illuminating analysis of
"Urtod" Jeremy Adler has shown how the column of words that
comprise the poem assumes the character of a monument and thus
conveys in its visual image "the relentlessly linear and irreversible
progression of life through time"[38] that its title also denotes.
The effect of the triangle shape, on the other hand, is to create
both a rhythmically and visually dynamic impression.[40] Although
"Freudenhaus" is not triangular in its lay-out as a whole, as is
the case with a poem like "Verzweifelt", it nevertheless contains,
as my markings make clear, triangular components, as to a lesser
extent does Holz's poem.

At a superficial level, therefore, these two poems are not dissimilar.
And yet, as even the most cursory reading must reveal, they are
despite their rhythmic and visual similarity totally different in
intensity. For whereas Holz does little more than draw the contours
of a scene, Stramm paints a complete and striking picture, with
hardly a single word wasted or superfluous. The sheer detail that
Stramm condenses into the fifth and sixth lines, for example, almost
defies analysis: the prostitutes are creatures who have renounced
their natural being as women and mothers, whose wombs open not in

order to bring forth life but to facilitate death through abortion
and who have therefore forfeited their souls, as is epitomised by
their raucous, unnatural laughter. All that in seven words! Whereas
Holz's poem contains hardly an image of note - and "grau das Herz"
bearly escapes the status of cliché - by contrast virtually every
other word in "Freudenhaus" is rich in new and evocative connotations.
We have already noted the multiple nuances of "schamzerpört".
Similarly, "die Seuche" (line 2) denotes not only the physical
disease of the syphilitic prostitute, sitting legs apart at the
door-way, but also, by refusing to refer to her in human terms, the
mental or moral affliction caused by the inhuman depersonalisation of
existence in the brothel. Indeed, the unexpected engages our
attention within the first two words, for "lichte" could be either
an adjective or a noun, and "dirnen" either a noun (without a
capital letter) or a verbal neologism. Ultimately, I think the
meaning i s clear - candles in the brothel windows entice the
prospective clients - but the syntax remains ambiguous. It was
quite probably sentence structure of this type which led Holz, in
rejecting Schikowski's identification of him with Expressionism,
to declare:

> Man darf und soll in unserer durch die
> Jahrtausende gewordenen und Ring um Ring o r g a n i s c h
> gewachsenen Sprache n i c h t s "vernachlässigen",
> und schon gar "bewußt", und vollends am wenigsten den
> "l o g i s c h e n S a t z b a u". Nur da, wo sie
> ihn s e l b s t ... vernachlässigt, wo sie ihn
> s e l b s t nicht befolgt, soll man ihn a u c h und
> nicht befolgen. "Natürlich" und nicht "künstlich"![41]

Leaving aside for the moment the question of to what extent Holz
himself adhered to conventional syntax, we need only note that Stramm
rarely, if ever, dissolves syntax for its own sake. Rather, he tends
either to loosen grammatical relationships for the purpose of
ambiguity or to use alien grammar in order to produce what has been
termed the "grammatical metaphor".[42]

The poems "Eine Düne" and "Freudenhaus" may well have the same basis
or "Fundament", as Schikowski called it; but they are truly worlds

apart in intensity and effect, if not, however, in style. Moreover, Holz in fact wrote "Eine Düne" in 1893, i.e. prior to his real work on P h a n t a s u s. This is surely significant, for the surface-similarities with Stramm are as great, if not greater, in this poem than in any of the subsequent poetry. Thus, what P h a n t a s u s in all its development tells us about the relationship between Holz and Stramm is that although they may well have begun from a common starting-point, thereafter their respective paths were increasingly to diverge. After all, if one considers the two men's mature poetry, it would be difficult to imagine a greater contrast than that between the formalist prolixity of Holz's "Das Tausendundzweite Märchen" and the economy and intensity of Stramm's "Urtod". That is to say, their relationship is not the unproblematical one that has been commonly posited by numerous critics but a classic example of what I have referred to as a tendential relationship.

If the identification of P h a n t a s u s with Expressionism was one thing which Holz at least was at pains to refute, then another relationship which engaged his attention was that implicit in the criticism that his innovations had in fact "revolutionised" poetry out of existence and had produced what essentially was nothing more than elevated prose.[43] From the standpoint of the present, where the elision of genre distinctions has long since ceased to be regarded as an artistic heresy, the question of whether P h a n t a-s u s is or is not poetry concerns us far less than its possible relationship to other modes of writing. Holz's own view, however, was characteristically contradictory. For while in his more tolerantly modernist moments he professed it to be a matter of complete indifference to him how his work was categorised, on other occasions he reacted vehemently to the view that his poetry was to all intents and purposes only prose and thus might just as well be written as such.[44] Although as usual he does not confront the problem systematically, Holz suggests that there are three things which distinguish poetry in general, and his poetry in particular, from ordinary prose. The first is that "die Prosa kümmert sich um

Klangwirkungen überhaupt nicht."[45] As a generalisation this is
demonstrably untrue, a fact which perhaps Holz even sensed himself,
for he follows this bald assertion with the qualification, "wenig-
stens nicht um Klangwirkungen in dem Sinne, um den einzig es sich
hier drehen kann",[46] a statement which effectively collapses the
original distinction. Merely to assert that the acoustic effects of
poetry are somehow different from those of prose does little in
itself to illuminate the difference between the two. Equally
tenuous is the distinction, referred to earlier, that Holz makes
between the prose version of the sentence, "Der Mond steigt
hinter blühenden Apfelbaumzweigen auf", which "referiert nur",
and its poetic adaptation

>           Hinter blühenden Apfelbaumzweigen
>               steigt der Mond auf

which, according to Holz, "stellt dar". The problem with these
terms is that they are purely subjective. Whether a particular
sentence is thought to be "referierend" or "darstellend" depends
primarily on the recipient rather than on the application of
objective criteria. Holz himself admits as much when comparing the
old form of poetry to his new one:

> Bei der älteren Form liegt das Schwierige wesentlich in
> der Form selbst. Und dieses Schwierige läßt sich
> überwinden. Denn es ist im Grunde handwerklich. Bei
> der neueren Form setzt die Schwierigkeit bereits früher
> ein und sitzt hier tiefer. Sie besteht im Wesentlichen
> darin, daß man vor allem seine Vorstellung klar hat.[47]

Moreover, this holds equally true for the third distinction Holz
proposes, namely that only poetry reveals the words' "necessary"
or "natural" rhythm, for as Borcherdt remarks: "Es besteht ...
kein Zweifel, daß dieser 'notwendige' Rhythmus unter objektiven
Kriterien so nicht erfaßt werden kann und daß damit der höchsten
Subjektivität Tor und Tür geöffnet ist."[48]   Obviously, as
Schultz points out, even a sentence of prose has a rhythm,[49] but
in Holz's example the reason why the second version flows more
"naturally" is that the inversion makes the sentence appear both

visually and rhythmically more bi-partite and also emphasises,
again both rhythmically and typographically, the dynamic centre
of the sentence, "steigt".[50] However, there is no reason why this
sentence cannot be written in its inverted form, and thus with
approximately the same rhythmic effect, as prose. The main flaw
in Holz's argumentation would seem to be that he implies a
spuriously absolute polarity between "referierende Prosa" and
"darstellende Lyrik" which ignores the substantial middle ground
of what, to remain with Holz's terms, could be called "darstellende
Prosa". Moreover, the boundary between this and poetry is
sufficiently fluid to allow of a tendential relationship between
P h a n t a s u s  and certain forms of prose-writing. That is
to say, apart from that of the division of sentences into verse-
lines, it is quite possible to accommodate within the framework
of prose certain of the techniques which Holz developed in his
poetry.

The one which undoubtedly has the most relevance for prose-writing
is Holz's technique of "differentiation", since, it is commonly
claimed, this provides the formal basis for one of the most
important prose-innovations of modern literature, the stream-of-
consciousness. Emrich, for example, writes as follows of Holz's
attempt to convey in language the kaleidoscopic structure of
subjectivity:

>Um den unmittelbaren, lebendigen Ausdruck des
>Vorstellungsbildes zu erreichen, muß die Sprache
>bis zum äußersten differenziert und nuanciert werden,
>was zu einer ungeheuerlichen Aufschwellung von
>Attributen führt, die immer genauer, immer treffender
>das Vorstellungsbild einfangen wollen;  die
>Sprachmittel verselbständigen sich; entsprechend
>verliert die Thematik des Werkes alle gewohnten
>Konturen. Die gesamte Vorstellungswelt des Menschen
>zieht kaleidoskopartig in ständigem Wechsel an uns
>vorüber, unmittelbar alles, was überhaupt gefühlt,
>gedacht, geträumt, erinnert werden kann, wird
>sprachlich gestaltet, ohne irgendeinen Orientierungspunkt
>geistiger, sittlicher oder auch nur räumlicher oder
>zeitlicher Art ... Das gilt nicht nur für Arno Holz,
>sondern für alle modernen Dichter, die den "inneren

Monolog", das heißt die Abbildung der gesamten viel-
schichtigen inneren Vorstellungswelt des Menschen ...
in den Mittelpunkt ihrer Kompositionsweise stellen.[51]

The resultant "assoziative(n) Logik"[52] of P h a n t a s u s's
"Ich ... ohne Kontur"[53] has led many critics to draw the parallel
with James Joyce. For instance, in one of the first post-war
attempts to re-assess the significance of Arno Holz, an article
entitled "Arno Holz und die Literatur der neuen Zeit" - which was
published, significantly, under the editorship of Alfred Döblin
in the journal D a s   g o l d e n e   T o r - points to the
similarities between certain passages in P h a n t a s u s and
Joyce's F i n n e g a n s   W a k e.[54] More differentiated, in my
view, is Schulz's more cautious comparison with its all-important
qualification that in many of Holz's passages - and in contrast to
Joyce - "der Sinn ... liegt suggestiv im Klang, Rhythmus, Ton und
ist als Denkzusammenhang nicht mehr zu fassen."[55] In my opinion,
however, the writer whose prose-work offers the best comparison
with P h a n t a s u s is Alfred Döblin.

Döblin's view of Holz, in fact, was never a fixed or static one and
nowhere, perhaps, is this better illustrated than in his evaluation
of P h a n t a s u s. However, when in 1929 he bemoans the fact
that writers do not appear to have learned anything from that work,
the implication is clearly that he, Döblin, has.[56] Moreover, if, as
an essay in the following year makes clear,[57] the lesson that Döblin
drew from P h a n t a s u s was at that time in fact a critical
one, then it is equally true to say that ten years earlier at any
rate his response was a less qualified one, and that to a certain
extent the stylistic influence of P h a n t a s u s can be detected
in Döblin's own early prose-work, such as B e r g e, M e e r e   u n d
G i g a n t e n.

At this time the idea on which Döblin's work centred was the all too
familiar concept of "Natur". His sole task as an artist, Döblin
wrote in 1920, was: "Ausweiten die Fühl- und Denkweise; im

190

engsten Andrang an die Natur, an die herumliegenden und mit mir wachsenden Realitäten selber wachsen".[58] Accordingly he could describe his utopian novel B e r g e, M e e r e u n d G i g a n t e n as a " 'Sang' an die große Natur"[59] whose main theme was "die Schrankenlosigkeit der Natur, ihr Wuchern und Überwuchern".[60] Moreover, the relationship to language that corresponds to this epic vision was conceived of by Döblin in identical terms to those which he was later to apply to P h a n t a s u s:

> Ich liebe sonst Knappheit. Hier (i.e. in B e r g e, M e e r e u n d G i g a n t e n, R.B.) konnte ich Impulsen rein sprachlicher Art nicht widerstehen. Es ging ins Weite, Farbige. Es war, als wenn sich alles autonom machen wollte, und ich mußte auf der Hut sein. Das hohe Niveau mancher Partien, ihr feiernder hymnischer Charakter, trug dazu bei. Ich will auch gestehen, daß ich das Gefühl hatte, nicht im Gebiet eigentlicher oder gewöhnlicher Prosa mehr zu sein, im Sprachlichen. Wohin die Reise geht, weiß ich nicht. Die alten Versformen scheinen mir unmöglich.[61]

The following passage from the novel indicates, moreover, that the stylistic characteristics which prompted Döblin to this statement recall in some ways the style of the earlier P h a n t a s u s:

> Die fleischernen blühenden welkenden Menschenwesen lagen über dem südlichen Faltenland Europas ... Gebirgsmassen Höhenzüge Senken bewegte die Erde unter ihnen und um sie. Im Strömen zog das weiße Wasser hin, füllte Seenbecken. Braune und grüne Pflanzengeschöpfe drangen aus dem Boden. Büsche und Wälder bauten sich längs der Donau auf, längs des Dnjepr und Don. Urwälder und Moraste von der atlantischen Küste bis zu den südlichen Pusten. Auf ihnen girrten schluchzten starben Feldblumen Gräser Vögel. Über die Flächen krochen schwammen mit nackten schuppigen beharrten Leibern Tiere, gaben nicht Ruhe um sich zu greifen, aufzunehmen, sich zu entleeren. Bis der Boden, das wandlungssüchtige Wasser, die verzehrende Luft sie ganz wieder hatte. Die Scharen der Menschen in Ruhe und Tod, in Werben und Brautkämpfen, unter Vulkanausbrüchen und Ertränkungen. Hielten sich aneinander fest, schwanden tränend hin, Schwall über Schwall, Mutter und Kind Mutter und Kind, Geliebter und Geliebte. Und immer sehnsüchtig die Gase der Luft in die Lungenbläschen hinein, an die kleinen Zellen, die Kerne, das weiche Protoplasma,

immer anzegogen und weiter gegeben. Und wenn die Herzen
stillstanden, die Zellen sich trennten und auflösten,
waren sie neue Seelen, zerfallendes Eiweiß Ammoniak
Aminosäuren Kohlensäure und Wasser, Wasser das sich in
Dampf verwandelte.[62]

The first thing that strikes one in this passage is that trait of
Holz's writing which Strohschneider-Kohrs termed its
"Verwörtlichungswillen",[63] namely the accumulation of nouns and
adjectives aiming at defining as closely as possible the qualities
of a particular phenomenon. Thus, man is described in the first
sentence as "fleischern", "blühend" and "welkend", adjectives which
are designed, presumably, to indicate that he too is just a part
of, rather than something distinct from, nature. More common than
the series of adjectives and adverbs favoured by Holz is the
proliferation of nouns, which could be seen as an influence of
Futurism.[64] What clearly is reminiscent of P h a n t a s u s,
however, is the rhythm of Döblin's prose, its abrupt, staccato
character reflected in the simple structure of its sentences and the
relative absence of subordinate clauses. Such sentences, as an
example from the quoted passage shows, could be quite easily adapted
to the "Mittelachse" structure and rhythm of Holz's P h a n t a s u s:

Über

die Flächen

krochen schwammen

mit nackten schuppigen beharrten Leibern

Tiere,

gaben nicht Ruhe

um sich zu greifen, aufzunehmen, sich zu entleeren.

Just as Robert Musil could say in a review of M a n a s that
Döblin's poetry was more like "normal prose",[65] so perhaps we could
agree with Döblin's own view of B e r g e, M e e r e u n d
G i g a n t e n that it was "nicht im Gebiet ... gewöhnlicher Prosa".
If it is possible to postulate an "area" where poetry and prose over-
lap such that the two are virtually indistinguishable from each other,

then it would seem that it is precisely there that works such as
this, and possibly  P h a n t a s u s  too, must be located

By the time of Holz's death, however, Döblin's enthusiasm for
P h a n t a s u s  had changed towards an attitude of critical
distance which saw the work as a symptom of the underlying weakness
in Holz's position as an author who was writing "mit den
Produktionsmitteln der Revolution für das Bürgertum":

> Der Vorkämpfer der Eroberung der Natur ... dreht den
> Kopf beiseite und sagt 'Phantasus' ... Es erfolgt ein
> sonderbarer Waffenstillstand.  In diesen 'Phantasus'
> wird die halbe Realität hineingestopft, Historie,
> Geographie, Literatur, - entfernte Realität, - und dann
> gewinnt über diese Realität die Kunst, das Kunsthandwerk
> die Oberhand, in einer ungeheuren Weise.  Es liegt geradezu
> ein dialektischer Prozess vor.  Die Sprachtechnik Holzens
> war geschaffen, um der Eroberung der Natur zu dienen.
> Jetzt wird eine abgedämpfte, literarische Realität
> herangezogen, über sie läßt man weggehen und wuchern -
> diese neue Sprachtechnik, den freisten Rhythmus, den neuen
> Ton, der für den Naturalismus gefunden war, - und wir haben
> vor uns, vielleicht, vielleicht, formalen Naturalismus,
> aber auch l'art pour l'art! Wir sind am Gegenpol.[66]

This quotation is important for two reasons:  firstly, although
referring to  P h a n t a s u s, its point is not directed exclusively
at Holz  for, as Leo Kreutzer has suggested,[67] there was undoubtedly
an element of self-criticism on Döblin's part.  After all, if,
according to Döblin's criteria,  P h a n t a s u s  is "removed from
reality", then is that not equally true of his own early work?
More importantly for our immediate purpose, however, Döblin also
indicates the other direction in which the relational tendencies
of  P h a n t a s u s  point, even though now  the term "l'art pour
l'art" might seem rather imprecise for a mode of literature whose
relationships to  P h a n t a s u s, based on the formalist autonomisation of language, are many and substantial.

Given the underlying aim of Holz's "revolutionisation" of poetry
- namely "eine Lyrik, die auf jede Musik durch Worte als Selbstzweck

verzichtet" – it may seem perverse to relate him to a type of
writing which would appear to represent the diametrical opposite
of that aim. And in view of his comments on Expressionist poetry
we can be quite sure that he himself would have regarded it as
anything but a compliment. But as this study has repeatedly
shown, the relation between intention and effect in Holz's work
is rarely unproblematical. Few critics would disagree that the
basic motivation for Holz's development of language was the drive
for ultimate immediacy. There clearly comes a point in
P h a n t a s u s, however, where his preoccupation with the means
to that end, language, actually obscures, if not negates that
aim; a point that is, where language ceases to represent reality
in any meaningful sense but contains or becomes, so to speak, its
own autonomous reality. Käte Hamburger has described this process
well in D i e  L o g i k  d e r  D i c h t u n g:

> Die Objekte ... verschwinden unter den Wörtern, die
> sich selbständig machen und als Vokalklänge existent,
> eigenwertig und eigenweltlich bleiben. Die Aussagen
> in diesem Stück, auf Substantive und Attribute,
> auf Wörterreihen reduziert, sind aus dem Objektpol
> weggezogen und zueinander geordnet. Doch wird dadurch
> nicht dieser verdunkelt. Eben weil der Prozeß ein
> rein sprachlicher, sozusagen sinnhintergrundloser und
> nur das Verhältnis von zu beschreibendem Ding und
> beschreibender Sprache das Thema des Textes ist, erhält
> sich der Objektpol deutlich. Dies widerspricht nicht
> der Formulierung, daß das Objekt in den Wörtern
> verschwindet, verwörtlicht wird oder werden soll. Es
> ist die Absicht dieser lyrischen Aussage, das Objekt
> in den 'Impressionen', die die Wörter erwecken, wider-
> stehen zu lassen, Impressionen, die als durch
> den Gegenstand hervorgerufene zu verstehen sind ...
> Und so gesehen liegt diese Dingdichtung nahe an der
> Grenze zur mitteilenden Aussage.[68]

Seen from this standpoint it matters relatively little whether
Holz's verbal monsters, his "Wortkaskaden",[69] are understood as
a celebration of the power of language or as an attempt to
combat its impotence. Moreover, the parallels with contemporary
writing in this area are numerous. Arno Schmidt's constitution
of the world as language in his radical texts is an obvious
example. The polyglot idiolect, in which Holz occasionally

indulges, as in the following passage, has almost become a trade-
mark of Schmidt's writing:

Schwein!

Cochong! Cotschine!
Mallatsch!
Porku!! Pork!
Pick!!
Domutz!! Farken!!

Swinja! Swinsko!

Swin!

Porkatschjo!!![70]

Moreover, even if one preferred, as Tony Phelan does, to view
Schmidt's prose as rationalist narrative, in which his almost
overriding concern is "with the psychology of the experiencing
subject" and in which "consciousness and the dialectical
relationship between the exterior and interior world provide both
the matter and the form of his fiction",[71] then this need not
dissuade us from comparison with P h a n t a s u s, for such a
description could apply equally well to Holz. Similarly, when one
reads in the introduction to the U l t i m i s t i s c h e r
A l m a n a c h, the programme of a neo-Dadaist group, that "der
Ultimist arbeitet mit an der Evolution der von Willkür und anti-
quierten Zufallsnormen beherrschten metrischen und strophischen
Gedichtformen zu einer Wortkunst aus immanenter Gesetzlichkeit",[72]
then such a statement sounds suspiciously familiar. These
suspicions are confirmed when the acknowledged debt of the "Ultimisten"
to tradition is formulated in the following fashion:

ARNO HOLZ
HAT DIE LYRIK
zu Beginn des 20. Jahrhunderts

durch die Anwendung der typographischen Mittelachsenform

in seinen Riesenpoem "Phantasus"

REVOLUTIONIERT.

Der Ultimismus leitet daraus

den Begriff der "polyphonen Poesie" ab, das heißt:

DIESER SATZ

kann von links nach rechts ("linear")

und gleichermaßen von oben nach unten ("polyphon")

gelesen werden, indem man die kurzen Zeilen,

bestehend aus nicht mehr als drei Wörtern

die ohnehin die Mittelachse markieren,

typographisch hervorhebt und optisch

ISOLIERT.

-: dadurch ergibt sich als Skelett des ganzen Gebildes

eine "zweite Stimme", ein "Gedicht im Gedicht",

eine Ahnung dessen, was Novalis

vielleicht als "Poesie der Poesie" vorgeschwebt haben mag;

erst in dieser konzentrierten Gestalt

befriedigt der so sich offenbarende geheime  Sinn des Gedichts

DIE ULTIMISTEN

+

ARNO HOLZ

HAT DIE LYRIK

REVOLUTIONIERT

DIESER SATZ

ISOLIERT

DIE ULTIMISTEN[73]

Nor should it surprise us that a group of writers of considerably
greater eminence, namely the "Wiener Gruppe", expressly name Holz
as the founder of the tradition to which they affiliate themselves.[74]
The dialect poems of Artmann and Achleitner, Max Bense's idea of
advertisements as text-material, the sound poems and the technique
of "surface translation"[75] of Ernst Jandl and the structuring of
material for visual effect, which is so characteristic of concrete
poetry as a whole:  all of these find their anticipation in Holz's

P h a n t a s u s.  In view of this it is surely hardly coincidental
that references to Holz among experimental writers are not uncommon.
It is significant, too, that of such references one of the most
unequivocal is by Helmut Heißenbüttel, arguably the foremost
practitioner of contemporary experimental writing in Germany, whose
work and affinities to Holz may in this context be justifiably viewed,
therefore, as representative of a whole range of writers associated
with the labels, experimental prose and concrete poetry.

"Vater Arno Holz" is the title of an article by Heißenbüttel, commemora-
ting the centenary of Holz's birth and it is clear that one of the
reasons why he considers Holz of such significance as to merit the
title "Vater der Moderne"[76] is to be found in their relationship to
tradition.  To Heißenbüttel the uncritical and epigonic acceptance of
conventional form and traditional aesthetic criteria can constitute
nothing less than a "Sperre zwischen Leser und literarischem Werk"[77]
and what Holz sought to effect was, as it were, "eine Demokratisierung
der Poesie",[78] that is to say, the emancipation of poetry from the
traditional "hierarchy" of metre, rhyme and verse.  To these
Heißenbüttel would add one further representative of the "geheimer
Leierkasten", namely the symbol.  In an essay written in 1963 he
refers to Hegel's definition of the symbol in the V o r l e s u n g e n
ü b e r   d i e  Ä s t h e t i k  as "die Beziehung der Außenwelt auf
das Innere des Bewußtseins", an idea, he maintains, which has
dominated poetry since Romanticism but which due to the complexity of
language and experience in the twentieth century is no longer
adequate for a form of poetry turning its back on subjectivity.[79]
Although Holz does not expressly reject the symbol as such, the
effect of his technique of "differentiation" or "nuancierende(s)
Benennen"[80] is to militate against the symbolic usage of words.
Moreover, when he remarks of his poetry that "wenn ich einfach und
schlicht ... "Meer" sage, so klingt's wie "Meer"; sagt es Heine in
seinen Nordseebildern, so klingt's wie "Amphitrite" ",[81] then the
implication is that for Holz words are concrete and signify only
their "reales Äquivalent".

197

What unites Heißenbüttel and Holz above all, however, is their
relationship to language in that both approach it not as an
incontestable given but as something whose power has been eroded
by tradition and conventional usage.  Thus, just as a contemporary
of Holz's could describe Holz's work as constituting a "Reinigung
der Kunstmittel",[82] so Eugen Gomringer can describe the ultimate
aim of concrete poetry as "der große Reinigungsprozeß".[83]  By the
latter is meant the attempt to distil from language those layers
of meaning which convention has superimposed upon it so that the
resultant residue can serve as the embryo in the genesis of a reformed,
meaningful language.  This residual "Rumpfsprache" Heißenbüttel
describes as follows: "Wenn ich Rumpfsprache sage, dann heißt es,
daß ich versuche, die Sprache von dem, was manipulierbar ist, zu
reinigen und versuche, auf Grund dieser Rumpfsprache sozusagen
eine gereinigte Sprache herzustellen".[84]  This claim of concrete
poetry to direct social relevance clearly goes beyond anything that
Holz envisaged, but equally clearly his more modest proposition that
the revolutionisation of German literature could only follow from
the rejuvenation of its language is nevertheless still an a priori
assumption for Heißenbüttel.  Moreover, if Holz's work was
predicated on the realisation of the changed relationship between
language and reality, then Heißenbüttel could be said to extend
that realisation even further:

> Realistisch wäre eine Literatur, die in ihren Modellen
> den unauflösbaren Zusammenhang zeigte zwischen der
> faktisch veränderten Welt und der Unmöglichkeit diese
> Veränderung direkt und unreflektiert zu benennen....[85]
> ich versuche nicht mit Sprache Realität oder Vorstellungen
> zu beschreiben, mit Sprachbildern, Symbolen, Metaphern zu
> Realität und Vorstellung mich zu verhalten, sondern ich
> versuche, aus der Sprache herauszuholen, herauszulocken,
> was als Realitätsspur darin aufbewahrt ist und was erst
> Realität hier und jetzt heißen kann.[86]

From this follow two ideas that apply equally well to P h a n t a s u s
as to concrete poetry:  firstly, the recognition that the boundaries
of poetry's language are virtually infinite - in this respect
P h a n t a s u s could be seen as the embodiment of Max Bense's

view that "alle herstellbaren Texte aus Wörtern bestehen, die
Wörter eines umfassenden Gesamttextes sind, der also aus allen
Wörtern der Sprache besteht"[87] - and secondly, the proposition that,
to use Gomringer's words, poetry is a reality in itself, not a poem
about one.[88] If the term "concrete poetry" refers to anything,
then it is to the tendency to emphasise the materiality of
language which, as noted earlier, emerges almost willy-nilly in
Holz's P h a n t a s u s.

In an article defining the character of concrete poetry Heißenbüttel
maintains that it can be considered primarily from two points of
view, namely "Reduktion und die Überschreitung von medialen
Begrenzungen"[89] and to a greater or lesser extent both these
tendencies are reflected in P h a n t a s u s. Of the two by far
the most important for concrete poetry is that of reduction.
Semantically this entails a gross contraction of content while
at the same time giving birth to new particles of language in the
attempt to open up whole new vistas of meaning in the individual
word or word-chain. Syntactically it involves turning away from the
dictates of the traditional "subject-object-predicate" scheme in
favour of less formalised syntactic patterns. This increases the
evocative power of individual words and makes redundant those
elements which have a purely syntactical function and thus convey
nothing in themselves. It is significant, therefore, that
Heißenbüttel himself identifies a similar effect in P h a n t a s u s,
namely the reduction of words to "Was in quasi atomarer Bedeutungs-
speicherung sich in ihnen gesammelt hat."[90] Although I would argue
that words in P h a n t a s u s never quite achieve the complete
autonomy that they often do in concrete poetry, it is nevertheless
clear that Holz's technique of the rhythmic and visual isolation
of words is a significant anticipation of the reduction process, as
in the following example from P h a n t a s u s:

Wie,

wie ... wie

war das doch? ... wie ... wie ... wie ... spann sich das?

wie ... wie,

wie?[91]

As was indicated earlier, the "Mittelachse" itself has only rarely
been imitated by other writers, but the patterns which it generated
provide a clear model for the typography of experimental writing.
Thus, in the above example the diamond shape, constructed out of
the single word "wie", marks an obvious anticipation of one of
concrete poetry's most common visual devices, the constellation.
Gomringer describes it in the following terms:

> die einfachste gestaltungsmöglichkeit der auf dem wort
> beruhenden dichtung;  in ihr sind zwei, drei oder mehr,
> neben oder untereinandergesetzten worten – es werden
> nicht zu viele sein – eine gedanklich-stoffliche
> beziehung gegeben ... die konstellation ist eine
> ordnung und zugleich ein spielraum mit festen größen ...
> ein aufbauprinzip der konstellation ... ist die
> unmittelbare wiederholung eines wortes.  sie bewirkt
> die beharrung und momentane konzentration und ein
> plötzliches bewußtwerden der besonderheit einer
> bestimmten wortmaterie.[92]

In Heißenbüttel's text "Sprechwörter" he forms a similar type of
constellation but whereas Holz used only the single word "wie",
Heißenbüttel bases it on a five-word phrase:

| wie | die | so | kann | man |
|-----|-----|----|------|-----|
| wie | die | so |      | man |
|     |     |    | kann | man |
|     | die | so |      |     |
| wie | die |    |      |     |
|     | die |    |      | man |
|     |     |    | kann |     |
|     |     | so |      |     |
| wie | die |    |      |     |
|     | die |    |      | man |
|     |     | so |      |     |
| wie |     |    |      | man |
|     | die |    | kann | man |

```
                              kann
         die
wie      die                                        man
         die                    kann                man
                    so          kann                man
         die
wie      die                                        man
                    so          .
wie      die
         die                                         man
wie                 so          kann
         die                    kann                man
                    so
wie                 so
```

wie die so kann man[93]

Another technique of Holz's that is commonly deployed in concrete
poetry is the construction of word-chains or word-associations.  The
following is a typical example from  P h a n t a s u s:

überfliessende, überquellende, überflutende

überschwellende

überströmende, überschäumende

überdrängende,

überwallende, überwogende,

überirdische

überparadiesische, überelysische

Liebeslust

Liebeswonne, Liebesseligkeit,

Liebesbeglücktheit, Liebesentrücktheit, Liebesverzücktheit

Liebesversunkenheit, Liebesertrunkenheit[94]

This offers an obvious parallel with a text such as "vokabulär" which contains similar progressions based on synonyms and association:

halten freilegen

frei wovon frei

wozu Freigeist

Freischarler Frei-

tod Freiheit Ell-

bogenfreiheit frei-

lich Freiligrath

Freiheit

Gleichheit und

Brüderlichkeit

gleich

gleichgesinnt

gleichgesonnen


gleichgemacht

gleichmachen

gleichrichten

gleichschalten

gleichgültig

gleichwertig

gleichgewichtig

Gleichgewicht     etc.[95]

Yet another structure frequently used in concrete poetry is the
permutation in which words, syllables or word-order are varied from
line to line. Holz too comes close to this form when in  D i e
B l e c h s c h m i e d e  he constructs a long sequence in blocks
of twenty lines which is in effect a permutation on the words
"Worte sind ..." and which concludes as follows:

Worte prahlen! Worte prunken!
Worte sind die gemeinsten Halunken!
Worte quälen dich bis aufs Blut!

Wort sind die schlimmste Brut!
Worte sind die protzigsten Protzer!
Worte sind die rotzingsten Schmarotzer!
Worte sind Plebs! Worte sind Pöbel!
Worte Mob! Worte Möbel!
Worte sind Gänse, die gackern und schnattern!
Worte sind Fledermäuse, die flattern!
Worte sind kribbelnde, wibbelnde Milben!
Worte sind weiter nichts, als Silben![96]

This structure is almost identical to a text such as Heißenbüttel's
"die Zukunft des Sozialismus" which is composed of blocks of thirteen
lines that are permutated according to a similar principle as in the
opening block:

    niemand besitzt was
    niemand beutet aus
    niemand unterdrückt
    niemand wird ausgebeutet
    niemand wird untergedrückt
    niemand gewinnt was
    niemand verliert was
    niemand ist Herr
    niemand ist Sklave
    niemand ist Vorgesetzter
    niemand ist Untergebener
    niemand ist einem was schuldig
    niemand tut einem was[97]

Admittedly the experimentation with language by many contemporary
writers is more extreme than even Holz aspired to. Nevertheless, many
of the techniques which form the basis of that experimentation
(such as reduction, combination, constellation and permutation)
unmistakably find their prefiguration in Holz's work.

The second major characteristic of concrete poetry which
Heißenbüttel identified was what he called "die Überschreitung
von medialen Begrenzungen"; that is to say, the aim of concrete
poetry is quite often an intentional break in communication. I
have already referred to the fact that at times P h a n t a s u s
too is virtually impenetrable and in this respect it is worth
noting that for Holz this was by no means an undesirable effect.
Thus he boasts: "Wer das Gesamte mit allen seinen vielhundert
Einzelheiten nicht mindestens zwölfmal hat auf sich wirken lassen,
wird hinter dieses Gesamte mit seinen vielhundert Einzelheiten nie
kommen!"[98]Similarly, when in a favourite analogy Holz compares his
poetic structures to a musical score, adding that he has thus
provided only the notes and not their realisation as music,[99] then
clearly he is seeking the active involvement of the reader in the
same way as concrete poetry often demands participation in the
structuring of the text in that it does not fall within the
immediate bounds of intelligbility as accepted by the reader. As
far as concrete poetry is concerned, however, the difficulty in
comprehension derives mainly from its rejection of conventional
syntax. Moreover, this is not meant to be understood merely as a
form of word-play, for many such writers consider accepted grammar
as a major determinant of the relationship between language and
reality, a relationship which, of course, they are attempting to
modify. Thus Heißenbüttel, for example, submits that our interpretation of reality is pre-determined by the basic structure of our
language,namely the syntactical model of subject-object-predicate:

> Dieses Grundmodell besagt, daß die sprachliche Auseinander-
> setzung mit der Welt unter der Voraussetzung geschieht, daß
> es immer etwas gibt, auf das sich alles bezieht und etwas
> anderes, das diesem Bezugspunkt gegenübersteht, beides aber
> in Form von Aktions- und Verhaltensweisen miteinander
> verbunden ist.[100]

Accordingly concrete poetry tends either to loosen the conventions
of grammar - one common example being the elimination of the finite
verb and the predominance of infinitives - or to obliterate

syntactical relationships altogether so as to heighten the autonomy
of the individual words.

Holz's theoretical writings contain no such critical analysis
of the effect of syntax.  Indeed, the only occasion where he refers
to it at all is his defence of syntactical logic against the
linguistic attacks perpetrated upon it by the Expressionists.  This
has led certain observers to the conclusion that Holz operated quite
consistently within the framework of conventional grammar;  as
Fauteck glibly puts it, "seine Syntax war intakt, weil die Wirklichkeit für ihn noch intakt war".[101]  To see the issue purely in
absolute terms of rejection or acceptance of traditional syntax,
however, is in my view somewhat misleading since it gives no
indication of the way in which Holz, in his literary practice as
opposed to his theory, was concerned to modify or extend accepted
grammatical possibilities.  That is to say, in  P h a n t a s u s
Holz achieves less the grammatical liberation of the word that
concrete poetry seeks than a general blurring of syntactical contours.
There are basically two things which create this impression.  Firstly,
the effect of many of the linguistic innovations discussed so far
is to dilute the consistency of the syntactical base.  To take one
example:  the technique of content-compression in word-combinations
such as "wenn der Dampfer radschaukelt" or "augenweitaufgerissen",[102]
which are really abbreviations for, respectively, "wenn das Rad des
Dampfers schaukelt" and "seine Augen sind weit aufgerissen", may not
pose too many semantic problems, at least in these examples, but
it does nevertheless engender a certain grammatical opacity.  Moreover,
when the process is extended in such a manner as to produce verbal
monsters like the aforementioned "Baumriesenwipfelblütengigantenschmetterlinge", then the result quite clearly contravenes any
meaningful notion of grammatical norms.  Indeed, this very technique
is often used in concrete poetry, as in Heißenbüttel's text
"Bremen wodu" which is based solely on this principle and ends as
follows:

obihrdasdagetanhabtmeinich

obwirdasdagetanhabenmeinstdu

obihrdasallezusammengetanhabtmeinich

obwirdasallezusammengetanhabenmeinstdu

obihrdasallezusammeninBremengetanhabt

weißtdudennicht

wasweißichnicht

daßwirdasda

daßihrdasdagetanhabt

jadaßwirdassallezusammengetanhaben

allezusammen

jadahabenwirdasallezusammengetan

inBremen

jadahabenwirdasallezusammeninBremengetan

unddassokurzvorWeihnachten[103]

The example quoted from P h a n t a s u s of "radschaukelt" also illustrates the second and more important way in which Holz erodes syntactical logic. In the "Nachlaß" version the basis of the sentence is: "Unter mir...radschaukelt sich der Dampfer querschräg ...über die...Havel." However, this is merely the skeleton of the sentence, for the dots here in fact represent its expansion by means of synonym-extension and adjectival and adverbial qualification to a length of some seventeen pages. Similarly, Holz's coveted "longest sentence of all time" in "Das Tausendundzweite Märchen", although nominally retaining the "subject-predicate-object" scheme, only comes to the "pivot" of the sentence, a one-syllable verb, on the final page of its seven hundred and forty-three lines![104] That is to say, in P h a n t a s u s the l o g i c of grammar is observed - and in the first P h a n t a s u s in more or less transparent manner - but the sheer accumulation of linguistic elements in the later versions dissolves, if not at times totally collapses any real sense of syntactical relationship between those elements. Indeed, it is this which has led Schmidt-Henkel to speak, possibly

in terms more appropriate to the practitioners of concrete poetry,
of Holz's "pervertiertes Syntaxverständnis".[105]  In fact, however,
it is one of the most successful representatives of German experimental writing, Jürgen Becker, who has best described Holz's
relationship to conventional syntax:

> Hier wirkte in Holzens Verfahren ein besonderer Widerspruch.
> So streng er seine Satzgerüste baute, so chaotisch
> gerieten sie. Was er ins Schema quetschte, arbeitete an
> seiner Zerstörung. Nicht umsonst. Nicht ohne Grund.
> Holz...haderte mit dem Subjekt-Objekt-Schema des Satzbaus;
> seine Imaginationen, seine Phantasie, sein Erlebnis der
> Realität ging über die Nutzmöglichkeiten dieses Schemas
> hinaus. Denn es bedeutet einen vorgegebenen Modus der
> Erfahrung und des Ausdrucks; es verhindert eine spontane
> Sprechweise; es unterschlägt der Sprache, was ihr zu
> vermitteln es vorgibt. Holz gab diesem Schema recht und
> wendete es loyal an; aber indem er dies tat, indem er seine
> Möglichkeit bis zum Exzeß ausnutzte, machte er es zum
> Labyrinth, oder zur Farce. Nicht der Satzkünstler, sondern
> der Saboteur konstruierte Sätze seitenweise.[106]

Heißenbüttel's relationship to syntax, however, is clearly less
ambiguous. And if its rejection in his work is one form of "die
Übereschreitung von medialen Begrenzungen", then there is another
technique which contributes nearly as much to this effect and which
I have already referred to as constituting an important element in
Holz's writing also, namely the collage. Montage and collage play
an important role in concrete poetry in general,but in respect to
Heißenbüttel's work there is one variation which is of particular
importance since it establishes a further point of contact with
Holz. I refer to the quotation-collage. The role of quotation,
in fact, is crucial for any attempt to come to terms with Heißenbüttel's
conception of literature as his joint reflections with Heinrich
Vormweg on the subject make clear:

> Realistisch wäre eine Literatur, die Welt und Sachen
> im abgelösten Sprachzitat zu verdoppeln suchte und in
> dieser Verdoppelung zeigte, daß wir nicht sinngebend
> und ordnend in die Welt einzudringen vermögen, es
> sei denn im Sinne der spezialwissenschaftlichen
> Statistik oder Fotographie...Nur indem wir den im Wort

> gespeicherten Sachbezug  z i t i e r e n,  vermögen
> wie uns dem zu nähern, was man außerhalb der Sprache
> Welt nennen könnte.[108]

Consequently, the material for many of Heißenbüttel's later texts
is composed of quotation, but the work which most spectacularly
translates this aim into literary practice is his "novel"
D'A l e m b e r t s   E n d e, which consists almost in its
entirety of extended quotation-collage. A good example of this
method is the episode entitled "Zweites Kunstgespräch"[109] in which
the characters function solely as the mouthpieces of figures such
as Marx, Benjamin, Marcuse, Warhol etc. In his study of this
subject entitled  C r o s s-R e a d i n g   u n d   C r o s s-
T a l k i n g  which, incidentally, locates Holz as one of the
earliest exponents of the quotation-collage, Karl Riha describes
D i e   B l e c h s c h m i e d e   as a vast mosaic of quotations.[110]
Indeed, Holz's own description of the work's genesis indicates how
closely his method of composition resembles Heißenbüttel's in
D'A l e m b e r t s   E n d e:

> Die Form, auf die ich gerade bei dieser Arbeit eine
> besondere Bedeutung lege, wird eine höchst
> eigentümliche werden...ich beabsichtige mit ihr ein
> riesiges Mosaik...Um das Werk, wie es mir vorschwebt,
> niederzuschreiben, werde ich die kolossale Mühe
> nicht scheuen dürfen, die gesamte einschlägige
> Literatur der letzten zehn, fünfzehn Jahre bis heute
> auf die neuesten Erscheinungen nochmal durchzugehen,
> und zwar gründlich bis auf eine Legion von Exzerpten.
> Denn es ist mein Ehrgeiz, in dieses Buch möglichst
> dokumentar, möglichst die ganze Verschrobenheit
> eines ganzen Zeitalters zu sperren.[112]

However, we have no need of recourse to Holz's other work to
illustrate his use of this technique, for the episode in
P h a n t a s u s  called "Großer Dichtermittwochnachmittag in
meiner Feuerstuhlbude" contains a similar mosaic in miniature as
quotation upon quotation is wrenched from its literary context only
to finish on a somewhat familiar note:

                    "Kreusa, Schatzkind,
Rabenvieh!" "Auch dies, auch dies ist Popelsie!"
        "Greift kühn dem Zeitrad in die
                        Nabe!
                       "Tod
                  dem Getue, dem
Gehabe!" "Zu Brei, zu Mus matscht jeden Greis am Stabe!"
        "Nichts von Verträgen, nichts von
                    Übergabe!"
        "Umbläfft von Schimpf, umkläfft von
Blague", "von nun ab bis zum jüngsten Tage"
        "Sein oder Nichtsein, das ist hier die
                    Frage!" "Verzage
                       nicht,
                    du Häuflein
        klein!" "In neue Schläuche neuen Wein!"
                    "Kommen Se
            rein, kommen Se rein, kommen Se rein,
                    kommen Se
                       rein!"
        "Die Kunst hat die Tendenz, die Natur zu
                    sein!" 113

In the same way as it is possible to attribute a satirical function
to the section referred to in D'A l e m b e r t s   E n d e, namely
that of highlighting the way in which intellectual cut and thrust
can within the context of the "Kulturindustrie" so easily
degenerate into a process  whereby the participants merely go
through the motions of debate and name-dropping replaces any real
exchange of ideas, so too this passage from P h a n t a s u s
could be seen as an extended literary joke at the expense of the
very tradition from which Holz sought to break away.  But if, as
Schulz does, one sees Holz's use of quotation in general as
"nicht immer nur literarisches Zitat, sondern die für Holz
unwiderstehliche Reproduktion einmal irgendwo Gelesenen oder

Gehörten"[114], then clearly it must be considered primarily as a
formal technique whose significance transcends any immediate
satirical purpose and which, as such, fulfils a function similar
to that of the quotation-collage in Heißenbüttel's work.

Heißenbüttel's overall relationship to Holz could be described as
that of the critical and discriminating admirer, as he himself
acknowledges: "Arno Holz kann für den, der richtig sucht, eine
Fundgrube sein. Man muß in seinem Werk graben wie in einem
Steinbruch."[115] Textual comparison indicates, moreover, that
Heißenbüttel, to use his phrase, h a s searched in the right
places, for his work clearly develops and refines certain
techniques and principles that were initiated in P h a n t a s u s.
This does not mean that he was without criticisms of the work:
"...im "Phantasus" - Zyklus zeigt sich, daß die Zerteilung und
Häufung von Wortmaterial in sich selber steckenbleibt. Das
geschieht, weil Holz gegen alle Möglichkeiten, sein Material aus
sich sinnvoll zu organisieren blind bleibt."[116] Heißenbüttel's
criticism of P h a n t a s u s is significant because it alludes
to the major difference between his work and that of Holz, a
difference whose origins must be located in a fundamental epistemological divergence. Once again it is Käte Hamburger who identifies
the source of this divergence when she discusses the role of
subjectivity in experimental poetry:

> Wird aber das lyrische Ich nicht bloß als "Subjekt" in
> dem personenhaften Sinne dieses Begriffes, sondern als
> Aussagesubjekt fixiert, so wird gerade dadurch...der
> Begriff der Subjektivität aus der Theorie der Lyrik
> eliminiert, und es wird möglich, auch die modernsten
> Formen und Theorien der Lyrik, wie etwa Text und
> Texttheorie, unter ihren Gattungsbegriff zu fassen.[117]

Thus, in Heißenbüttel's texts when we encounter an "Ich" at all,
then it is as a consciousness that no longer relates to an
unfettered, all embracing subjectivity and which acknowledges the
ultimate relativity of all responses. Subjectivity, which
formerly was conducive to "eine Dichtung des persönlichen und

hedonistischen Ausdrucks",[118] is redefined and thus emanates from an "Ich" whose status is reduced purely to that of "Aussagesubjekt". Bearing in mind the virtual solipsism of P h a n t a s u s it is clear that Heißenbüttel actually reverses the subject-object relationship that obtains in Holz's poetry. Indeed, Walter Hinderer could be describing this very polarity when he says of Heißenbüttel: "Doch nicht das literarische Objekt soll hier im Subjekt aufgelöst werden, sondern umgekehrt das Subjekt im Objekt".[119]

The other significant difference between Holz and Heißenbüttel is less easy to define but basically it concerns their relationship to language. The following quotation - which is, in fact, part of a review of Jürgen Becker's R ä n d e r - illustrates the nature of this difference:

> Becker's difficulties of communication do not really stem from those of language but from the fact that he challenges language to do things which are contrary to its nature...Time and time again one finds that the writer who rebels ostensibly against the clichés of language rebels in fact against language itself and thus leaves himself no way out except silence.[120]

If we interpret the term "silence" in a broad sense to mean rejection of conventional language, then clearly both parts of this statement apply to Heißenbüttel as well as to Becker and many others. However, much though Holz may have at times challenged language to do things contrary to its nature, it is surely inconceivable that P h a n t a s u s represents, in however broad a sense, a literary "silence". Thus, when Becker in turn says of Holz "nicht der Artist jonglierte sondern der Sprachlose zahlte heim dem System, das seine Sprachlosigkeit verwaltet",[121] then this statement arguably applies more to Becker himself or writers such as Heißenbüttel than to Arno Holz. For, in truth, Holz's attitude to language is not as straightforward as Becker would have it; it is much more ambivalent, contradictory even. Nor should this really surprise us given that Holz was writing prior to the development of any real science or philosophy of language from which later writers

211

such as Heißenbüttel have so clearly drawn so much of their understanding of language. In this respect Heinrich Vormweg provides a useful framework within which to locate Holz when, in the course of analysing the widespread questioning of language in the sixties, he makes the distinction between the precoccupation with language in modern writing and that of the Baroque period:

> Der Unterschied zwischen der Prosa des frühbarocken
> Autors und den modernen Texten...scheint ein Unterschied
> der Vitalität und Selbstsicherheit zu sein. Fischart
> überläßt sich mit spontaner Lust den Wörten...als fasse
> er mit ihnen lauter Sachen, Dinge...Die neuen Texte
> haben dafür...meist etwas Zauderndes, Bewußtes, analytisch
> Grübelndes, Experimentelles.[122]

The curious thing about Holz is that he occupies a middle position between these two poles in that his work embraces both tendencies. It both conveys and derives from a delicate balance between doubt and confidence, between the celebration of the power of language, on the one hand, and the denial of its efficacy, on the other. For whereas Holz's reflections were prompted by the recognition of the inherently epigonic nature of a literature that evinced an uncritical acceptance of language, he still saw as primary the relationship between words and their "reales Äquivalent", even though he further recognised that the mediation of that relationship in literature was becoming increasingly problematical. Not for nothing does Holz write at one point in P h a n t a s u s:

In

dampfem Zimmer

gebückt zwischen Büchern

Tage

Wochen, Monate

saß ich, sann

ich ... und ... schrieb!

Dinge,die mich, einst geschmerzt, Dinge, die mich, einst bewegt, Dinge
von vor tausend Jahren, Dinge, die noch niemals waren

```
                    Dinge
               Dinge, Dinge
                Dinge!

                    Das
                  dumpfe,
             karge, einsam enge
                 Zimmer,
          der Stuhl, der Tisch, der
   gelbe Lampenkreis ... die ... bleichtoten Bücher
                    ein
      Meer, ein ... Wust ... ein Berg
                 Papier,
             Papier, Papier
                   und
       "Dinge"..."Dinge"..."Dinge",
              "Dinge"!!¹²³
```

The manner in which Holz straddles the two co-ordinates of Vormweg's comparison becomes even more evident when he pursues the distinction in respect of the way that words are used in modern writing: "(Worte) dienen...offensichtlich nicht dazu, Gedanken, Erlebnisse, Empfindungen, innere Zustände des Autors zu transportieren, sondern es ist ihnen Eigenkraft, Eigenwelt zugeschrieben. Sie dienen nicht, sie haben Autonomie".[124] While this is undoubtedly the case with writers such as Heißenbüttel, the fact remains that it is not so with Holz. In P h a n t a s u s words are intended in the first instance to convey subjective experience and yet, as we have seen, they do at times also acquire willy-nilly a degree of autonomy. Indeed, Jürgen Becker expresses this paradox when defining the contemporary significance of P h a n t a s u s:

> Als der durchgeführte Versuch einer Komposition, die
> Sprache autonom macht und zugleich den fortwährend
> wechselnden Erfahrungskomplexen anmißt, leitet der
> "Phantasus" eine Tendenz der zeitgenößischen Literatur
> ein.[125]

This description applies equally well to Becker's own work, a
fact which is significant because it helps explain a certain lack
of differentiation in the above statement. For where Becker is
wrong, in my opinion, is that he conflates the two separate strands
he identifies in P h a n t a s u s  into the  o n e  tendency
in contemporary literature;  whereas, in fact, there too they often
retain a separate identity.  Thus, the paradox remains that
although Becker's work, for example, shares the two tendencies of
P h a n t a s u s,  textual analysis reveals that a relationship
of substantial identity exists not with Becker but with concrete
poetry, in particular with the work of Heißenbüttel, which evinces
only the one tendency.  That is to say, the real relationship which
P h a n t a s u s  suggests is one with the literary autonomisation
of language.  Nevertheless, as I shall argue in my final chapter,
Becker is undoubtedly  right to point to Holz's literary mediation
of subjectivity as a crucial reason for his subsequent resonance in
modern literature.  Where he is wrong is to identify  P h a n t a s u s
as the sole or even the most important realisation of the subjectivist
mode.

## CONCLUSION

In a moment of uncharacteristically accurate self-assessment Holz once said of himself: "ich litt noch nie an Selbstunterschätzung".[1] Indeed, one indication of the degree of Holz's self-centredness is provided by his apparent inability to appreciate any writer other than himself, for his extensive theoretical writings and letters contain only one serious attempt to examine the work of another author, namely his essay on Zola. Moreover, even this served only as the springboard for his own ideas. The overriding impression created by the endless polemics and acrimonious disputes with erstwhile collaborators and contemporaries is of a man so utterly convinced as to the uniqueness of his literary achievements as to deny totally any contribution that others may have made to his artistic development. One can hardly wonder, then, that the relationship between Holz and the critics was anything but an easy one. Indeed, it is external factors such as this – and, in particular, Holz's social and economic circumstances – which, Helmut Scheuer argues in his biographical study, help to explain Holz's relative lack of success.[2]

More relevant for the purposes of this study, however, are the possible reasons for the revival of interest in Holz. If we assume that the publication of Holz's work in the sixties was either the catalyst for or the symptom of this revival rather than its direct cause, then we must account for it by identifying in general terms what were the particularly "modern" aspects of his work, by defining, that is to say, in what way Holz was, to use his own expression, "ahead of his time". The key to this problem can, I believe, be found in Holz's theoretical writings, even though this need in no sense commit us to Holz's own assertion that "es ist bei einem Künstler von vornherein das Zeichen einer gewissen Inferiorität, wenn er sich mit Gedanken über seine Kunst nicht abgibt".[3] Admittedly, it is true that Holz's theory is at times banal, diffuse, ambiguous and, above all, unnecessarily polemical. Nevertheless, it is also the case that most major reassessments of his work have begun by examining the main propositions of his aesthetic theory. Moreover, even if, as Pascal believes, such analyses have in

the process possibly attributed to Holz's writings a subtlety and
complexity which they do not in reality possess,[4] then nevertheless
their value must be located in the fact that Holz succeeded in theorising,
however inadequately, certain major problems that have also confronted
later writers.

The first of these is Holz's persistent concern with form, for above
all it was his recognition that older forms could not resolve all the
problems of his time that identifies him potentially as a radically
modern writer. It is not totally coincidental, therefore, that it is
in the sixties, i.e. at a time when traditional assumptions about
literature were increasingly being called into account and when new
alternatives, particularly in respect to form, were continually being
sought, that a proper appreciation of Holz's work begins to emerge.
It is perhaps no coincidence either that it is in the sixties also
that we find the first real acknowledgement in Germany of another - and,
it must be said, much more important - theoretician, Walter Benjamin,
for his work is similarly underpinned by the view that radical formal
change is the essential prerequisite for the transformation or
"revolutionisation" of the work of art as such. After all, it was
Holz who wrote that "man revolutioniert eine Kunst also nur, indem man
ihre Mittel revolutioniert",[5] but such a formulation could belong
just as easily to Benjamin's pioneering essay "Der Autor als Produzent",
which exercised such a considerable influence over many German writers
in the sixties. One such writer is Helmut Heißenbüttel who, when
discussing the historical location of the emergence of a significant
formal awareness, provides a further perspective on Holz's claim to
modern relevance:

> Für die Literatur des 19. Jahrhunderts besitzt die Kategorie des
> Inhaltlichen eine wesentliche Bedeutung. Inhalt als etwas
> Ablösbares, etwas Erzählbares. Literatur im 19. Jahrhundert
> hat den Aspekt: Inhalt, in eine Form gegossen. Form erscheint
> als etwas Gegebenes, als etwas Überliefertes...Für die
> Literatur im 19. Jahrhundert gilt wesentlich die Zweiteilung
> in Form und Inhalt, Stil und Gehalt usw. Diese Zweiteilung
> ist eine Eigenschaft der Literatur im 19. Jahrhundert.

> In der Opposition gegen diese Zweiteilung läßt sich
> ein Ansatzpunkt für die Literatur des 20. Jahrhunderts
> erkennen. Die Opposition ist aggressiv. Sie reduziert
> den Inhalt und löst die Form in ihren traditionellen
> Erscheinungsweisen auf. Sie ist getragen von der
> Intention einer neuen Sprechmöglichkeit. Diese neue
> Sprechmöglichkeit wird gesehen in der Rückführung
> und Rückbesinnung der Sprache auf sich selbst. In
> dieser Rückbesinnung wird die Frage nach Form und
> Inhalt gegenstandslos.[6]

Holz's development would appear to encapsulate the transition which
Heißenbüttel suggests. For, as we have seen, the lesson Holz drew
from the content-orientatedness of B u c h   d e r   Z e i t was the
recognition of the primacy of form, as reflected, for example, in
his view "daß der Naturalismus eine Methode ist, eine
D a r s t e l l u n g s a r t und nicht etwa 'Stoffwahl'",[7] while the
prefigurement of Heißenbüttel's "Rückführung der Sprache auf sich
selbst" can, as was suggested in the previous chapter, be clearly
found in the autonomisation of language in P h a n t a s u s. From
this point of view, therefore, it would appear that the most
grandiose of Holz's claims, namely that his work constituted a landmark
between two epochs, is not without a certain validity.

Holz's work bridges the two centuries in another way, however, and
that is in the literary expression it gives to the previously almost
unexplored realm of subjectivity. That is to say, it marks not only
the recognition of the changed nature of the reality that confronted
writers at the end of the nineteenth century, but also the realisation
of the necessity for the literary representation of that reality to
change accordingly. It thus stands at the beginning of the development
of a literary mode which increasingly came to reject the nineteenth
century realist tradition's emphasis on the external and the objective
in favour of an internalised perspective that redefines reality as the
inner and the subjective. In Holz's theory the clearest prescription
of such an internalised view of reality is represented by the following
crucial proposition:

> Ich gestalte und forme die 'Welt', sagte ich mir,
> wenn es mir gelingt, den Abglanz zu spiegeln, den
> sie mir in die 'Seele' geworfen. Und je reicher,
> je mannigfaltiger, je vielfarbiger ich das tue, um
> so treuer, um so tiefer, um so tiefer, um so
> machtvoller wird mein Werk.[8]

In his creative writing this assumed two forms: the subjectivist
prose-works provide a poly-perspectival representation of reality
that increasingly threatens the view of a single, secure and
unchallengeable reality, while  P h a n t a s u s,  with its absorption of the external world into the experience of a single
imagination, effectively dissolves the distinction between the
subject and object.  This intensification of the subjectivised
perspective is certainly one major aspect of the way German
literature has developed in the twentieth century.  Moreover, one
need only consider the views of a writer such as Jürgen Becker to
appreciate the relevance of Holz to that development, for he, more
clearly than any other writer, stresses the mediation  of experience
as the key to a portrayal of reality:

> ich möchte die Dinge authentisch haben, wie ich sie
> erlebt habe-d.h. nicht nur konkret auf der Straße,
> sondern wie ich sie durchs Denken erlebt habe, wie ich
> sie in der Phantasie erlebt habe, so möchte ich sie
> eigentlich genau rekapitulieren in der Sprache.[9]

Similarly, Becker gives the following description of one of his own
texts:

> Dieser Text demonstriert nur die Bewegungen eines
> Bewußtseins durch die Wirklichkeit und deren
> Verwandlung in Sprache.  Bewußtsein:  das ist meines
> in seinen Schichten, Brüchen und Verstörungen;
> Wirklichkeit:  das ist die tägliche, vergangene,
> imaginierte.  Sie lesen nur Mitteilungen aus meinem
> Erfahrungsbereich.[10]          •

Reality for Becker is not just inner reality as such but his  o w n
experience,  "Mitteilungen aus  m e i n e m  Erfahrungsbereich".
If we bear in mind Becker's description of Holz's  P h a n t a s u s

as "sein Versuch, die totale Realität und ihre Erscheinungsweise
im dichtenden Bewußtsein sprachlich zu demonstrieren" in which
reality is transformed into "einen sprachlichen Kosmos,der das Bewußtsein dessen, der da redete,genau reflektierte",[11] then it is clear that
Becker marks the summation of a subjectivist tradition in German literature whose origins he himself locates in the work of Arno Holz.

In conclusion, it remains only to summarise in what particular forms
those two general tendencies of Holz's work can be translated into
concrete literary relationships. Earlier I·suggested a distinction
between three types of relationship and surveying the literary
criticism on Holz one cannot escape the conclusion that the type
most commonly suggested - although not explicitly categorised
as such - is the parallel. Admittedly, the diversity of Holz's work
allows for an almost infinite number of possible parallels, but some
of the writers who have been proposed in this connection - Wyndham
Lewis, Pinter, Kafka,[12] to name but three - stretch even this
flexible category beyond its limits. For the sake of clarity,
therefore, I would give just one textual example to illustrate the
type of relationship that I understood by the term:

oliven

azuren, orangen, lasuren

königsblau,bischofsblau,himmelblau,fliederblau,enziablau,veilchenblau,
kornblumenblau, vergißmeinnichtblau,

mondblau, nachtblau,

ultramarin,

meergrün, glasgrün, apfelgrün, blaßgrün, resedagrün,
graßgrün

vitriolgrün, lauchgrün, eidechsgrün,

hauchgrün

kaffeebraun, zimmetbraun, tabackbraun, bronzebraun,

rostbraun,

kastanienbraun,

maulwurfsgrau, eselsgrau, schiefergrau,

<pre>
          aschgrau, bleigrau,
            beinschwarz,
        lilienweiß, silberweiß
              goldgleiß[13]
</pre>

The following passage from Günter Grass's H u n d e j a h r e
offers an interesting comparison with these lines from
P h a n t a s u s:

> Diesmal waren es nicht nur SA-Uniformen. Auch das Zeug
> einiger simpler Parteigenossen fand sich darunter. Aber
> alles war braun; nicht das Braun sommerlicher
> Halbschuhe; kein Nüßchenbraun Hexenbraun; kein braunes
> Afrika; keine geriebene Borke, Möbel nicht, altersbraun;
> kein mittelbraun sandbraun; weder junge Braunkohle noch
> alter Torf, mit Torfspaten gestochen; keine Frühstücks-
> schokolade, kein Morgenkankaffee, den Sahne erhöht; Tabak,
> so viel Sorten, doch keine so bräunlich wie; weder das
> augentrügerische Rehbraun noch das Niveaubraun zweier Wochen
> Urlaub; kein Herbst spuckte auf die Palette, als dieses
> Braun; Kachbraun, allenfalls Lehmbraun, aufgeweicht, kleistrig,
> als das Parteibraun, SA-Braun, Braun aller Braunbücher,
> Braunen Häuser, Braunauer Braun, Evabraun als dieses Uni-
> formbraun, weit entfernt von Khakibraun   Braun aus tausend
> pickligen Ärschen auf weiße Teller geschissen, Braun aus Erbsen
> und Brühwurst gewonnen, nein nein, ihr sanften Brunetten,
> hexenbraun nüßchenbraun, standet nicht Pate, als dieses Braun
> gekocht, geboren und eingefärbt, als dieses Dunghaufenbraun -
> ich schmeichle noch immer - vor Eddi Amsel lag.[14]

The surface similarities between these two passages are immediately
evident, particularly in respect of their general playing with and
permutation of words, such as to allow one to speak of a certain
stylistic resemblance between some elements of Grass's writing and
Holz's poetry. However, even at the level of these two extracts,
clear differences are also discernible. In Holz's passage, which
initially seeks to evoke the visual beauty of various species of
birds, the sheer magnitude of his catalogue of colours (fifty-nine
different shades in all) renders almost impossible any conceptualisation of the phenomena by the reader with the result that ultimately
the value of the words does not extend beyond their individual acoustic
and rhythmic qualities. With Grass, on the other hand, even if one

were to abstract the passage from its overall context, one would still derive from it a strong sense of the critique of Nazism which, amongst other things, informs the novel as a whole. Although, paradoxically, certain of Grass's statements on the relation between form and content are more extreme than those of Holz,[15] the fact nevertheless remains that his work is rarely legitimated by linguistic vigour alone. In other words, a comparison between Grass and Holz would reveal certain limited stylistic similarities but no substantial point of intersection[16] and it is in this sense that I would wish to designate such a case as a p a r a l l e l.

The second category that was identified was what I termed a t e n d e n t i a l  r e l a t i o n s h i p and the clearest example of this would seem to be Holz's relationship to Expressionism. B u c h  d e r  Z e i t prefigures from the viewpoint of content the Expressionists' concern with the metropolis, but it is only with that generation that the theme becomes central in a way that profoundly influences form. Paradoxically, in the case of Holz's later poetry the converse is true. Holz's "revolutionisation" of poetry provided the formal basis which certain Expressionist poets such as August Stramm and Herwath Walden were able to develop, but the intensity of the ideas which they sought to express was such as to extend their poetry on to a level qualitatively different from that which Holz achieved in P h a n t a s u s.

As with the parallel numerous other tendential relationships can be suggested with Holz's work, but in my opinion the type which indicates most clearly his significance for modern German literature is that which I have described as a  r e l a t i o n s h i p  o f  s u b s t a n t i a l  i d e n t i t y. This is particularly the case since, in general, such relationships go beyond the level of comparison with an individual writer and point rather to specific m o d e s of writing that have developed in the twentieth century. This study has identified three such tendencies which, generally speaking, could be called the objectivist, the subjectivist and the formalist modes. In an essay characterising the development

of German literature since the inception of capitalist industrialisation, Michael Scharang has argued that the effect of the social
developments attendant on it was to deprive literature of its
traditional narrative basis, thus leaving the writer, broadly
speaking, with two possible approaches.  The first alternative
Scharang describes as follows:

> Legt der Autor...Wert darauf, reale Verhältnisse, die
> schwer durchschaubar sind, von denen der Allgemeinheit
> ein falsches Bild gemacht wird oder die überhaupt der
> allgemeinen Erfahrung durch Manipulation vorenthalten
> werden, der allgemeinen Erfahrung zuzuführen,
> gleichgültig ob diese Arbeit den Charakter von Kunst
> hat oder nicht, so wird sich seine Methode einerseits
> aus der Struktur jener Verhältnisse ergeben, die er
> darstellen will, andererseits aus seiner Absicht,
> sie erfahrbar zu machen.  Ein solcher Autor will etwas
> zeigen, etwas dokumentieren.  Da er das sprachlich tut,
> wird er nach sprachlichem Material suchen, das
> i n   m ö g l i c h s t   u n m i t t e l b a r e r
> B e z i e h u n g   z u   b e s t i m m t e n   r e a l e n
> V e r h ä l t n i s s e n  steht, und dieses
> d o k u m e n t i e r e n.[17] (my emphasis)

In locating the historical origins of the documentary mode in
Naturalism, i.e. at the onset of industrialisation in Germany, and
in defining its primary characteristic as a linguistic method which
aims for the most immediate reproduction of reality possible,
Scharang alludes to the relationship between reportage and the
objectivist tendency of Holz's prose-writing which is the first of
the three significant modes of writing in Holz's work.  The second
is represented by the other choice which, according to Scharang,
faces the modern author:

> Legt er Wert darauf, etwas zu machen, das deutlich den
> Charakter von Kunst hat,...so wird seine Frage nach der
> Methode immer eine Frage nach der Sprach-Methode sein.
> Der Autor wird die Sprache, die ein Mittel seiner
> Arbeit ist, verabsolutieren und zum Zweck seiner Arbeit
> erklären.  Er wird dem Funktionieren der Sprache
> nachgehen, seine Einsicht in dieses Funktionieren zur
> Methode erheben.[18]

This concern with language for its own sake corresponds to the formalist tendency in Holz's late poetry which prefigures the contemporary experimental prose-writing and concrete poetry of such figures as Heißenbüttel, Mon, Ror Wolf and members of the Wiener Gruppe. Holz's work can thus be seen to embrace both the alternatives that, according to Scharang, exist for the modern writer. And yet, Holz's work itself reveals that Scharang's framework is too narrow, for it ignores the subjectivist tradition which includes, amongst others, Alfred Döblin, Jürgen Becker and the New Realism of Dieter Wellershoff and the Kölner Schule and which, analysis has shown, finds such excellent prefigurement in Holz's subjectivist writing. As mentioned earlier, recent criticism has tended to focus on P h a n t a s u s as the major source of Holz's contemporary relevance but, in my opinion, it is his contribution to this tradition, in the shape of the subjectivist style of consequential Naturalism, which marks his greatest significance for modern German literature. Indeed, looking at Holz's career as a whole, one is left with the slightly sad thought that had he devoted but a fraction of the time he spent on P h a n t a s u s to the further development of his prose-writing,he might well have joined the ranks of Germany's major modern novelists and thus achieved the elusive success which he so clearly sought throughout his artistic life.

The following abbreviations will be used to refer to the two
editions of Holz's work:

DW   = D a s  W e r k,  ed. Hans. W. Fischer, Berlin,
          1924-5,  10 Volumes.

W    = W e r k e,  ed. Wilhelm Emrich and Anita Holz,
         Neuwied, 1961-4, 7 Volumes.

# I N T R O D U C T I O N

1. DW X, p.I.

2. cf. "Ich schätze das, was ich für die Entwicklung unserer
   deutschen Literatur bisher geleistet, für wichtiger, als
   jede andre Einzelleistung eines betreffenden Zeitgenossen..",
   B r i e f e  E i n e  A u s w a h l,  ed. Anita Holz and
   Max Wagner, Munich, 1948, p.137.

3. ibid., p.211.

4. cf. "ich litt noch nie an Selbstunterschätzung", DW X,
   p.533.

5. W VII, p.453, (published originally in P r o t e s t  u n d
   V e r h e i ß u n g,  Frankfurt a.M., 1960, pp.155-168, here,
   p.155).

6. ibid., p.471 (P r o t e s t  u n d  V e r h e i ß u n g,
   p.168).

7. This is true of nearly all the recent studies of Holz to
   which I will refer in the course of this study.

8. "An Interview with Pierre Macherey", R e d  L e t t e r s
   No.5, London, 1977, p.3.

9. DW X, p.534.

10. cf. "Denn Parallele bedeutet im genauen Sinn ihres Begriffs,
    daß nicht die geringste Berührung der beiden Erscheinungen
    vorliegt, ..." Käte Hamburger, P h i l o s o p h i e  d e r
    D i c h t e r,  Stuttgart, 1966 , p.180f.

11. The group consisted of Paul Ernst, Rolf Wolfgang Martens,
    Reinhard Piper, Robert Reß and Georg Stolzenberg.  It was
    responsible for various volumes imitating Holz's "Mittelachse"
    poetry from the Saßenbach Verlag which published the original
    P h a n t a s u s  volumes, hence the name.

1.  Ursula Münchow, D e u t s c h e r  N a t u r a l i s m u s, Berlin, 1968, p.31.

2.  It may be as well to try and clarify the relationship between working-class and socialist literature as it may otherwise appear that I use the terms interchangeably and without differentiation. This is not the place to discuss at length the possible meaning of the term "working-class literature" but, in short, I would argue that it must be seen as one component within the broader category of "socialist literature". That is to say, I do not believe that the ultimate determinant of working-class literature is, as is commonly assumed, the author's social origin or the literary content of the work, but rather the specific function ascribed to and fulfilled by the literature in question w i t h i n a  p a r t i c u l a r  h i s t o r i c a l  c o n t e x t. (For elaboration of this argument cf. Florian Vassen "Über die Brauchbarkeit des Begriffs 'Arbeiterdichtung'" in: A r b e i t e r d i c h t u n g. A n a l y s e n–B e k e n n t– n i s s e–D o k u m e n t a t i o n e n, Wuppertal, 1973, pp.117-131). For this reason I would argue that B u c h d e r  Z e i t  can be seen as a significant contribution not only to the tradition of a socialist literature as a whole in Germany but also to the development of working-class literature in particular.

3.  cf. Jost Hermand, D e r  S c h e i n  d e s  s c h ö n e n L e b e n s, Frankfurt, 1972, p.32.

4.  ibid., p.37.

5.  M o d e r n e  D i c h t e r–C h a r a k t e r e, ed. Wilhelm Arent, Berlin, 1885.

6.  DW I, p.7 and p.9.

7.  ibid., p.55.

8.  ibid., p.16.

9.  ibid., p.19.

10.  ibid., p.28.

11.  ibid., p.28.

12.  ibid., p.77.

13.  ibid., p.78.

14.  ibid., p.78.

15.  ibid., p.74f.

16.  ibid., p.63.

17.  ibid., p.67f.

18.  ibid., p.134.

19. Hermand, op.cit., p.37.

20. Holz, B r i e f e, p.66.

21. DW I, p.18.

22. ibid., p.19.

23. ibid., p.20.

24. ibid., p.22.

25. ibid., p.23.

26. ibid., p.23.

27. ibid., p.34.

28. ibid., p.8.

29. Hermann Ploetz, "Arno Holz der Deutsche", O s t d e u t s c h e
    M o n a t s h e f t e, January 1934, p.334.

30. DW I, p.224.

31. Alfred Klein, "Zur Entwicklung der sozialistischen
    Literatur in Deutschland 1918-33", in: Irmfried Hiebel
    (ed.), L i t e r a t u r d e r A r b e i t e r k l a s s e,
    Berlin, 1971, p.23f.

32. Arno Holz and Oskar Jerschke, D e u t s c h e W e i s e n,
    L e i p z i g, 1884.

33. Holz, B r i e f e, p.59.

34. Holz, B r i e f e, p.66f. Similarly Holz's positive
    response to the founding of the Weimar Republic shows that
    as regards his general political views he maintained, in this
    respect at least, a degree of consistency:

    > Die Zuversicht, daß die Revolution - vorausgesetzt,
    > daß unser Volk nicht unter die Fuchtel irgendeiner
    > abermaligen Gewaltherrschaft gerät - für seine Geistigen
    > keinen Zusammenbruch, sondern den Anfang eines
    > neuen sozialen Aufbaues bedeutet, teile ich.
    > (Arno Holz 10.1.1919)

    This statement appeared in a pamphlet entitled "Für das neue
    Deutschland" (published by Otto Elsner A-G Berlin, 1919)
    in which various personalities such as Gerhart Hauptmann,
    Thomas Mann, Heinrich Mann and Fritz von Unruh were
    invited to express their view on the founding of the
    Republic and on the assumption of power by a socialist
    government. The document was made available to me by the
    Arno Holz Archive in Berlin.

35. DW I, p.78.

36. Holz, B r i e f e, p.67.

37. Ernst Troeltsch, S c h r i f t e n, Tubingen, 1912,
    Vol.I, p.84.

38. DW I, p.XI.

39. ibid., p.38.

40. ibid., p.X.

41. ibid., p.XI.

42. ibid., p.47.

43. Holz, B r i e f e, p.67.

44. DW I, p.XII.

45. ibid., p.22.

46. Holz, B r i e f e, p.75f.

47. DW I, p.48.

48. ibid., p.46.

49. Georg Fülberth, P r o l e t a r i s c h e  P a r t e i
u n d  b ü r g e r l i c h e  L i t e r a t u r, Neuwied
and Berlin, 1972; Herbert Scherer, B ü r g e r l i c h-
o p p o s i t i o n e l l e  L i t e r a t u r  u n d
s o z i a l d e m o k r a t i s c h e  A r b e i t e r-
b e w e g u n g  n a c h 1890, Stuttgart, 1974.

50. Heinrich Hart, "Die Moderne", D e r  K u n s t w a r t,
IV (1890-1), Munich, p.149.

51. cf. Johannes Schlaf who identified with socialism as an
expression of sympathy with the lower classes but who
rejected it as an ideology. See Johannes Schlaf,
A u s  m e i n e m  L e b e n, Halle, 1941, p.38f.

52. DW I, p.359f.

53. Franz Servaes, "Nietzsche und der Sozialismus", F r e i e
B ü h n e, III 1892, Berlin p.205.

54. Klaus R. Scherpe, "Der Fall Arno Holz. Zur sozialen und
ideologischen Motivation der naturalistischen Literatur-
revolution", in: Gert Mattenklott and Klaus R. Scherpe
(ed.), P o s i t i o n e n  d e r  l i t e r a r i s c h e n
I n t e l l i g e n z  z w i s c h e n  b ü r g e r l i c h e r
R e a k t i o n  u n d  I m p e r i a l i s m u s, Kronberg,
1973, pp.121-178, here p.137.

55. For a more balanced account of the relationship of Naturalism
and socialism, see: Jost Hermand and Richard Hamann,
N a t u r a l i s m u s, Munich, 1972, p.209ff; Friedrich
Kummer, D e u t s c h e  L i t e r a t u r g e s c h i c h t e
d e s  19. u n d  20. J a h r h u n d e r t s, Dresden,
1922, Vol.2, p.244f; Ursula Münchow, op.cit., p.147ff;
John Osborne, T h e  N a t u r a l i s t  D r a m a  i n
G e r m a n y, Manchester, 1971, p.56ff; Roy Pascal,
F r o m  N a t u r a l i s m  t o  E x p r e s s i o n i s m,
London, 1973.

56. For a more detailed discussion of this and other similar debates, see Osborne, op.cit., pp.62-65.

57. ibid., p.63.

58. cf. my discussion of this in Chapter 2(i), p.87ff.

59. Georg Lukács, "Franz Mehring 1846-1914", in: B e i t r ä g e z u r G e s c h i c h t e d e r Ä s t h e t i k, Berlin, 1954, p.318-403.

60. Franz Mehring, G e s a m m e l t e S c h r i f t e n, ed. Höhle, Koch and Schleifstein, Berlin, 1960-67, Vol.XI, p.449.

61. ibid., p.135.

62. Paul Ernst, "Mehrings Lessing-Legende und die materialistische Geschichtsauffassung", D i e N e u e Z e i t, ed. Karl Kautsky, (1883-1914) 1-32, No.12, p.7.

63. See Fülberth, op.cit., p.53.

64. Pascal, op.cit., p.185.

65. Klein, loc.cit., p.23f.

66. Armin Kesser, "Die Arbeiterlyrik der SPD", D i e L i n k s k u r v e 4Jg., Berlin, 1932, No.10, pp.14-19, here p.15.

67. Mehring, op.cit. p.234.

68. ibid., p.234.

69. ibid., p.135.

70. ibid., p.563.

71. Gerald Stieg and Bernd Witte, A b r i ß e i n e r G e s c h i c h t e d e r d e u t s c h e n A r b e i t e r - l i t e r a t u r, Stuttgart, 1973, p.25.

72. cf. Münchow, op.cit., p.31.

73. A r n o H o l z u n d s e i n W e r k. D e u t s c h e S t i m m e n z u s e i n e m 60. G e b u r t s t a g, ed. Friedrich Avenarius, Berlin, 1923, p.56.

74. ibid., p.53.

75. Alfred Döblin, A u f s ä t z e z u r L i t e r a t u r. Olten and Freiburg, 1963, p.138.

76. ibid., p.141.

77. G e r h a r t S c h u l z, A r n o H o l z. D i l e m m a e i n e s b ü r g e r l i c h e n D i c h t e r l e b e n s, Munich, 1974, p.29.

78. Döblin, op.cit., p.145.

79. ibid., p.143.

80. ibid., p.145.

81. ibid., p.141.

82. ibid., p.145.


CHAPTER I (ii)

1. DW I,p.534.

2. The Poetical Works of William Wordsworth, ed. Thomas Hutchinson, London, 1913, p.269.

3. Walter Benjamin, Baudelaire, ein Lyriker im Zeitalter des Hochkapitalismus, ed. Rolf Tiedemann, Frankfurt a.M., 1969.

4. A more detailed account of the effects of industrialisation on German society is given by Ralf Dahrendorf, Gesellschaft und Demokratie in Deutschland, Munich, 1971, pp.39-55. See also Pascal, op.cit., p.124ff.

5. Pascal, op.cit., p.124.

6. DW I, p.52.

7. ibid., p.115.

8. ibid., p.117.

9. Hermand and Hamann, Naturalismus, p.66.

10. Ernst Stadler, Dichtungen (2 Vols.), ed. Karl Ludwig Schneider, Hamburg o.J., 1954, Vol.I, p.152.

11. Pascal, op.cit., p.143.

12. Fritz Hoffmann, "Nachwort", in: Fritz Hoffmann, Joachim Schreik, Manfred Wolter (ed.), Über die großen Städte, Berlin, 1967, p.476.

13. Johannes R. Becher, "Brief an Walter Rheiner 24.5.1920", in: K. Edschmid (ed.), Briefe der Expressionisten, Frankfurt a.M., 1954, p.22.

14. DW I, p.98.

15. ibid., p.100.

16. ibid., p.92.

17. ibid., p.97.

18. Stadler, Dichtungen, Vol.I, p.189.

19. Helmut Uhlig, "Von Ästhetizismus zum Expressionismus in Ernst Stadler, Georg Heym und Georg Trakl", in: Hermann

Friedmann and Otto Mann (ed.), E x p r e s s i o n i s m u s: G e s t a l t e n   e i n e r   l i t e r a r i s c h e n B e w e g u n g, Heidelberg, 1956, p.101.

20. In fact, the whole verse from "Berliner Frühling" is quoted as a motto for the book. Here, "Vorwort", in: I m s t e i n e r n e n   M e e r, ed. Oskar Hübner and Johannes Moegelin, Berlin, 1910, p.IX.

21. Q u a d r i g a, Vierteljahresschrift der Werkleute auf Haus Nyland, Jena, 1912-14, p.48.

22. DW I, p.103.

23. Stadler, D i c h t u n g e n, Vol.I, p.175.

24. Heine Rölleke, D i e   S t a d t   b e i   S t a d l e r, H e y m   u n d   T r a k l, Berlin, 1966, p.103.

25. DW I, p.77.

26. Gerrit Engelke, D a s   G e s a m t w e r k, Munich, 1960, p.51.

27. ibid., p.95.

28. Georg Heym, D i c h t u n g e n   u n d   S c h r i f t e n, (5 Vols.), ed. Karl Ludwig Schneider, Hamburg, 1960, Vol.I, p.349.

29. cf. Schulz, op.cit., p.27.

30. DW I, p.97.

31. M o d e r n e   D i c h t e r-C h a r a k t e r e, p.136.

32. DW I, p.86.

33. ibid., p.57 and p.77.

34. ibid., p.78 and p.85.

35. See Osborne, op.cit., for detailed discussion (pp.69-73).

36. Wilhelm Bölsche, H i n t e r   d e r   W e l t s t a d t, Leipzig, 1901, p.viii (quoted by Osborne, op.cit. p.69).

37. DW I, p.III.

38. Rölleke, op.cit., p.160.

39. DW X, p.534.

40. Döblin, op.cit., p.138.

41. Helmut Scheuer, A r n o   H o l z   i m   l i t e r a r i s c h e n L e b e n   d e s   a u s g e h e n d e n   19. J a h r h u n-d e r t s (1883-1896), Munich, 1971, p.22.

42. DW I, p.53ff.

43. DW I, p.121.

44. ibid., p.37.

45. cf. Pascal, op.cit., p.143.

46. DW I, p.108.

47. ibid., p.107.

48. ibid., p.117.

49. cf. Keith Bullivant and Hugh Ridley, I n d u s t r i e  u n d  d e u t s c h e  L i t e r a t u r 1830-1914, Munich, 1976, p.214.

50. Schulz, op.cit., p.24.

51. cf. So betrachtet liegt dem Kampf gegen den Naturalismus... ein antisozialistischer Affekt zugrunde...Denn schließlich ist der Naturalismus die erste moderne Kunstbewegung überhaupt, die sich mit den sozialen, politischen und wissenschaftlichen Konsequenzen des heutigen Industriezeitalters zu beschäftigen beginnt ...Eine solche Revolte gegen alles Schreinkünstlerische mußte bei der sorgfältig manipulierten Kulturpolitik der wilhelminischen Ära notwendig auf scharfen Widerstand stoßen. So dumm waren die herrschenden Klassen schon damals nicht, um eine Bewegung wie den Naturalismus einfach passieren zu lassen. Und so wurde der Naturalismus nicht nur in Deutschland, sondern in allen europäischen Ländern um 1900 durch einen von oben geforderten Symbolismus ersetzt.

    Hermand, D e r  S c h e i n  d e s  s c h ö n e n  L e b e n s, p.38.

52. This is expressed above all in the two essays, "Der Geist des naturalistischen Zeitalters" and "Vom alten zum neuen Naturalismus. Akadamie-Rede über Arno Holz", (in: A u f s ä t z e  z u r  L i t e r a t u r, pp.62-83 and pp.138-144).

53. Pascal, op.cit., p.278.


C H A P T E R  2

1. Arno Holz and Johannes Schlaf, N e u e  G l e i s e, Berlin, 1892.

2. Quotations from this will be given from Arno Holz, D a s  W e r k, Vol.10, (DW X), Berlin, 1925.

3. Gero von Wilpert, S a c h w ö r t e r b u c h  d e r  L i t e r a t u r, Stuttgart, 1969, p.700.

4. Marianne Kesting, E n t d e c k u n g  u n d  D e s t r u k-t i o n, Munich, 1970, p.175.

5. cf. "Arno Holz und die moderne Kunst", in: Wilhelm Emrich, P r o t e s t  u n d  V e r h e i ß u n g, Frankfurt, 1960, pp.155-168.

6.     Pascal, op.cit., p.60.

7.     cf. Siegwart Berthold, "Der sogenannte 'konsequente Naturalismus' von Arno Holz und Johannes Schlaf", Phil. Diss., Bonn, 1967, p.50.

8.     In the original N e u e  G l e i s e volume the title "Die papierne Passion" actually embraces four sketches:  the title sketch, "Krumme Windgasse 20.", "Die kleine Emmi" and "Ein Abschied".  Strictly speaking, only the first two sketches belong to this category  and "Die kleine Emmi", in particular, reveals a marked subjectivist tendency.  Similarly, "Die Familie Selicke" is in one sense a category on its own, since it is a drama rather than a prose-work.  However, the important thing for the present discussion is to draw the distinction between two t y p e s  of writing and in so far as these types exist in a pure form, they are represented by  "Die papierne Passion" and "Ein Tod", on the one hand, and by "Papa Hamlet" and "Der erste Schultag", on the other.

C H A P T E R  2 (i)

1.     cf. Scherpe, loc.cit., p.159.

2.     Holz, B r i e f e, p.262.

3.     cf. DW X, p.105.

4.     ibid., p.59.

5.     ibid., p.64.

6.     ibid., p.69.

7.     ibid., p.72f.

8.     Osborne, op.cit., p.42.

9.     DW X, p.159.

10.    ibid., p.80.

11.    ibid., p.83.

12.    ibid., p.131.

13.    Scherpe, loc.cit., p.157.

14.    Roy Pascal, "Consequential Naturalism". (Lecture, Warwick University, November, 1972).

15.    W. Rasch, "Zur dramatischen Dichtung des jungen Gerhart Hauptmann", in: F e s t s c h r i f t  f ü r  F.R. S c h r ö d e r, Heidelburg, 1959, p.245.

16.    Osborne, op.cit., p.42.

17.  Wyndham Lewis, T h e   W r i t e r   a n d   t h e
     A b s o l u t e, quoted in: Walter Allen, T h e
     E n g l i s h   N o v e l, London, 1954, p.248.

18.  Heinrich Hart, "Literarische Erinnerungen", G e s a m m e l t e
     W e r k e  (4 Vols.), ed. Julius Hart, Berlin, 1907,
     Vol.III, p.69.

19.  Pascal, op.cit., p.60.

20.  Fritz Martini, D a s   W a g n i s   d e r   S p r a c h e,
     Stuttgart, 1954, p.109.

21.  DW X, p.64.

22.  Günther Mahal, N a t u r a l i s m u s, Munich, 1975,
     p.169.

23.  DW X, p.330.

24.  Gerhard Fricke, G e s c h i c h t e   d e r   d e u t s c h e n
     D i c h t u n g, Hamburg and Lubeck, 1961, p.329.

25.  cf. Mahal, op.cit., p.169, and Hermand and Hamann,
     N a t u r a l i s m u s, pp.250-264.

26.  DW X, p.189.

27.  ibid., p.253.

28.  N e u e   G l e i s e, p.204.

29.  See below, p.105ff.

30.  N e u e   G l e i s e, p.19.

31.  A term coined by Franz Servaes and gratefully accepted by
     Holz, cf. DW X, p.254.

32.  ibid., p.214.

33.  N e u e   G l e i s e, p.14.

34.  ibid., p.204.

35.  ibid., p.208.

36.  ibid., p.215f.

37.  Hermand and Hamann, N a t u r a l i s m u s, p.253.

38.  ibid., p.252.

39.  DW X, p.254.

40.  N e u e   G l e i s e, p.158f.

41.  Scherpe, loc.cit., p.170.

42.  DW X, p.232.

43.  "Sie schildern auch wie ein Kleinmaler, wie einer, der
     keine distance hat, sondern aus nächster Nähe mit der Lupe
     beobachtet;..." Letter from Gerhart Hauptmann to Holz and
     Schlaf, 12.2.1889, a copy of which is available in the Arno
     Holz Archive in Berlin.

44.  H. H. Borcherdt, "Einführung" to Holz, B r i e f e, p.21.

45.  DW X, p.254.

46.  Martini, op.cit., p.120.

47.  ibid., p.122.

48.  Roy Pascal, "Arno Holz, Der erste Schultag. The Prose-Style
     of Naturalism", in: H. Siefken and A. Robinson (ed.),
     E r f a h r u n g   u n d   Ü b e r l i e f e r u n g,
     Festschrift for C.P. Magill, Cardiff, 1974 and "The Prose
     of Papa Hamlet. The Irrepressible Narrator", (unpublished
     manuscript, pp.1-23).

49.  Martini, op.cit., p.114.

50.  See below, p.101f.

51.  N e u e   G l e i s e, p.149.

52.  cf. Martini, op.cit., and Roy C. Cowen, D e r
     N a t u r a l i s m u s, Munich, 1975, p.94.

53.  DW X, p.330.

54.  ibid., p.222.

55.  David Turner, "D i e   F a m i l i e   S e l i c k e   and the
     Drama of Naturalism", in: J. M. Ritchie (ed.), P e r i o d s
     i n   G e r m a n   L i t e r a t u r e, London, 1969,
     Vol.2, p.207.

56.  ibid., p.208.

57.  Mahal, op.cit., p.214.

58.  Schulz, op.cit., p.52.

59.  Mahal, op.cit., p.213.

60.  ibid., p.208.

61.  N e u e   G l e i s e, pp.8-10.

62.  Mahal, op.cit., p.209f.

63.  ibid., p.214.

64.  ibid., p.209.

65.  ibid., p.210.

66.  Gerhart Hauptmann, V o r   S o n n e n a u f g a n g.
     S o z i a l e s   D r a m a, Berlin, 1889, p.3.

67.  cf. Berthold, op.cit., pp.137-144; C.F.W. Behl and
     Felix A. Voigt, C h r o n i k   v o n   G e r h a r t
     H a u p t m a n n s   L e b e n   u n d   S c h a f f e n,
     Munich, 1957, p.27ff.

68.  Osborne, op.cit., p.38.

69.  Pascal, "The Prose of Papa Hamlet", (p.1f).

70. Roy Johnson, "The Proletarian Novel", L i t e r a t u r e
    a n d  H i s t o r y,  No.2, London, 1975, pp.84-95,
    here p.90.

71. ibid., p.93.

72. Hermand and Hamann, N a t u r a l i s m u s,  p.8.

73. ibid., p.250.

74. Martini, op.cit., p.115.

75. Martin Walser, "Ein Nachwort zur Ergänzung", in: Ursula
    Trauberg, V o r l e b e n, Reinbek, 1970, p.195.

76. ibid., p.196.

77. Günter Wallraff, N e u e  R e p o r·t a g e n, U n t e r-
    s u c h u n g e n  u n d  L e h r b e i s p i e l e,
    Reinbek, 1974, p.134.

78. Erika Runge, F r a u e n.  V e r s u c h e  z u r
    E m a n z i p a t i o n, Frankfurt, 1969, p.266.

79. Reportage is a term belonging originally to the realm of
    journalism ("Publizistik") which was taken over into
    literature in Germany in the twenties; cf. below
    Lukács's discussion of reportage as a literary technique,
    p.91f.

80. Wilpert, op.cit., p.636.

81. Siegfried Kracauer, D i e  A n g e s t e l l t e n,
    (1929), Frankfurt a.M., 1971, p.16.

82. Quoted by Reinhard Dithmar in: G ü n t e r  W a l l r a f f s
    I n d u s t r i e r e p o r t a g e n, Kronberg, 1973,
    p.67.

83. Günter Wallraff, V o n  e i n e m  d e r  a u s z o g·u n d
    d a s  F ü r c h t e n  l e r n t e, Munich, 1970, p.37f.

84. Wallraff, N e u e  R e p o r t a g e n, p.133f.

85. Klas Ewert Everwyn, "Beschreibung eines Betriebsunsfalls",
    in: Fritz Hüser (ed.), A u s  d e r  W e l t  d e r
    A r b e i t, Neuwied, 1966,pp.37-48.

86. ibid., p.42ff.

87. ibid., p.42.

88. ibid., p.38.

89. ibid., p.48.

90. DW X, p.45.

91. cf. "Hervorragendes Mittel der Dokumentation ist die
    Montage, sie soll über die bloße Wiedergabe von zufälligen
    Realitätsausschnitten hinausgehen". Wallraff, N e u e
    R e p o r t a g e n, p.134.

92.    Lukács's critique of Naturalism, while it is articulated at
       many points in the body of his writings, is expressed at
       its most concise in the essay, "Kunst und objektive Wahrheit"
       (in: G e o r g  L u k á c s.  W e r k e, Vol.4, Neuwied and
       Berlin, 1971). In my exegesis, therefore, I shall draw
       primarily on the concepts used there. It is significant,
       however, that when he does expressly mention Holz, it is to
       note the f o r m a l  achievement of his contribution to
       Naturalism: "Es ist das Verdienst von Holz und Schlaf,
       daß sie die Tendenz der Naturwahrheit, den Aufstand gegen die
       lebensferne Künstlichkeit der damals herrschenden
       Literatur theoretisch und praktisch auf eine Stilform brachten".
       Georg Lukács, "Der deutsche Naturalismus", in: S c h r i f t e n
       z u r  L i t e r a t u r s o z i o l o g i e, Neuwied and
       Berlin, 1961, p.456.

93.    Georg Lukács, G e s c h i c h t e  u n d  K l a s s e n-
       b e w u ß t s e i n, Amsterdam, 1923, p.21.

94.    Lukács, "Kunst und objektive Wahrheit", loc.cit., p.620.

95.    Georg Lukács, "Reportage oder Gestaltung? Kritische
       Bemerkungen anläßlich des Romans von Ottwalt", D i e
       L i n k s k u r v e IV, 7, 8, 1932, pp.23-30, pp.26-31.

96.    cf. Rob Burns, "The Theory and Organisation of Revoluntionary
       Working-Class Literature", in: Keith Bullivant (ed.),
       C u l t u r e  a n d  S o c i e t y  i n  t h e  W e i m a r
       R e p u b l i c, Manchester, 1977, pp. 122-49.

97.    Lukács, "Reportage oder Gestaltung?", loc.cit., p.27.

98.    ibid., p.27.

99.    Walter Benjamin, "Das Kunstwerk im Zeitalter seiner
       technischen Reproduzierbarkeit", in: I l l u m i n a t i o n e n,
       Frankfurt, 1969, p.170.

100.   See, for example, Siegrfried Kracauer's analysis of the film
       in which he uses familiar terms such as "surface approach",
       the recording of "thousands of details without connecting
       them", "kaleidoscopic arrangement" and which includes a line
       of criticism so often directed at Naturalism: "This
       symphony fails to point out anything, because it does not
       uncover a single significant context". Siegfried Kracauer,
       F r o m  C a l i g a r i  t o  H i t l e r, Princeton,
       1947, pp.182-187.

101.   George Lukács, "Erzählen oder beschreiben?", in: G e o r g
       L u k á c s.  W e r k e, Vol.4, p.226.


C H A P T E R  2 (ii)

1.     Arno Holz, "Eine neue  Dramaturgie. II", in: D e r
       s o z i a l i s t i s c h e  A k a d e m i k e r, 2.Jg., No.7,
       Berlin, 1896, pp.432-437. (The essay is available in copy-form
       in the Arno Holz Archive).

2.  cf. the quotation on p.85.

3.  Raymond Williams, K e y w o r d s, Glasgow, 1976, p.184.

4.  Hans-Georg Rappl, "Die Wortkunstheorie von Arno Holz",
    Phil.Diss., Cologne, 1957.

5.  DW X, p.130f.

6.  cf. a letter of 10.2. 1889 : "Des Photographen? Wieder so
    ein 'Stichwort'!...Aber nur wenige mögen existieren, die
    gedankenhöhler, als grade dieses sind. So eine Blindheit!
    Wie kann ein 'Hirn' 'photographieren'!?" (B r i e f e,
    p.84); or a letter of 2.6.1896 where Holz rejects the term
    "Nachahmung": "in dem heutigen strikten Sinn...D i e s e r
    Begriff und 'Kunst'. Puh. Dann allerdings hätten die Gegner
    nur zu recht!" (B r i e f e, p.104f).

7.  Emrich, op.cit., p.155.

8.  Emrich, for example, writes:

    > Um jede Verwechslung mit naturalistischen Vorstellungen
    > zu vermeiden, hat Arno Holz später die Formel...
    > abgeändert...Er beseitigt also die Worter "wieder"
    > und "Reproduktionsbedingungen", um sich abzusetzen
    > von seinen Kritikern, die ihm vorwarfen, nach seiner
    > Theorie solle die Kunst die Natur nur fotographisch
    > genau abbilden". (Emrich, op.cit., p.156,
    > footnote I).

9.  DW X, p.186f.

10. ibid., p.139.

11. ibid., p.11.

12. Emrich, op.cit., p.156.

13. Schulz, op.cit., p.45.

14. DW X, 198f.

15. Osborne, op.cit., p.41.

16. DW X, p.187.

17. Pascal, "The Prose of Papa Hamlet", (p.18).

18. Käte Hamburger, D i e  L o g i k  d e r  D i c h t u n g,
    Stuttgart, 1968, p.73.

19. In his typology Stanzel terms this the "personal" perspective
    in contradistinction to the other narrative modes of
    authorial and first person perspective. This is a useful
    categorisation provided that the distinction between voice
    and perspective is asserted within the personal type; cf.
    F. K. Stanzel, D i e  t y p i s c h e n  E r z ä h l-
    s i t u a t i o n e n  i m  R o m a n, Vienna and
    Stuttgart, 1955.

20. cf. the first four chapters which comprise Part 1 of Roy
    Pascal, The  D u a l  V o i c e, Manchester, 1977, pp.1-32.

21.    ibid., p.31.

22.    Pascal, "The Prose of Papa Hamlet", (p.18).

23.    cf. ibid., (p.21) and the historical survey of the critical
       assessment of the technique in T h e  D u a l  V o i c e.

24.    DW X, p.41.

25.    ibid., p.45.

26.    ibid., p.336.

27.    N e u e  G l e i s e, p.197.

28.    ibid., p.174f.

29.    Pascal, "Arno Holz, Der erste Schultag", loc.cit., p.160.

30.    The sketch "Die kleine Emmi" provides another good example
       of this technique.  Here the perspective is consistently
       Emmi's mediated as in "Der erste Schultag" more through
       perspectivised narration than free indirect style.

31.    Borcherdt, loc.cit., p.19.

32.    Osborne, op.cit., p.49.

33.    Pascal, "Arno Holz, Der erste Schultag", p.161f.

34.    N e u e  G l e i s e, p.172.

35.    ibid., p.111.

36.    ibid., p.122.

37.    ibid., p.115.

38.    ibid., p.117.

39.    ibid., p.126.

40.    ibid., p.113.

41.    ibid., p.129.

42.    ibid., p.147.

43.    Pascal "The Prose of Papa Hamlet", (p.13).

44.    ibid., (p.13A). Pascal is thus challenging the conventional
       definition of the inner monologue which always demands the
       first person form and the present tense and which thus sees
       the inner monologue as a contrast to "erlebte Rede" (cf.
       Wilpert, op.cit., p.355).  Although, strictly speaking, the
       more clumsy term "indirect inner monologue" or the unwieldy
       "inner monologue in the form of the indirect speech" would
       be more accurate, therefore, Pascal is, to my mind,
       essentially right in his view that such passages merit the
       term monologue.

45.    N e u e  G l e i s e, p.121.  Schulz compares this with the
       actual monologue from  H a m l e t  (Act II, Scene 2)
       as found in the translation by A. W. Schlegel:

Ich habe seit kurzem-ich weiß nicht wodurch-alle
meine Munterkeit eingebüßt, meine gewohnten Übungen
aufgegeben; und es steht in der Tat so übel um
meine Gemütslage, daß die Erde, dieser treffliche
Bau, mir nur ein kahles Vorgebirge scheint, seht
ihr, dieser herrliche Baldachin, die Luft, dies
wackre umwölbende Firmament, dies majestätische
Dach mit goldnem Feuer ausgelegt: kommt es mir
doch nicht anders vor, als ein fauler, verpesteter
Haufe von Dünsten. Welch ein Meisterwerk, ist der
Mensch! wie edel durch Vernunft! wie unbegrenzt
an Fähigkeiten! In Gestalt und Bewegung wie
bedeutend und wunderwürdig! im Handeln wie ähnlich
einem Engel! im Begreifen wie ähnlich einem Gott!
die Zierde der Welt! das Vorbild der Lebendigen!
Und doch, was ist mir diese Quintessenz von Staube?
Ich habe keine Lust am Manne - und am Weibe auch nicht,
wiewohl ihr das durch euer Lächeln zu sagen scheint.
(Schulz, op.cit., p.245).

46.  Pascal, "The Prose of Papa Hamlet", (p.13A).

47.  Walter Sokel, D e r   l i t e r a r i s c h e
     E x p r e s s i o n i s m u s   i n   d e r   d e u t s c h e n
     L i t e r a t u r   d e s   20.   J a h r h u n d e r t s,
     Munich, 1970, p.31.

48.  Pascal, "The Prose of Papa Hamlet", (p.14).

49.  Pascal, "Arno Holz, Der erste Schultag", loc.cit., p.160.

50.  Pascal, "The Prose of Papa Hamlet", (p.14f).

51.  N e u e   G l e i s e, p.119.

52.  ibid., p.114.

53.  ibid., p.140.

54.  ibid., p.117f.

55.  Pascal, "The Prose of Papa Hamlet", (p.8).

56.  N e u e   G l e i s e, p.149.

57.  ibid., p.128.

58.  Pascal, "Arno Holz, Der erste Schultag", loc.cit., p.159.

59.  Pascal, "The Prose of Papa Hamlet", (p.7).

60.  Osborne, op.cit., p.49.

61.  Holz, B r i e f e, p.83.

62.  Pascal, "The Prose of Papa Hamlet", (p.15).

63.  N e u e   G l e i s e, p.114.

64.  ibid., p.152.

65.  Fritz Martini, "Nachwort" to the Reclam edition of
     P a p a   H a m l e t, Stuttgart, 1970, p.114.

66. N e u e  G l e i s e, p.130.

67. For analysis of this passage and the exact location of
    the quotations from  H a m l e t  that comprise it, see:
    Dieter Schickling, "Interpretationen und Studien zur
    Entwicklung und geistesgeschichtlichen Stellung des
    Werkes von Arno Holz", Phil. Diss., Tubingen, 1965, pp.88-90.

68. Martini, "Nachwort", loc.cit., p.117.

69. Reproduced in the  N e u e  G l e i s e volume, pp.94-104.

70. Martini, "Nachwort", loc.cit., p.117.

71. Martini, D a s  W a g n i s  d e r  S p r a c h e, p.110.

72. N e u e  G l e i s e, op.cit., p.160.

73. Martini, D a s  W a g n i s  d e r  S p r a c h e, pp.118-121.

74. Pascal, "The Prose of Papa Hamlet", (p.16).

75. The actual  H a m l e t  quotations are as follows:

    Act 2, Scene 2, Hamlet: "Laßt uns eine Probe eurer Kunst sehen.
                            Wohlan! eine pathetische Rede".
    Act 1, Scene 4, Hamlet: "Und meine Seele, kann es der was tun,
                            Die ein unsterblich Ding ist..."

76. Richard Hinton Thomas, "The Commitment of German Studies",
    (an inaugural lecture delivered in the University of
    Birmingham on 14th October, 1965, pp.3-5).

77. Richard Hinton Thomas and Keith Bullivant, L i t e r a t u r e
    i n  U p h e a v a l, Manchester, 1974, p.2.

78. Osborne, op.cit., p.47.

79. Martini, D a s  W a g n i s  d e r  S p r a c h e, p.117f.

80. ibid., p.118.

81. ibid., p.123.

82. Peter Weiss, D e r  S c h a t t e n  d e s  K ö r p e r s
    d e s  K u t s c h e r s, Frankfurt a.M., 1960 (the edition
    quoted here is edition suhrkamp 53, 5. Auflage, 1971).

83. Dieter Wellershoff, E i n  s c h ö n e r  T a g, Cologne
    and Berlin, 1966.

84. Elias Canetti, A u f z e i c h n u n g e n 1942-1948,
    Munich, 1965, p.8f.

85. Weiss, ed.cit., p.31f.

86. Osborne, op.cit., p.46f.

87. Pascal, "Arno Holz, Der erste Schultag", loc.cit., p.157.

88. Weiss, ed.cit., p.61.

89. Osborne, op.cit., p.46.

90. Weiss, ed.cit., p.68.

91.     ibid., p.7.

92.     ibid., p.14.

93.     ibid., p.71f.

94.     ibid., p.73.

95.     ibid., p.88.

96.     ibid., p.48.

97.     ibid., p.10.

98.     Rose Zeller, "Peter Weiss. D e r  S c h a t t e n  d e s
        K ö r p e r s  d e s  K u t s c h e r s. Erzähler und Autor",
        in: Z e i t s c h r i f t  f ü r  d e u t s c h e  P h i l o-
        l o g i e, 87, (1968), p.643ff.

99.     Weiss, ed.cit., p.9.

100.    ibid., pp.25-27.

101.    ibid., p.71.

102.    ibid., p.14.

103.    Karl Krolow, "Porträt strenger Isoliertheit", D e u t s c h e
        R u n d s c h a u, June 1963, No.6, p.61ff.

104.    In a review of Papa Hamlet (in: D a s  M a g a z i n  f ü r
        d i e  L i t e r a t u r  d e s  I n  u n d  A u s l a n d e s
        58.Jg., Dresden, 2 November 1889, No.45, p.713). Kaberlin
        calls the sketches "Neurealistische Novellen", thus
        anticipating by some seventy years Wellershoff's term.

105.    cf. his second and third novels, D i e  S c h a t t e n-
        g r e n z e  and  E i n l a d u n g  a n  a l l e.

106.    Dieter Wellershoff, L i t e r a t u r  u n d  V e r ä n-
        d e r u n g,  Cologne and Berlin, 1969, p.22.

107.    ibid., p.22.

108.    Robert Burns, "Ein schöner Tag – Neuer Realismus oder
        psychologisierter Naturalismus?", in: Richard Hinton Thomas
        (ed.), D e r  S c h r i f t s t e l l e r  D i e t e r
        W e l l e r s h o f f, Cologne and Berlin, 1975, p.17.

109.    Martini, D a s  W a g n i s  d e r  S p r a c h e, p.125.

110.    Burns, "Ein schöner Tag – Neuer Realismus oder psycholo-
        gisierter Naturalismus?", loc.cit., pp.19-25.

111.    Wellershoff, L i t e r a t u r  u n d  V e r ä n d e r u n g,
        p.96.

112.    Burns, "Ein schöner Tag – Neuer Realismus oder psycholo-
        gisierter Naturalismus?", loc.cit., p.27.

113.    Wellershoff, L i t e r a t u r  u n d  V e r ä n d e r u n g,
        p.103.

114.    Wellershoff, E i n  s c h ö n e r  T a g, p.195.

115. ibid., p.99.

116. Wellershoff, L i t e r a t u r   u n d  V e r ä n d e r u n g, p.90.

117. Günter Zehm, "Ein deutscher 'Nouveau Roman'. Dieter Wellershoffs Werk aus seiner Kölner Schule", D i e  W e l t d e r  L i t e r a t u r, 22 September 1966.

118. Wellershoff, L i t e r a t u r  u n d  V e r ä n d e r u n g, p.89.

119. ibid., p.27.

120. Burns, "Ein schöner Tag – Neuer Realismus oder psychologisierter Naturalismus?", loc.cit., p.32.

121. Wellershoff, E i n  s c h ö n e r  T a g, p.34.

122. ibid., p.115.

123. ibid., p.13.

124. ibid., p.75.

125. ibid., p.48.

126. Hamburger, D i e  L o g i k  d e r  D i c h t u n g, p.73.

127. Wellershoff, E i n  s c h ö n e r  T a g, p.153.

128. ibid., p.125.

129. ibid., p.15.

130. ibid., p.190f.

131. Letter to Richard Hinton Thomas, Cologne, 5.3.75., p.1f.

132. Schulz, op.cit., p.47; cf. Martini: "Kunst wird (for Holz, R.B.) als eine Methode und als eine Funktion zum Erkenntnisakt", W a g n i s  d e r  S p r a c h e, p.113.

C H A P T E R  2  (iii)

1. Herbert Scherer, "The Individual and the collective in Döblin's B e r l i n  A l e x a n d e r p l a t z", in: Keith Bullivant (ed.), C u l t u r e  a n d  S o c i e t y  i n t h e  W e i m a r  R e p u b l i c, pp.56-70, here p.65.

2. cf. the essays "Grabrede auf Arno Holz", "Vom alten zum neuen Naturalismus. Akademie-Rede über Arno Holz" and "Einführung in eine Arno Holz-Auswahl", in: Alfred Döblin, A u f s ä t z e  z u r  L i t e r a t u r, pp.133-138, pp.138-145 and pp.145-163 respectively.

3. cf. "Manche sind der Meinung, daß das, wovon hier die Rede ist, überhaupt kein besonderer Geist, keine plastisch wirkende Kraft sei, sondern nur eine mit Wissenschaft verbrämte

Handfertigkeit...Es ist grotesk, aber begreiflich, daß sogar
Funktionäre des neuen Geistes ihn für materialistisch halten".
Alfred Döblin, A u f s ä t z e   z u r   L i t e r a t u r,
p.67.

4.  ibid., p.145.

5.  ibid., p.136.

6.  ibid., p.139.

7.  cf. "Als rigoröser Naturalist, hinter dem ein materialistischer
    Sozialismus stand,..." ibid., p.161.

8.  cf. the links Döblin wished to establish between Naturalism
    and the Labour Movement:

    mit der sozialen Welle und der Arbeiterbewegung
    konnte zwar der Naturalismus auftreten, die
    Arbeiterbewegung konnte den Naturalismus gebären,
    aber sie konnte ihn nicht am Leben erhalten...
    das starke deutsche Bürgertum konnte zwar die Geburt
    des Naturalismus nicht verhindern, aber es vermochte
    ihn langsam zu erdrücken.

    ibid., p.141.

9.  ibid., p.154.

10. Quotations will be given from the edition B e r l i n
    A l e x a n d e r p l a t z,  Munich, 1969 (7. Auflage).

11. Döblin, A u f s ä t z e   z u r   L i t e r a t u r, p.109.

12. ibid., p.107.

13. ibid., p.132.

14. ibid., p.154.

15. ibid., p.157.

16. Döblin, B e r l i n   A l e x a n d e r p l a t z,  ed.cit.,
    p.412.

17. ibid., p.105.

18. Erich Hülse, "Alfred Döblins  B e r l i n   A l e x a n d e r-
    p l a t z", in: Rolf Geißler (ed.), M ö g l i c h k e i t e n
    d e s   m o d e r n e n   d e u t s c h e n   R o m a n s,
    Frankfurt a.M., 1962, pp.45-101.

19. Döblin, A u f s ä t z e   z u r   L i t e r a t u r,  p.113.

20. ibid., p.132.

21. ibid., p.130.

22. Döblin, B e r l i n   A l e x a n d e r p l a t z,  ed. cit.,
    p.414.

23. ibid., p.163.

24. ibid., p.345.

25. Döblin, A u f s ä t z e  z u r  L i t e r a t u r, p.136.

26. ibid., pp.111-112.

27. ibid., p.123.

28. Döblin, B e r l i n  A l e x a n d e r p l a t z, ed.cit., p.117.

29. ibid., p.118f.

30. ibid., pp.55-57.

31. ibid., p.43.

32. Döblin, A u f s ä t z e  z u r  L i t e r a t u r, p.106.

33. ibid., p.132.

34. Hülse, loc.cit., p.74.

35. Döblin, B e r l i n  A l e x a n d e r p l a t z, ed.cit., p.95.

36. Martini, D a s  W a g n i s  d e r  S p r a c h e, p.370.

37. Döblin, B e r l i n  A l e x a n d e r p l a t z, ed.cit., p.76f.

38. Martini, "Nachwort", loc.cit., p.117.

39. Hermann Meyer, D a s  Z i t a t  i n  d e r  E r z ä h l-
k u n s t, Stuttgart, 1967, p.11.

40. Döblin, A u f s ä t z e  z u r  L i t e r a t u r, p.177f.

41. Albrecht Schöne, "Alfred Döblins B e r l i n
A l e x a n d e r p l a t z", in: Benno von Wiese (ed.),
D e r  d e u t s c h e  R o m a n.  V o m  B a r o c k  z u r
G e g e n w a r t, Düsseldorf, 1963, Vol.2, p.323.

42. Walter Jens, S t a t t  e i n e r  L i t e r a t u r-
g e s c h i c h t e, Tübingen, 1957, p.25.

43. Döblin, B e r l i n  A l e x a n d e r p l a t z, ed.cit., pp.19-23.

44. ibid., p.31.

45. ibid., p.69.

46. ibid., p.83.

47. ibid., p.75f.

48. Martini, D a s  W a g n i s  d e r  S p r a c h e, p.343.

49. Döblin, A u f s ä t z e  z u r  L i t e r a t u r, p.114.

50. Döblin, B e r l i n  A l e x a n d e r p l a t z, ed.cit., p.88.

51. ibid., p.7.

52. On one occasion in "Papa Hamlet" Holz achieves a similar
effect.  Section II opens with the famous "Sein oder Nichtsein"

quotation but the typographical presentation is such as to create the effect of a caption rather than of the actual text of the chapter. (N e u e  G l e i s e, p.112).

53.     Döblin, B e r l i n  A l e x a n d e r p l a t z, ed. cit., p.410.

54.     Walter Muschg, "Nachwort" to B e r l i n  A l e x a n d e r-p l a t z, ed.cit., pp.415-430.

55.     Schöne, loc.cit., p.322.

56.     Volker Klotz, D i e  e r z ä h l t e  S t a d t, Munich, 1969, p.413.

57.     Döblin, A u f s ä t z e  z u r  L i t e r a t u r, p.132.

58.     Martini, D a s  W a g n i s  d e r  S p r a c h e, p.343.

59.     Döblin, A u f s ä t z e  z u r  L i t e r a t u r, p.136.

C H A P T E R  3  (i)

1.     The various editions of P h a n t a s u s  will be referred to according to the following abbreviations:

        S = Berlin, Saßenbach, 1898/99 (Facsimile of the
            original edition, Gerhard Schulz, Stuttgart, 1968,
            no page numbers)
        I = Leipzig, Insel-Verlag, 1916
        DW = Berlin, Dietz, 1924/25, Volumes 7-9
        W = Neuwied, Luchterhand, 1961-64, Volumes 1-3

2.     Emrich, op.cit., p.163.

3.     W I, p.328.

4.     See Franz Kleitsch, "Der "Phantasus" von Arno Holz", Phil.Diss., Berlin, 1940.

5.     Rappl., op.cit., p.31.

6.     Emrich, op.cit., p.156f.

7.     DW X, p.621.

8.     ibid., p.534.

9.     ibid., p.498.

10.    ibid., p.489.

11.    ibid., p.490.

12.    ibid., p.639f.

13.    ibid., p.650.

14.    ibid., p.537f.

15.    ibid., p.649.

16.    ibid., p.493 and p.693.

17.  ibid., p.503.

18.  ibid., p.529 and p.510.

19.  ibid., p.691.

20.  ibid., p.538.

21.  ibid., p.502.

22.  ibid., p.501.

23.  ibid., p.538f.

24.  ibid., p.494.

25.  cf. "kein Mittel ist umfassender als das Wort. Es ersetzt,.. bis zu einem gewissen Grade jedes übrige Mittel". ibid., p.189.

26.  See, for example, Schulz, op.cit., p.83.

27.  Ingrid Strohschneider-Kohrs, "Sprache und Wirklichkeit bei Arno Holz", P o e t i c a  I, (1967), p.47.

28.  DW X, p.341.

29.  ibid., p.498f.

30.  Schulz, op.cit., p.83.

31.  DW X, p.190.

32.  ibid., p.186f.

33.  ibid., p.187.

34.  ibid., p.198f.

35.  Emrich, op.cit., p.158.

36.  Rappl, op.cit., p.49f.

37.  Emrich, op.cit., p.161.

38.  DW X, p.650.

39.  ibid., p.653.

40.  Leopold Demler, "Arno Holz, Kunst und Natur", Phil.Diss., Vienna, 1938, p.25.

41.  DW X, p.651.

42.  ibid., p.605.

43.  ibid., p.642.

44.  ibid., p.651f.

45.  Introduction to P h a n t a s u s, New York and London, 1968, p.xxxvi.

46.  W I, p.7.

47.  Schickling, op.cit., p.172.

48.  DW X, p.653.

49. cf. Der da redet, ist das Ich des Arno Holz; aber dieses Ich versteht sich als eine Versammlung von Personen, historischen Figuren, Wunschhelden, Untieren, Traumtänzern, Terroristen, Idyllikern, Sängern, Schreihälsen, Spieß- bürgern, Teppichhändlern, Sternguckern etc. Dieses jeweils verwandelte Ich konkretisiert alle Erfahrungen, Imaginationen, Träume, "Alles durchrann mich". Holz gab im "Phantasus" die Darstellung dessen, was in seinem Bewußtsein wohnte, rumorte oder schlief.

    Jürgen Becker, "Das Riesen-Phantasus-Nonplusultra-Poem", D e u t s c h e   Z e i t u n g, No.161, 14/15 July 1962, p.19.

50. DW X, p.651.

51. ibid., p.502f.

52. ibid., p.656.

53. Hartwig Schultz, V o m   R h y t h m u s   d e r   m o d e r n e n   L y r i k.   P a r a l l e l e   V e r s s t r u k t u r e n   b e i   H o l z,   G e o r g e,   R i l k e,   B r e c h t   u n d   d e n   E x p r e s s i o n i s t e n, Munich, 1970, p.100.

54. Donald Davie, A r t i c u l a t e   E n e r g y, London, 1955, p.126.

55. Schultz, op.cit., p.101.

56. Karl Turley, A r n o   H o l z.   D e r   W e g   e i n e s   K ü n s t l e r s, Leipzig, 1935, p.68f.

57. DW X, p.620f.

58. Käthe Lichtenstern, "Der Phantasus von Arno Holz in seiner formalen Entwicklung", Phil.Diss., Vienna, 1936, p.119.

59. ibid., p.120.

60. DW X, p.623.

61. ibid., p.574.

62. ibid., p.659.

63. ibid., p.657.

64. Arno Holz, P h a n t a s u s.   Z u r   E i n f ü h r u n g, Berlin, 1922, p.26.

65. I, p.12.

66. DW VII, p.7.

67. DW IX, pp.1264-9.

68. Holz, B r i e f e, p.210.

69. DW X, p.660f.

70. DW X, "Vorwort", p.III.

71. Robert Reß, D i e   Z a h l   a l s   f o r m e n d e s

W e l t p r i n z i p, Berlin, 1926. For discussion of this work see Schulz, op.cit., p.232.

72.    cf. DW X, p.710 and "Vorwort" p.111.

73.    ibid., "Vorwort", p.111.

74.    Kleitsch, op.cit., p.68f.

75.    ibid., p.26.

76.    Rappl., op.cit., p.78.

77.    Holz, B r i e f e, p.233.

78.    W I, p.7f.

79.    I, p.7.

80.    DW X, p.670.

81.    Döblin, A u f s ä t z e  z u r  L i t e r a t u r, p.137.

82.    Quoted in: Hans Fischer, A r n o  H o l z. E i n e  E i n f ü h r u n g  i n  s e i n  W e r k, Berlin, 1924, p.123.

83.    DW X, p.651.

84.    W I, p.64.

85.    S, (p.81).

86.    Schulz, op.cit., p.219.

87.    S (p.88).

88.    W I, p.175.

89.    Gerhard Schmidt-Henkel, M y t h o s  u n d  D i c h t u n g, Bad Homburg, 1967, p.146.

90.    DW VIII, p.780.

91.    DW VII, p.81.

92.    I, p.6.

93.    Holz, B r i e f e, p.265.

94.    I, p.204, and p.265.

95.    DW IX, pp.1190-2.

96.    W III, p.363.

97.    Kleitsch, op.cit., p.70.

98.    ibid., p.70.

99.    Schulz, op.cit., p.214.

100.    W III, p.85f.

101.    cf. W II, p.455 and p.95ff.

102.    Schulz, op.cit., pp.211-223.

103. W III, p.301f.

104. Holz, B r i e f e, p.247.

105. Cowen, op.cit., p.234.

106. Schulz, op.cit., p.181 and p.199.

107. Rappl., op.cit., p.89.

108. Döblin, A u f s ä t z e   z u r   L i t e r a t u r, op.cit., p.161.


C H A P T E R  3 (ii)

1. Strohschneider-Kohrs, loc.cit., p.64f.

2. ibid., p.65.

3. "Nachwort", P a p a   H a m l e t, ed.cit., p.105.

4. DW X, p.690.

5. ibid., p.693.

6. ibid., p.695.

7. ibid., p.694.

8. See above, pp. 156-168.

9. Heinrich Fauteck, "Arno Holz", N e u e   R u n d s c h a u 77, 1963, p.466.

10. Armin Arnold, D i e   L i t e r a t u r   d e s E x p r e s s i o n i s m u s, Stuttgart, 1966, p.7.

11. Walter Muschg, V o n   T r a k l   z u   B r e c h t, Munich, 1961, p.62.

12. Alfred Döblin, A r n o   H o l z.  D i e   R e v o l u t i o n d e r   L y r i k.  E i n e   E i n f ü h r u n g   i n   s e i n W e r k   u n d   e i n e   A u s w a h l, Wiesbaden, 1951. The poems by Stramm included in this volume as "Literarische Parallelen" are "Schwermut" and "Patrouille" (p.128).

13. Schultz, op.cit., p.106f.

14. ibid., p.126.

15. ibid., p.106.

16. See "Anhang", in: August Stramm, D a s   W e r k, edited by René Radrizzani, Wiesbaden, 1963, p.430.

17. ibid., p.430f.

18. Quoted by Emrich, op.cit., p.166f.

19. ibid., p.166f.

20. Quoted by Radrizzani, loc.cit., p.431.

21. ibid., p.441.

22. Schultz, op.cit., p.126.

23. F. J. Schneider, D e r   e x p r e s s i v e   M e n s c h   u n d   d i e   d e u t s c h e   L y r i k   d e r   G e g e n w a r t, Stuttgart, 1927, p.44.

24. Emrich, op.cit., p.162.

25. J. J. White, "Some Significant Features of the Typography and Lay-out of August Stramm's Poetry, (unpublished article), (p.439).

26. cf. Radrizzani, loc.cit., p.439.

27. Quoted by Radrizzani, loc.cit., p.427.

28. August Stramm, D a s   W e r k, p.45 and p.52.

29. ibid., p.14.

30. DW X, p.503.

31. Charles Olson, S e l e c t e d   W r i t i n g s, ed. Robert Creeley, New York, 1950, p.19.

32. White, op.cit., (p.17).

33. Jeremy Adler, "Towards a reassessment of "Urtod"." (unpublished article) (p.6).

34. ibid., (p.31).

35. M o d e r n e r   M u s e n-A l m a n a c h   a u f   d a s   J a h r 1893, ed. Otto Julius Bierbaum, Munich, 1892, p.74.

36. August Stramm, D a s   W e r k, p.14.

37. Referred to, for example, by Holz himself, DW X, p.618.

38. Quoted in Arnold, op.cit., p.39.

39. Adler, op.cit., (p.48).

40. cf. White, op.cit., (p.19f).

41. DW X, p.694f.

42. cf. White, op.cit., (p.31).

43. cf. Andreas Heusler, D e u t s c h e   V e r s g e s c h i c h t e, Vol.III, Berlin and Leipzig, 1929, p.314 and Hans Stoltenberg, "Arno Holz, sein Kreis und sein Werk", in: N a c h r i c h t e n   d e r   G i e s s e n e r   H o c h s c h u l g e s e l l s c h., Giessen, 1930, Vol.7, p.15ff.

44. cf. DW X, p.504 and p.658.

45. ibid., p.538.

46. ibid., p.538.

47. ibid., p.547.

48. Introduction to Holz, B r i e f e, p.26.

49. Schultz, op.cit., p.121.

50. ibid., p.123ff.

51. "Zur Ästhetik der modernen Dichtung", Emrich,op.cit., p.129f.

52. Dietrich, "Arno Holz und die Literatur der neuen Zeit", D a s  g o l d e n e  T o r,  ed. Alfred Döblin, 2.Jg., 1947, No.3/4, p.219.

53. Ludwig Pesch, D i e  R o m a n t i s c h e  R e b e l l i o n  i n  d e r  m o d e r n e n  L i t e r a t u r  u n d  K u n s t, Munich, 1962, p.115.

54. Dietrich, loc.cit., p.218f.

55. Schulz, op.cit., p.227.

56. Döblin, A u f s ä t z e  z u r  L i t e r a t u r, p.137.

57. "Vom alten zum neuen Naturalismus", in: A u f s ä t z e  z u r  L i t e r a t u r, cf. p.144f.

58. "Bekenntnis zum Naturalismus", D a s  T a g e b u c h, I, 1920, p.1600f.

59. Alfred Döblin, B r i e f e, Olten and Freiburg, 1970, p.123.

60. A u f s ä t z e  z u r  L i t e r a t u r, p.372.

61. ibid., p.354f.

62. Alfred Döblin, B e r g e  M e e r e  u n d  G i g a n t e n, Berlin, 1924, p.588f.

63. Strohschneider-Kohrs, loc.cit., p.65.

64. For discussion of the influence of Futurism on Döblin, see Arnold, op.cit., pp.80-107.

65. Robert Musil, "Alfred Döblins Epos", B e r l i n e r  T a g e b l a t t, 10 June 1927, quoted in: Leo Kreutzer, A l f r e d  D ö b l i n, Stuttgart, 1970, p.111.

66. A u f s ä t z e  z u r  L i t e r a t u r, p.143f.

67. Kreutzer, op.cit., p.110.

68. Hamburger, D i e  L o g i k  d e r  D i c h t u n g, p.208.

69. Schulz,op.cit., p.227.

70. W II, p.293.

71. Tony Phelan, R a t i o n a l i s t  N a r r a t i v e  i n  s o m e  W o r k s  o f  A r n o  S c h m i d t, Occasional Papers in German Studies No.2, Warwick University, 1972, p.9.

72. U l t i m i s t i s c h e r  A l m a n a c h, ed. Klaus M. Rarisch, Cologne, 1965, p.14.

73. ibid., p.14f.

74. "Vorwort", D i e  W i e n e r  G r u p p e, ed. Gerhard Rühm, Reinbek, 1967, p.9.

75. See L. W. Forster, T h e  P o e t ' s  T o n g u e s, Cambridge, 1970, p.91.

76. Helmut Heißenbüttel, Ü b e r  L i t e r a t u r, Munich, 1970, p.32.

77. ibid., p.118.

78. ibid., p.33.

79. Helmut Heißenbüttel, "Kriterien für den Begriff des Gedichts im 20. Jahrhundert", S p r a c h e  i m  t e c h n i s c h e n  Z e i t a l t e r, ed. Walter Höllerer, 1963, Heft 9/10, (pp.774-777) here p.776.

80. P. Hartmann, D a s  W o r t  a l s  N a m e, Cologne and Opladen, 1958, p.57, quoted by Strohschneider-Kohrs, loc.cit., p.61.

81. DW X, p.501.

82. Schikowski, quoted in DW X, p.697.

83. Eugen Gomringer, w o r t e  s i n d  s c h a t t e n, Reinbek, 1969, p.279.

84. Quoted in: Robert A. Burns, C o m m i t m e n t, L a n g u a g e  a n d  R e a l i t y: a n  i n t r o d u c- t i o n  t o  t h e  w o r k  o f  H e l m u t  H e i ß e n b ü t t e l. Occasional Papers in German Studies, No.7, Warwick University, 1975, p.34f.

85. Helmut Heißenbüttel and Heinrich Vormweg, B r i e f w e c h s e l  ü b e r  L i t e r a t u r, Neuwied and Berlin, 1969, p.28f.

86. Helmut Heißenbüttel, Z u r  T r a d i t i o n  d e r  M o d e r n e, Neuwied and Berlin, 1972, p.51.

87. Max Bense, E i n f ü h r u n g  i n  d i e  i n f o r m a- t i o n s t h e o r e t i s c h e  Ä s t h e t i k, Reinbek, 1969, p.120.

88. Gomringer, op.cit., p.281.

89. Helmut Heißenbüttel, "Anmerkungen zur konkreten Poesie", in: T e x t  +  K r i t i k, 25, Konkrete Poesie I, ed. Heinz Ludwig Arnold, Munich, 1970, p.19.

90. Helmut Heißenbüttel, "Literatur und Wissenschaft", A k z e n t e, 1965, Heft 2, p.183.

91. W I, p.22.

92. Gomringer, op.cit., p.280 and p.284.

93. Helmut Heißenbüttel, D a s  T e x t b u c h, Neuwied and Berlin, 1967, p.222.

94.  W III, p.507.

95.  D a s  T e x t b u c h,  p.255.

96.  DW IV, p.737ff.

97.  D a s  T e x t b u c h,  p.159.

98.  Holz,  P h a n t a s u s.  Z u r  E i n f ü h r u n g,  p.26.

99.  DW X, p.503f.

100.  Ü b e r  L i t e r a t u r,  p.208.

101.  Fauteck, loc.cit., p.4-73.

102.  I, p.293 and p.51.

103.  D a s  T e x t b u c h,  p.131.

104.  cf. DW X, p.672f.

105.  Schmidt-Henckel, op.cit., p.138.

106.  Becker, loc.cit., p.19.

107.  See Franz Mon,  p r i n z i p  c o l l a g e,  Neuwied and
      Berlin, 1968 and Burns,  C o m m i t m e n t  L a n g u a g e
      a n d  R e a l i t y:  a n  i n t r o d u c t i o n  t o
      t h e  w o r k  o f  H e l m u t  H e i ß e n b ü t t e l,
      p.20f.

108.  B r i e f w e c h s e l  ü b e r  L i t e r a t u r,  p.28f.

109.  Helmut Heißenbüttel,  D'A l e m b e r t s  E n d e,  Neuwied
      and Berlin, 1970, pp.213-220.

110.  Karl Riha,  C r o s s - R e a d i n g  u n d  C r o s s -
      T a l k i n g,  Stuttgart, 1971, p.16.

111.  cf.  Z u r  T r a d i t i o n  d e r  M o d e r n e,  pp.369-374.

112.  Holz,  B r i e f e,  p.113.

113.  W III, p.85f.

114.  Schulz, op.cit., p.214.

115.  Ü b e r  L i t e r a t u r,  p.34.

116.  ibid., p.33.

117.  Hamburger,  D i e  L o g i k  d e r  D i c h t u n g,  p.189.

118.  Berold van der Auwera, "Theorie und Praxis Konkreter Poesie",
      in:  T e x t  +  K r i t i k,  30, Konkrete Poesie II,
      Munich, 1971, p.34.

119.  Walter Hinderer, "Zur Situation der westdeutschen
      Literaturkritik", in: Manfred Durzak (ed.),  D i e
      d e u t s c h e  L i t e r a t u r  d e r  G e g e n w a r t.
      A s p e k t e  u n d  T e n d e n z e n,  Stuttgart, 1971,
      p.311.

120.  T i m e s  L i t e r a r y  S u p p l e m e n t,  10 January,
      1969.

121.  Becker, loc.cit., p.19.

122.  Heinrich Vormweg, "Die Renaissance des Barock",
      F r a n k f u r t e r   H e f t e,   June 1966, p.418.

123.  W I, p.372ff.

124.  Vormweg, loc.cit., p.418.

125.  Becker, loc. cit., p.19.


C O N C L U S I O N


1.    DW X, p.533.

2.    Scheuer, op.cit., p.163.

3.    DW X, p.368.

4.    Pascal, "Arno Holz, Der erste Schultag", loc.cit., p.154.

5.    DW X, p.490.

6.    Ü b e r   L i t e r a t u r, p.9.

7.    DW X, p.271.

8.    ibid., p.651.

9.    Jürgen Becker, interview with Reinhard Lettau, in: Werner
      Koch (ed.), S e l b s t a n z e i g e.   S c h r i f t-
      s t e l l e r   i m   G e s p r ä c h,   Frankfurt a.M., 1971,
      p.83.

10.   Quoted in  V o r z e i c h e n,   ed. Hans Magnus Enzensberger,
      Frankfurt a.M., 1962, p.16.

11.   Becker, "Das Riesen-Phantasus-Nonplusultra-Poem",
      loc.cit., p.19.

12.   References to these writers can be found in, respectively,
      Hans Hennecke, D i c h t u n g   u n d   D a s e i n,   Berlin,
      1950, p.176; Herbert Pfeiffer, "Pinters Höhlen-Trio. Im
      Theater am Kurfurstendamm: Der Hausmeister, B e r l i n e r
      M o r g e n p o s t,   20.3.1962; Emrich, op.cit., p.168.

13.   W III, p.359.

14.   Günter Grass, H u n d e j a h r e,   Neuwied and Berlin,
      1963, p.234f.

15.   cf. Der Inhalt ist der unvermeidliche Widerstand, der
      Vorwand für die Form...Es kommt nicht auf das Was an, nur,
      auf das  W i e.  Der Inhalt stört nur ist Konzession fürs
      Publikum, die Kunst will  d i e   F o r m   a n   s i c h.

      Günter Grass, Ü b e r   m e i n e n   L e h r e r   D ö b l i n
      u n d   a n d e r e   V o r t r ä g e,   Berlin, 1968, p.56f.

16.   In his essay entitled "Arno Holz, Alfred Döblin, Günter
      Grass.  Zur Tradition von politischer Dichtung in Deutsch-
      land",  (Moderna Sprak, Stockholm, 1972)  Manfred Durzak
      attempts to locate this point of intersection in the
      political development of Holz and Grass.  While it would
      be inappropriate to comment here on the validity of this
      political relationship, I would nevertheless point out
      that Durzak does not develop his analysis to establish
      any substantial  s t y l i s t i c  relationship between
      the two writers.

17.   Michael Scharang, E i n e r  m u ß  i m m e r  p a r i e r e n,
      Darmstadt and Neuwied, 1973, p.9.

18.   ibid., p.9.

# BIBLIOGRAPHY

This bibliography divides into four sections:

256

I. THE WORK OF ARNO HOLZ

Reference will be made only to that part of Holz's work which is relevant for the purpose of this study. There are, however, two editions of his work which are as follows:

D a s   W e r k,   ed. Hans. W. Fischer, Berlin, 1924-5
                   10 Volumes.

    Vol.1   : Buch der Zeit (1924)
    Vol.2   : Dafnis (1924)
    Vol.3-4 : Die Blechschmiede (1924)
    Vol.5   : Sozialaristokraten. Sonnenfinsternis (1924)
    Vol.6   : Ignorabimus (1925)
    Vol.7-9 : Phantasus (1925)
    Vol.10  : Die neue Wortkunst (1925)

W e r k e,   ed. Wilhelm Emrich and Anita Holz, Neuwied,
             1961-4 7 Volumes.

    Vol.1-3 : Phantasus (1961-2)
    Vol.4   : Sozialaristokraten. Sonnenfinsternis.
             Ignorabimus (1962)
    Vol.5   : Buch der Zeit. Dafnis. Kunsttheoretische
             Schriften (1962)
    Vol.6-7 : Die Blechschmiede I (1963-4)

D e u t s c h e   W e i s e n   (Arno Holz and Oscar Jerschke),
                   Berlin and Leipzig, 1884.

D i e   K u n s t.   I h r   W e s e n   u n d   i h r e
                   G e s e t z e,   Berlin, 1891.

D i e   K u n s t.   I h r   W e s e n   u n d   i h r e
                   G a s e t z e,   Berlin, 1892.

N e u e   G l e i s e.   Gemeinsames von Arno Holz und Johannes
                   Schlaf, Berlin, 1892.

P h a n t a s u s.   Faksimiledruck der Erstfassung, ed.
                   Gerhard Schulz, Stuttgart, 1968.

P h a n t a s u s,   Mit einer Einführung von Jost Hermand,
                   New York and London, 1968.

P h a n t a s u s,   Leipzig, 1916.

P h a n t a s u s,   Zur Einführung, Berlin, 1922.

D i e   b e f r e i t e   d e u t s c h e   W o r t k u n s t,
                   Vienna and Leipzig, 1921.

D e r   e r s t e   S c h u l t a g,   (revised version), Berlin,
                   1922.

B r i e f e. E i n e A u s w a h l, ed. Anita Holz and
    Max Wagner, with an introduction by
    H. H. Borcherdt, Munich, 1948.

A r n o H o l z. D i e R e v o l u t i o n d e r L y r i k.
    Eine Einführung in sein Werk und eine Auswahl,
    ed. Alfred Döblin, Wiesbaden, 1951.


II.    SECONDARY LITERATURE ON HOLZ

Avenarius, Friedrich, A r n o H o l z u n d s e i n
            W e r k. D e u t s c h e S t i m m e n z u
            s e i n e m 6 0. G e b u r t s t a g e.
            Berlin, 1923.

Becker, Jürgen, "Das Riesen-Phantasus-Nonplusultra-Poem",
            D e u t s c h e Z e i t u n g, No.161,
            14/15 July 1962, p.19.

Berthold, Siegwart, "Der sogenannte "konsequente Naturalismus"
            von Arno Holz und Johannes Schlaf", Phil.Diss.,
            Bonn, 1967.

Brandstetter, Alois, "Gestalt und Leistung der Zeile im
            "Phantasus" von Arno Holz", W i r k e n d e s
            W o r t 16 (1966), pp.13-18.

Closs, August, "Arno Holz. New Forms in German Lyric",
            T h e P o e t r y R e v i e w 21 (1930),
            No.2, pp.99-110.

Cohen, Fritz Gerhardt, "Social and Political Concepts in the
            Works of Arno Holz", Phil.Diss., Iowa, 1955.

Demler, Leopold, "Arno Holz, Kunst und Natur", Phil.Diss.,
            Vienna, 1938.

Dietrich, "Arno Holz und die Literatur der neuen Zeit",
            D a s g o l d e n e T o r, (1947), No.3/4,
            pp.214-226.

Döblin, Alfred, "Grabrede auf Arno Holz" (1929),
            "Vom alten zum neuen Naturalismus. Akadamierede
            über Arno Holz" (1930),
            "Einführung in eine Arno-Holz-Auswahl" (1951)

            all in : A u f s ä t z e z u r L i t e r a t u r,
            Olten and Freiburg, 1963, pp.133-138, pp.138-
            145 and pp.145-163 respectively.

Durzak Manfred, "Arno Holz, Alfred Döblin, Günter Grass. Zur
            Tradition von politischer Dichtung in
            Deutschland", M o d e r n e S p r å k,
            Stockholm, 1972, pp.1-21.

Emrich, Wilhelm,   "Die Struktur der modernen Dichtung",
                   "Zur Ästhetik der modernen Dichtung",
                   "Arno Holz und die moderne Kunst" (also
                   published as the "Nachwort" in Holz,
                   W e r k e, Vol.7, pp.453-471),
                   all in: P r o t e s t   u n d
                   V e r h e i ß u n g,  Frankfurt a.M.,
                   1960, pp.111-122, pp.123-134 and
                   pp.155-168, respectively.
                   "Arno Holz - sein dicherisches Experiment,
                   N e u e   D e u t s c h e   H e f t e   10
                   (1963), No.94, pp.43-58.

Fauteck, Heinrich, "Arno Holz", N e u e   R u n d s c h a u
                   77 (1963), pp.459-476.

Fischer, Hans W., A r n o   H o l z.   E i n e   E i n f ü h -
                   r u n g   i n   s e i n   W e r k,  Berlin,
                   1924.

Geisendörfer, Karl, "Motive und Motivgeflecht im "Phantasus"
                   von Arno Holz", Phil.Diss., Würzburg, 1962.
                   "Die Entwicklung eines lyrischen Weltbildes
                   im "Phantasus" von Arno Holz",
                   Z e i t s c h r i f t   f ü r
                   d e u t s c h e   P h i l o l o g i e
                   82 (1963), pp.231-248.

Heißenbüttel,      "Vater Arno Holz", in:  Ü b e r
Helmut,            L i t e r a t u r,  Munich, 1970, pp.32-35.

Heselhaus, Clemens,"Arno Holz: Der Phantasus-Rhythmus", in:
                   D e u t s c h e   L y r i k   d e r
                   M o d e r n e   v o n   N i e t z s c h e
                   b i s   Y v a n   G o l l,  Düsseldorf,
                   1961, pp.166-177.

Kesting, Marianne, "Arno Holz - ein behinderter Neuerer",
                   in: E n t d e c k u n g   u n d
                   D e s t r u k t i o n,  Munich, 1970,
                   pp.172-188.

Kleitsch, Franz,   "Der "Phantasus" von Arno Holz",
                   Phil.Diss., Berlin, 1940.

Lichtenstern,      "Der Phantasus von Arno Holz in seiner
Käthe,             formalen Entwicklung", Phil.Diss., Vienna,
                   1936.

Martini, Fritz,   "Arno Holz, Papa Hamlet", in: D a s
                   W a g n i s   d e r   S p r a c h e,
                   Stuttgart, 1954, pp.99-132.

"Nachwort" to Arno Holz and Johannes Schlaf,
P a p a  H a m l e t.  E i n  T o d,
Stuttgart, 1963.
"Nachwort" to Arno Holz and Johannes Schlaf,
D i e  F a m i l i e  S e l i c k e,
Stuttgart, 1966.

Mehring, Franz,  ("Arno Holz") 1898, "Der Fall Holz". 1896,
("Arno Holz") 1900, in: G e s a m m e l t e
S c h r i f t e n,  Berlin, 1961, Vol.11,
pp.200-210, pp.230-237 and p.522 respectively.

Milch, Werner,  A r n o  H o l z.  T h e o r e t i k e r -
K ä m p f e r - D i c h t e r,  Berlin, 1933.

Pascal, Roy,  "Arno Holz, 'Der erste Schultag'.  The
Prose-Style of Naturalism", in:  J. Siefken
and A. Robinson (ed.),  E r f a h r u n g
u n d  Ü b e r l i e f e r u n g,  Festschrift
for C.P. Magill, Cardiff, 1974.
"The Prose of Papa Hamlet.  The Irrepressible
Narrator", (unpublished manuscript), pp.1-23.

Pesch, Ludwig,  D i e  R o m a n t i s c h e  R e b e l l i o n
i n  d e r  m o d e r n e n  L i t e r a t u r
u n d  K u n s t,  Munich, 1962, pp.110-115.

Ploetz, Hermann,  "Arno Holz der Deutsche",  O s t d e u t s c h e
M o n a t s h e f t e,  January 1934, pp.333-
337.

Rappl, Hans-  "Die Wortkunstlehre von Arno Holz",
Georg,  Phil.Diss., Cologne, 1957.

Reß,  Robert,  A r n o  H o l z  u n d  s e i n e
k ü n s t l e r i s c h e,  w e l t -
k u l t u r e l l e  B e d e u t u n g,
Dresden, 1913.

Scherpe,  "Der Fall Arno Holz", in:  Gert Mattenklott
Klaus R.,  and Klaus R. Scherpe (ed.), P o s i t i o n e n
d e r  l i t e r a r i s c h e n
I n t e l l i g e n z  z w i s c h e n
b ü r g e r l i c h e r  R e a k t i o n
u n d  I m p e r i a l i s m u s,  Kronberg,
1973, pp.121-178.

Scheuer, Helmut,  A r n o  H o l z  i m  l i t e r a r i s c h e n
L e b e n  d e s  a u s g e h e n d e n  1 9.
J a h r h u n d e r t s  (1 8 8 3-1 8 9 6).
Eine biographische Studie, Munich, 1971.

Schickling, Dieter,     "Interpretationen und Studien zur
                        Entwicklung und geistesgeschichtlichen
                        Stellung des Werkes von Arno Holz",
                        Phil.Diss., Tubingen, 1965.

Schmidt-Henkel,         "Arno Holz und der proteische Mythos
Gerhard,                des 'Phantasus'", in:  M y t h o s
                        u n d  D i c h t u n g,  Bad Homburg,
                        1967, pp.132-135.

Schulz, Gerhard,        "Sprache im "Phantasus" von Arno Holz",
                        A k z e n t e  18 (1971), pp.359-378.
                        A r n o  H o l z.  D i l e m m a
                        e i n e s  b ü r g e r l i c h e n
                        D i c h t e r l e b e n s,  Munich,
                        1974.

Strohschneider-Kohrs,   "Sprache und Wirklichkeit bei Arno
Ingrid,                 Holz",  P o e t i c a  1 (1967),
                        pp.44-66.

Turley, Karl,           A r n o  H o l z.  D e r  W e g  e i n e s
                        K ü n s t l e r s,  Leipzig, 1935.

Turner, David,          "Die Famile Selicke  and the Drama of
                        Naturalism", in:  J. M. Ritchie (ed.),
                        P e r i o d s  i n  G e r m a n
                        L i t e r a t u r e : T e x t s  a n d
                        C o n t e x t s,  London, 1969, Vol.2,
                        pp.193-219.

Zur Linde, Otto,        A r n o  H o l z  u n d  d e r  C h a r o n,
                        Großlichterfelde, 1911.


III.    GENERAL WORKS ON NATURALISM

Bahr, Hermann,          Z u r  Ü b e r w i n d u n g  d e s
                        N a t u r a l i s m u s,  (1898) ed.
                        G. Wunberg, Stuttgart, 1968.

Bleibtreu, Karl,        R e v o l u t i o n  d e r
                        L i t e r a t u r,  Leipzig, 1876.

Bölsche, Wilhelm,       D i e  n a t u r w i s s e n s c h a f t-
                        l i c h e n  G r u n d l a g e n  d e r
                        P o e s i e,  Leipzig, 1887.

Cowen, Roy C.,          D e r  N a t u r a l i s m u s.
                        K o m m e n t a r  z u  e i n e r
                        E p o c h e,  Munich, 1973.

Döblin, Alfred     "Der Geist des naturalistischen Zeitalters", in: A u f s ä t z e z u r L i t e r a t u r, Olten and Freiburg, 1963, pp.62-83.

Fülberth, Georg,     P r o l e t a r i s c h e P a r t e i u n d b ü r g e r l i c h e L i t e r a t u r, Neuwied and Berlin, 1972.

Furst, Lilian R., and Skrine, Peter, N.     N a t u r a l i s m, London, 1971.

Hart, Heinrich,     "Literarische Erinnerungen", G e s a m m e l t e W e r k e, ed. Julius Hart, Berlin, 1907, Vol.III.

Hermand, Jost and Hamann, Richard,     N a t u r a l i s m u s (Deutsche Kunst und Kultur von der Gründerzeit bis zum Expressionismus, Vol.2), Berlin, 1972.

Hermand, Jost,     "Der verdrängte Naturalismus", in: D e r S c h e i n d e s s c h ö n e n L e b e n s, Frankfurt a.M., 1972, pp.26-38.

Lubinski, Samuel,     D i e B i l a n z d e r M o d e r n e, Berlin, 1901.

Lukács, Georg,     W e r k e, (Vol.1: "Theorie des Romans" Vol.4: "Essays über Realismus") Neuwied and Berlin, 1967 and 1971. S c h r i f t e n z u r L i t e r a - t u r s o z i o l o g i e, Neuwied and Berlin, 1961.

Mahal, Günther,     N a t u r a l i s m u s, Munich, 1975.

Mehring, Franz,     G e s a m m e l t e S c h r i f t e n, ed. Höhle, Koch, Schleifstein, Berlin, 1960-63, 12 Vols.

Münchow, Ursula,     D e u t s c h e r N a t u r a l i s - m u s, Berlin (G.D.R.), 1968.

Osborne, John,     "Naturalism and the dramaturgy of the open drama", G e r m a n L i f e a n d L e t t e r s, XXIII (1969-70), pp.119-28. T h e N a t u r a l i s t D r a m a i n G e r m a n y, Manchester, 1971.

Pascal, Roy,            F r o m   N a t u r a l i s m   t o
                        E x p r e s s i o n i s m, London, 1973.

Ruprecht, Erich,        L i t e r a r i s c h e   M a n i f e s t e
                        d e s   N a t u r à l i s m u s.   1 8 8 0-
                        1 8 9 2, Stuttgart, 1962.

Scherer, Herbert,       B ü r g e r l i c h-o p p o s i t i o n e l l e
                        L i t e r a t e n   u n d   s o z i a l-
                        d e m o k r a t i s c h e   A r b e i t e r-
                        b e w e g u n g   n a c h   1 8 9 0.   Die
                        'Friedrichshagener' und ihr Einfluß auf
                        die sozialdemokratische Kulturpolitik,
                        Stuttgart, 1974.

Scheuer, Helmut         N a t u r a l i s m u s.   B ü r g e r-
(ed.),                  l i c h e   D i c h t u n g   u n d
                        s o z i a l e s   E n g a g e m e n t,
                        Stuttgart, Berlin, Cologne and Mainz, 1974.

Schulz, Gerhard,        "Naturalism", in: J. M. Ritchie (ed.),
                        P e r i o d s   i n   G e r m a n   L i t e r a-
                        t u r e,   London 1966, Vol.1, pp.199-225.

Soergel, Albert,        D i c h t u n g   u n d   D i c h t e r
                        d e r   Z e i t, Leipzig, 1911, Vol.I.

Thomas, Richard         "The Commitment of German Studies"  (an
Hinton,                 inaugural lecture delivered in the University
                        of Birmingham on 14th October 1965) pp.1-15.


V.    OTHER SECONDARY SOURCES

Adler, Jeremy,          "Towards a reassessment of 'Urtod'"
                        (unpublished article).

Arnold, Armin,          D i e   L i t e r a t u r   d e s
                        E x p r e s s i o n i s m u s.   S p r a c h-
                        l i c h e   u n d   t h e o r e t i s c h e
                        Q u e l l e n, Stuttgart, 1966.

Arnold, Heinz           T e x t   +   K r i t i k   25, Konkrete Poesie
Ludwig, (ed.)           I, Munich, 1970.
                        (ed.) T e x t   +   K r i t i k   30, Konkrete
                        Poesie II, Munich, 1971.
                        G r u p p e   61:   A r b e i t e r l i t e r a-
                        t u r  -  L i t e r a t u r   d e r
                        A r b e i t s w e l t ? Munich, 1971.

Bab, Julius,            A r b e i t e r d i c h t u n g, Berlin,
                        1929.

Benjamin, Walter,  "Krisis des Romans.  Zu Döblins 'Berlin
Alexanderplatz'", in: A n g e l u s
N o v u s.  A u s g e w ä h l t e
S c h r i f t e n  I I, Frankfurt a.M.,
1966, pp.437-443.
B a u d e l a i r e,  e i n  L y r i k e r
i m  Z e i t a l t e r  d e s  H o c h-
k a p i t a l i s m u s, ed. Rolf Tiedemann,
Frankfurt a.M., 1969.

Bense, Max,  E i n f ü h r u n g  i n  d i e  i n f o r-
m a t i o n s t h e o r e t i s c h e
Äs t h e t i k,  Reinbek, 1969.

Bullivant, Keith  I n d u s t r i e  u n d  d e u t s c h e
and Ridley, Hugh,  L i t e r a t u r  1 8 3 0-1 9 1 4, Munich,
1976.

Burns, Robert,  C o m m i t m e n t,  L a n g u a g e  a n d
R e a l i t y: a n  i n t r o d u c t i o n
t o  t h e  w o r k  o f  H e l m u t
H e i ß e n b ü t t e l, Occasional Papers
in German Studies No.7, Warwick University,
1975.
"Ein schöner Tag - Neuer Realismus oder
psychologisierter Naturalismus?", in:
Richard Hinton Thomas (ed.),  D e r
S c h r i f t s t e l l e r  D i e t e r
W e l l e r s h o f f, Cologne, 1975,
pp.15-39.
"The Theory and Organisation of Revolutionary
Working-Class Literature", in: Keith
Bullivant (ed.),  C u l t u r e  a n d
S o c i e t y  i n  t h e  W e i m a r
R e p u b l i c, Manchester, 1977,
pp.122-149.

Butler, Michael,  "Concrete Poetry and the crisis of language",
N e w  G e r m a n  S t u d i e s,  (1973),
Vol.1, pp.99-115.

Deutsche Akademie  Z u r  T r a d i t i o n  d e r
der Künste (ed.)  s o z i a l i s t i s c h e n  L i t e r a-
t u r  i n  D e u t s c h l a n d, Berlin
and Weimar, 1967.

Dithmar, Reinhard,  I n d u s t r i e l i t e r a t u r,
Munich, 1973.

Edschmid, Kasimir,  B r i e f e  d e r  E x p r e s s i o n i-
(ed.),  s t e n, Frankfurt, a.M.  and Berlin, 1964.

Endell, August,  D i e  S c h ö n h e i t  d e r  g r o ß e n
S t a d t, Stuttgart, 1908.

| | |
|---|---|
| von Hanstein, Adelbert, | D i e  s o z i a l e  F r a g e  i n d e r  P o e s i e, Leipzig, 1897. |
| Heißenbüttel, Helmut, | "Kriterien für den Begriff des Gedichts im 20. Jahrhundert", S p r a c h e  i m t e c h n i s c h e n  Z e i t a l t e r, ed. Walter Höllerer, (1963), Heft 9/10, pp.774-777. "Literatur und Wissenschaft",A k z e n t e, (1965) Heft 2, pp.171-191. W a s  i s t  d a s  K o n k r e t e  a n e i n e m  G e d i c h t?  Z w e i A n s ä t z e, Itzehoe, 1969. Ü b e r  L i t e r a t u r, Munich, 1970. Z u r  T r a d i t i o n  d e r  M o d e r n e. A u f s ä t z e  u n d  A n m e r k u n g e n 1964-71, Neuwied and Berlin, 1972. |
| Heißenbüttel, Helmut and Vormweg, Heinrich, | B r i e f w e c h s e l  ü b e r L i t e r a t u r, Neuwied and Berlin, 1968. |
| Heusler, Andreas, | D e u t s c h e  V e r s g e s c h i c h t e, Berlin and Leipzig, 1929, Vol.III. |
| Hiebel, Irmfried (ed.), | L i t e r a t u r  d e r  A r b e i t e r- k l a s s e, Berlin, 1971. |
| Hoffman, Fritz, | "Nachwort",in: Fritz Hoffmann, Joachim Schreik, Manfred Wolter (ed.), Ü b e r d i e  g r o ß e n  S t ä d t e, Berlin and Weimar, 1967. |
| Hülse, Erich, | "Alfred Döblins 'Berlin Alexanderplatz'", in: Rolf Geißler (ed.), M ö g l i c h- k e i t e n  d e s  m o d e r n e n d e u t s c h e n  R o m a n s, Frankfurt a.M., 1962, pp.45-101. |
| Jens, Walter, | S t a t t  e i n e r  L i t e r a t u r- g e s c h i c h t e, Tübingen, 1957. |
| Johnson, Roy, | "The Proletarian Novel", L i t e r a t u r e a n d  H i s t o r y No.2, London, 1975, pp.84-95. |
| Kesser, Armin, | "Die Arbeiterlyrik der SPD", D i e L i n k s k u r v e, 4Jg., Berlin, 1932, No.10 pp.4-19. |
| Klotz, Volker, | D i e  e r z ä h l t e  S t a d t, Munich, 1969. |

Koch, Hans,         F r a n z   M e h r i n g s   B e i t r a g
z u r   M a r x i s t i s c h e n   L i t e r a-
t u r t h e o r i e, Berlin, 1959.

Kracauer,          F r o m   C a l i g a r i   t o   H i t l e r,
Siegfried,        Princeton, 1947.
D i e   A n g e s t e l l t e n, (1930)
Frankfurt a.M., 1971

Kreutzer, Leo,    A l f r e d   D ö b l i n, Stuttgart,
1970.

Krolow, Karl,    "Porträt strenger Isoliertheit",
D e u t s c h e   R u n d s c h a u, June
1963, No.6.

Kummer,           D e u t s c h e   L i t e r a t u r-
Friedrich,        g e s c h i c h t e   d e s   19. u n d   20.
J a h r h u n d e r t s, Dresden, 1922.

Kühne, Peter,    A r b e i t e r k l a s s e   u n d
L i t e r a t u r. D o r t m u n d e r
G r u p p e   61. W e r k k r e i s-
l i t e r a t u r   d e r   A r b e i t-
s w e l t, Frankfurt a.M., 1972.

Leonhard, Kurt,  S i l b e, B i l d   u n d   W i r k l i c h-
k e i t. G e d a n k e n   z u
G e d i c h t e n, Eßlingen, 1953.

Lethen, Helmut,  N e u e   S a c h l i c h k e i t 1924-32,
S t u t t g a r t, 1970.

Links, Roland,   A l f r e d   D ö b l i n, L e b e n   u n d
W e r k, Berlin, 1965.

Martini, Fritz,  "Alfred Döblins 'Berlin Alexanderplatz'",
in: D a s   W a g n i s   d e r   S p r a c h e,
Stuttgart, 1954, pp.336-372.

Meyer, Hermann,  D a s   Z i t a t   i n   d e r   E r z ä h l-
k u n s t, Stuttgart, 1967.

Mon, Franz,      p r i n z i p   c o l l a g e, Neuwied and
Berlin, 1968.

Möbius Hanno,   A r b e i t e r l i t e r a t u r   i n   d e r
B R D, Cologne, 1970.

Muschg, Walter,  V o n   T r a k l   z u   B r e c h t, Munich,
1961.
"Nachwort" to Alfred Döblin, B e r l i n
A l e x a n d e r p l a t z, Munich, 1969.

Pallinowski, G.
Katrin,

"Die dokumentarische Mode", in:
L i t e r a t u r w i s s e n s c h a f t e n
u n d  S o z i a l w i s s e n s c h a f t e n.
G r u n d l a g e n  u n d  M o d e l l-
a n a l y s e n,  Stuttgart, 1971, pp.235-
314.

Pascal, Roy,

T h e  D u a l  V o i c e,  Manchester,
1977.

Phelan, Tony,

R a t i o n a l i s t  N a r r a t i v e
i n  s o m e  W o r k s  o f  A r n o
S c h m i d t,  Occasional Papers in
German Studies, Warwick University, 1972.

Promies, Wolfgang,

"Nachwort" to Fritz Hüser (ed.),  A u s
d e r  W e l t  d e r  A r b e i t,
A l m a n a c h  d e r  G r u p p e  61,
Neuwied, 1966, pp.371-395.

Raddatz, Fritz,

"In dieser machbar gemachten Welt",
M e r k u r  25. Jg., (1971), Heft 6,
pp.557-569.

Radrizzani, René,

"Anhang", in:  August Stramm,  D a s
W e r k,  Wiesbaden, 1963, pp.399-489.

Rarisch, Klaus,
M.,

U l t i m i s t i s c h e r  A l m a n a c h,
Cologne, 1965.

Riha, Karl,

C r o s s-R e a d i n g  a n d  C r o s s-
T a l k i n g,  Stuttgart, 1971.

Rothe, Wolfgang,

"Einleitung" to  D i e  G r o ß s t a d t-
l y r i k  v o m  N a t u r a l i s m u s
b i s  z u r  G e g e n w a r t,  Stuttgart,
1973, pp.5-36.

Rölleke, Heinz,

D i e  S t a d t  b e i  S t a d l e r,
H e y m  u n d  T r a k l,  Berlin, 1966.

Rumold, Rainer,

S p r a c h l i c h e s  E x p e r i m e n t
u n d  l i t e r a r i s c h e  T r a d i-
t i o n,  Frankfurt a.M. 1975.

Rülcker, Christoph,

I d e o l o g i e  d e r  A r b e i t e r-
d i c h t u n g. 1914-33, Stuggart, 1970.

Sagarra, Eda,

T r a d i t i o n  a n d  R e v o l u t i o n.
G e r m a n  L i t e r a t u r e  a n d
S o c i e t y  1830-1890, London, 1971.

Scherer, Herbert, "The Individual and the collective in Döblin's B e r l i n  A l e x a n d e r- p l a t z", in: Keith Bullivant (ed.), C u l t u r e  a n d  S o c i e t y  i n t h e  W e i m a r  R e p u b l i c, pp.56-70.

Schöne, Albrecht, "Alred Döblins 'Berlin Alexanderplatz'", in:  Benno von Wiese (ed.),  Der d e u t s c h e  R o m a n  v o m  B a r o c k b i s  z u r  G e g e n w a r t, Düsseldorf, 1963, Vol.2, pp.291-325.

Schultz, Hartwig, V o m  R h y t h m u s  d e r  m o d e r n e n L y r i k.  P a r a l l e l e  V e r s - s t r u k t u r e n  b e i  H o l z, G e o r g e, R i l k e, B r e c h t  u n d d e n  E x p r e s s i o n i s t e n, Munich, 1970.

Schwimmer, Helmut, "Erlebnis und Gestaltung der Wirklichkeit bei Alfred Döblin",Phil.Diss., Munich, 1960.

Sokel, Walter, D e r  l i t e r a r i s c h e  E x p r e s - s i o n i s m u s.  D e r  E x p r e s s i o n- i s m  i n  d e r  d e u t s c h e n  L i t e r a- t u r  d e s  20.  J a h r h u n d e r t s, Munich, 1970.

Stanzel, Franz K., D i e  t y p i s c h e n  E r z ä h l- s i t u a t i o n e n  i m  R o m a n, Vienna and Stuttgart, 1955.

Steinberg, Günter, E r l e b t e  R e d e, Goppingen, 1971.

Stieg, Gerald A b r i ß  e i n e r  G e s c h i c h t e and Witte, Bernd., d e r  d e u t s c h e n  A r b e i t e r- l i t e r a t u r, Stuttgart, 1973.

Thomas, Richard L i t e r a t u r e  i n  U p h e a v a l, Hinton and Manchester, 1974. Bullivant, Keith,

Uhlig, Helmut, "Von Ästhetizismus zum Expressionismus in Ernst Stadler, Georg Heym und Georg Trakl", in:  Hermann Friedmann and Otto Mann (ed.), E x p r e s s i o n i s m u s:  G e s t a l t e i n e r  l i t e r a r i s c h e n B e w e g u n g, Heidelberg, 1956, pp.84-115.

| | |
|---|---|
| Vormweg,<br>Heinrich, | D i e  W ö r t e r  u n d  d i e  W e l t,<br>Neuwied and Berlin, 1968.<br>E i n e  a n d e r e  L e s a r t.  Ü b e r<br>n e u e  L i t e r a t u r,  Neuwied and<br>Berlin, 1972. |
| White, J.J. | "Some Significant Features of the Typography<br>and Lay-out of August Stramm's Poetry",<br>(unpublished article). |
| Zehmn, Günter, | "Ein deutscher 'Noveau Roman'.  Dieter<br>Wellershoffs Werke aus seiner Kölner Schule",<br>D i e  W e l t  d e r  L i t e r a t u r,<br>22nd September, 1966. |
| Zeller, Rose, | "Peter Weiss.  'Der Schatten des Körpers<br>des Kutschers' Erzähler und Autor",<br>Z e i t s c h r i f t  f ü r  d e u t s c h e<br>P h i l o l o g i e  87 (1968), pp.643-676. |
| Zimmermann,<br>Felix, | "Die Widerspiegelung der Technik in der<br>deutschen Dichtung vom Goethe bis zur<br>Gegenwart", Phil.Diss., Leipzig, 1913. |
| Ziolkowski,<br>Theodore, | D i m e n s i o n s  o f  t h e  M o d e r n<br>N o v e l,  Princeton, 1969. |